The Next Available Operator

THE NEXT AVAILABLE OPERATOR

Managing Human Resources in Indian Business Process Outsourcing Industry

Edited by
Mohan Thite and Bob Russell

Response
Business books from SAGE
Los Angeles ▪ London ▪ New Delhi ▪ Singapore ▪ Washington DC
www.sagepublications.com

First published in 2009 by

 Response Books
Business books from SAGE
B1/I-1 Mohan Cooperative Industrial Area
Mathura Road, New Delhi 110 044, India

SAGE Publications Inc
2455 Teller Road
Thousand Oaks, California 91320, USA

SAGE Publications Ltd
1 Oliver's Yard, 55 City Road
London EC1Y 1SP, United Kingdom

SAGE Publications Asia-Pacific Pte Ltd
33 Pekin Street
#02-01 Far East Square
Singapore 048763

Published by Vivek Mehra for Response Books, typeset in 11/13pt Baskerville BE by Star Compugraphics Private Limited, Delhi and printed at Chaman Enterprises, New Delhi.

Library of Congress Cataloging-in-Publication Data Available

ISBN: 978-81-7829-932-7 (PB)

The SAGE Team: Reema Singhal, Abantika Banerjee, Anju Saxena and Trinankur Banerjee

To BRAND INDIA, on the success of which ride the hopes of a billion plus Indians.
Mohan Thite

To the hopes and aspirations of the workers in our study and their peers in Indian BPO.
Bob Russell

CONTENTS

LIST OF TABLES

LIST OF FIGURES

LIST OF ABBREVIATIONS

ASA	average speed of answer
BOSS	burn-out stress syndrome
BPO	business process outsourcing
BSE	Bombay Stock Exchange
CBPOP	Centre for Business Process Offshoring Professionals
CCs	call centres
CEO	chief executive officer
CSRs	customer service representatives
CVF	competing values framework
GSE	Global Skills Enhancement Curriculum
HRM	human resource management
IFAs	independent financial advisors
IJP	internal job promotion
INTUC	Indian National Trade Union Congress
IP	internet protocol
IT	information technology
ITeS	information technology enabled services
ITPF	Information Technology Professionals Forum
IVR	interactive voice response
KPI	key performance indicators
KPO	knowledge process outsourcing
MNCs	multinational corporations
NASDAQ	National Association of Securities Dealers Automated Quotation
NASSCOM	National Association of Software and Service Companies
NSE	National Stock Exchange (of India)
OCAI	organisational cultural assessment instrument

OHS	occupational health and safety
SIP	session initiated protocol
SLAs	service level agreements
R&D	research and development
UNI	Union Network International
UNITES Pro	Union of Information Technology Enabled Services Professionals

1

Introduction

Mohan Thite and Bob Russell

'Your call is important to us. Please hold the line and the next available operator will be with you shortly.' Most of us are familiar with this recorded message from call centres. It is also a message that has the potential to make or break a customer's relationship with an organisation, depending on how long one has to wait and how satisfactorily the call is resolved. In an increasingly global world, the call may be directed to just about anywhere, often without the knowledge of the customer. This book focuses on India, home to the largest number of off-shored call centres and commonly regarded as the 'electronic housekeeper of the world'.

In any service industry, customer service is mainly dictated by the quality of employees and call centres are no exception (Zeithaml et al. 1990). Despite technological advancements, the attitude and commitment of the customer service representatives (CSRs) are the key to 'customer delight'. Research on call centres indicates that where cost-minimisation is a dominant business approach, the work environment is generally fast-paced, routine, monotonous, tightly controlled and contains little scope for employee discretion. According to a recent global call centre study (Holman et al. 2007), the main distinction between such operations lies in the approach and philosophy taken towards human resource management (HRM). This includes decisions about the design of work, the adoption of progressive HR policies and practices and employee voice mechanisms, which are in turn influenced by institutional factors, business strategies and operational choices (Batt et al. 2005; Holman et al. 2007: 44). With outsourcing and offshoring being dominant trends in business process reengineering and India being a key player in business process outsourcing (BPO), it is very important to understand how BPO providers in India manage their human resources. The key message from recent empirical studies on Indian call centres/BPO is that human resources are at once the greatest strength and the greatest challenge confronting this new industry. Many of these studies are, however, based more on polemics and managerial rhetoric as opposed to systematic empirical investigation from different sides of the employment relationship. Currently, while there is a growing body of research on HRM in Indian call centres by several leading academics from around the world, there is no one publication that pulls these authors and their work together as a coherent, one stop source of information. This book intends to fill this important gap by advancing evidence-based understandings of the issues, challenges and strategies confronting HRM in the Indian call centre/BPO sector. It brings together significant, empirical and conceptual research work on employment relations in Indian call centres by leading academic researchers. These contributions are complemented by close-up views from industry practitioners and representatives in what we trust readers will find to be a useful compendium of cutting-edge work on these new work sites.

BACKGROUND

It has been exactly a decade since the first scholarly research on call centre work appeared (Baldry et al. 1998; Fernie and Metcalfe 1998). This kick-started a wide-ranging research effort that focused on such themes as working in the information economy and the nature of employment in new workplaces. Call centres continued to be popular venues for these endeavours, in part because of their rapid spread to the kinds of informational and service delivery activities that were generating so much new employment. As new workplaces they provided fruitful ground from which to study work and employment from a variety of theoretical perspectives and with a variety of interests in mind. Research on call centres began appearing in journals that were dedicated to the study of work and the labour process, HRM, technology and information systems, industrial and employment relations, management studies, sociology and organisational behaviour.[1] Three comprehensive edited collections have appeared over the last six years (Burgess and Connell 2006; Deery and Kinnie 2004; Holtgrewe et al. 2002), which along with the journal articles, have featured contributions on the nature of managerial control, employee representation, the gendering of work, the geography of work, organisational performance and employee behaviour in call centre work settings.

No sooner had the customer contact centre emerged than new lines of business that were specifically devoted to providing such services to other businesses sprang up. At first this was little remarked upon for the simple reason that the overwhelming majority of call centres remained internal business units. That is, they were established by pre-existing organisations (for example, banks, airlines, local councils, etc.) to meet their own requirements. What was obvious from the start was that in many cases they offered a new degree of spatial flexibility. They did not necessarily have to be contiguous to either business operations or to markets.[2] As a result, call centres quickly began to emerge in less highly populated regions, where unemployment was higher and labour and other costs such as building rents were cheaper (Richardson and Belt 2001; Richardson et al. 2000). This phenomenon of regionalisation or what some have referred to as 'near shoring' (see Carroll and Wagar in this volume) has been more or less contiguous with the growth of call centre employment, although it has been more apparent in some domestic markets rather than others.

It did not take long for these dynamics to extend beyond the national 'containers' in which they were first established. The same technologies that permitted info-service work to be hived off from other production operations and markets and sent to regional areas in search of cost advantages could be used to send such work offshore altogether. Just as call centres were becoming a trendy venue for research in the West, info-service work was on the move to even more 'far-away' locales in the East. For a variety of reasons, which are taken up in some of the chapters in this book, India was the largest recipient of this new investment in what is termed information technology enabled services (ITeS). This consists of both call centre and non-voice back-office services that are undertaken by the in-house operations of foreign multinational corporations (MNCs) (captives) as well as both foreign and domestic third-party providers. While the offshoring of interactive service work is certainly not restricted to India—the geography of info-service work is widely dispersed and includes the Philippines, China, South Africa, Israel and Malaysia—India has so far been the destination of choice and consequently undertakes the largest share of such work. This is the setting for this book.

STRUCTURE OF THE BOOK

Many of the contributions to this collection are either implicitly or explicitly concerned with the differences that the outsourcing of ITeS work makes. Put simply, does outsourcing require us to amend or re-think the conclusions that we have come to after a decade of research into such work in Western economies? The contributors to this book answer this important query in different but complementary ways. They adopt two different lines of enquiry. One examines the similarities and differences between call centre employment in India and in the Western countries from where outsourcing activity originates. This body of research focuses upon such matters as work designs and the expectations that are attached to them, HR practices and challenges and employee representation. A second related line of inquiry focuses upon the effects of such employment on the receiving economy and on the hundreds of thousands of workers who undertake it. To accommodate these divergent yet complementary approaches, the book is divided into three sections:

1. Indian Perspectives, presenting a front-line picture of employment relations and HRM in India.
2. Stakeholder Perspectives, focusing on the motives, strategic opportunities and constraints confronting management practitioners, trade unions and employees.
3. Comparative Perspectives, investigating the similarities and differences between Indian call centres and those located in a variety of other settings (United States, Canada and Australia).

We are fortunate in being able to present a unique volume that brings together chapters from well known academic contributors to the call centre literature and the voice of practitioners. We begin with the latter, with Catriona Wallace, an industry analyst, who sets the scene in India. Wallace's chapter provides a timely yet rich empirical 'curtain raiser' for the rest of the volume, benchmarking call centres in India with operations undertaken in other developed and developing locales. The overview that we get here is through the eyes of a critical consultant who is in a position to grapple with the challenges faced by this emerging industry and to draw our attention to likely developments over the coming years. In line with a major theme of the volume, Wallace's contribution pinpoints some of the unique HR issues that currently confront BPO in India.

The remaining chapters in this first section are all India-focused or present a perspective from within India. Thite and Russell present findings that combine employee surveys and detailed qualitative managerial interviews at four of India's largest outsourcing providers. To our knowledge, this is one of the largest sample surveys of BPO workers to have yet been conducted in India. They focus on core HR functions, including recruitment, training and retention practices and the oversight of occupational health and safety while going on to delve into the effects of these undertakings on various dimensions of employee engagement. The authors unearth a complex and contradictory situation in which strategic HR is successful in creating organisational engagement but largely unsuccessful in stemming a tide of attrition.

Further detail is added to this picture in the chapter by Budhwar, Malhotra and Singh. These authors employ data that has been gathered from open-ended qualitative interviews of workers at a large number of BPOs that are spread across both indigenous Indian firms and 'captive' multinational operations. Again, a mixed picture emerges that includes elements of job satisfaction with work design and organisational cultures, but also serious problems that are manifested in the high rates of attrition that preoccupy much of the HR function in BPOs.

While some of the chapters in this section are largely undertaken from the perspective of HR, Mirchandani provides a different optic by introducing us to a phenomenology of the BPO worker and integrating this within the larger context of global political-economy or what she refers to as 'globalisation from above'. Mirchandani provides rich evidence pertaining to the unique frustrations that participation in the BPO economy presents for a comparatively well off, university educated workforce as well as some of the ways in which such conditions are coped with. In doing so, she introduces a number of new theoretical constructs–locational masking, linguistic imperialism, temporal colonisation and scripted Taylorism–that further her project of attempting to understand BPO employment from the perspective of the worker. Her chapter elaborates upon the multidimensional challenges confronting HRM in this sector at the same time as it implicitly lays open a challenge to the HR project.

The chapters in the second section present analyses from the perspective of or are about different stakeholders in BPO activity. Again, we commence with a voice from the field, in this case HR practitioners from one of India's largest and most successful MNCs–Infosys. Readers ought to find this an informative chapter insofar as it provides a revealing look at how senior HR managers define issues and priorities in their work. The chapter highlights the dynamic quality of HR at Infosys BPO in meeting the business challenges of managing scale, execution, culture, risk, diversity and cost. It reveals the breadth and depth of progressive HR policies and practices that make firms like Infosys globally respected powerhouses and in the eyes of employees, 'compelling places to work'.

Until 2005, BPO firms in India were free of employee trade unions, in sharp contrast with Western call centres. Taylor, D'Cruz, Noronha and Scholarios, in their chapter, chart the founding and development of the Union of Information Technology Enabled Services Professionals (UNITES Pro) a new industry specific trade union which is charged with the mission of organising India's vast BPO sector. Through a unique large-scale survey of UNITES Pro members, the authors examine factors that are conducive to and obstacles to voluntarily joining a union in the Indian ITeS sector. The results provide a fascinating picture of existing union members in this sector, including their demographic characteristics, labour market intentions, the kinds of work they do, how they came to join the union and the reasons for doing so. Usefully, the authors present results separately for different types of BPO provider (for example, foreign captives, Indian third-party providers and domestic Indian centres). Specific sections of this chapter also examine union members' perceptions of working conditions, the role of HR in its relationship with employees and problems the union confronts in its organising plans.

The final chapter of Section Two examines the implications that outsourcing has for the management of careers through a detailed qualitative case study of a captive operation providing financial services to a UK-based parent company. Although captive operations are thought to offer better terms and conditions than Indian third-party and domestic providers, they have been particularly difficult to access for research purposes and consequently have been under-represented in academic research to date. In their chapter, Cohen, El-Sawad and Arnold probe into the meanings that are attached to commonplace notions such as careers and work–life balance. They find that these terms convey quite different things to workers in the context of Indian BPO work than they do to employees at a branch of the same company in the UK. Consequently, general theories of career management and work–life balance need to jettison the ethnocentricism that often informs what they take for granted. Cohen, El-Sawad and Arnold's contribution adds to our understanding of the subjective meanings that are attached by workers to the experience of working in an operation that carries out work on behalf of customers in the West in much the same manner as Mirchandani's chapter. It also presents a complementary approach to Russell and Thite's chapter that includes an analysis of an emerging occupational culture amongst BPO workers.

Section Three of the book introduces an explicitly comparative focus into the research agenda, but around different units of analysis and different themes. The contribution by Batt, Doellgast and Kwon provides a broad brushed comparative survey of American in-house, US-located outsourcers and Indian offshore providers (principally Indian-owned firms), focusing upon variation in work design/processes, training and development, compensation practices and the implications of this for attrition. Using establishment-level surveys, the authors are able to highlight contradictions that appear to be accentuated in the BPO employment model, including work design and monitoring practices which seem incongruent with the recruitment, selection and training regimes that are in place. This chapter raises the uncomfortable possibility of underemployment on a considerable scale, while introducing useful measurement constructs for the tasks it has set itself.

The following chapter by Russell and Thite covers comparable ground using employee surveys in the case study organisations introduced in Chapter Three and a matched sample taken from 20 different Australian call centres across a wide base of industries. The analysis of this chapter is informed by labour process and critical management theory and covers three substantive areas: work processes and required effort; job and employee skills; and participation in organisational culture and the effects of this on employee identities. Significant differences emerge around perceptions of expected work effort, different aspects of skill and the up-take of organisationally-sponsored culture with flow on effects onto the relationship between work and self-identity and actual behaviour in work. The implications are that BPO does differ substantially from domestic info-service operations. Such variation originates beyond HRM practice but may well demand quite different practices to those that have taken hold in Western operations.

Difference is also a key theme of the final chapter in the book by Carroll and Wagar where managerial perceptions across two units of one outsourcing company located in India and Canada respectively are compared. Indian managerial respondents attach greater importance to HR and its various functions, while the emphasis of organisational culture is differentially located at the two sites. Managers also perceive interesting differences in levels of employee satisfaction, stress and occupational health and safety, but not always in a manner that readers might expect. This study also introduces the neglected topic of managerial attrition into the discussion, an issue that is relevant to call centres in general and Indian BPO in particular.

The chapters in this collection, thus, cover some of the most important issues associated with the outsourcing of info-service work, including the labour process embedded in BPO, its control and management, the employment relations that are being constructed around it and the role of HRM in its rapid development. A notable strength of the collection is the diversity of theoretical paradigms, methodological approaches and consequently 'voices', which are represented in this volume. It is our hope that this will aid in deepening readers' understanding of managing human resources in a new and fast growing industry (info-services) and in a new context (offshoring).

NOTES

1. See Russell (2008) for a complete critical review of this genre of work.
2. Public sector contact centres, especially at local government or state level, are an exception to this point.

REFERENCES

Baldry, C., P. Bain, and P. Taylor. 1998. '"Bright Satanic Offices"': Intensification, Control and Team Taylorism', in P. Thompson and C. Warhurst (eds), *Workplaces of the Future*, pp. 163–83. Houndmills, UK: Palgrave.

Batt, R., V. Doellgast, H. Kwon, M. Nopany, and P. Nopany. 2005. *The Indian Call Centre Industry: National Benchmarking Report. Strategy, HR Practices and Performance*. Ithaca, New York: Cornell University.

Burgess, J. and J. Connell (eds). 2006. *Developments in the Call Centre Industry: Analysis, Changes and Challenges*. London: Routledge.

Deery, S. and N. Kinnie (eds). 2004. *Call Centres and Human Resource Management: A Cross-National Perspective*. Houndmills: Palgrave.

Fernie, S. and D. Metcalfe. 1998. *(Not) Hanging on the Telephone: Payment Systems in the New Sweatshops*. London: Centre for Economic Performance, London School of Economics and Political Science.

Holman, D., R. Batt, and U. Holtgrewe. 2007. 'The Global Call Centre Report: International Perspectives on Management and Employment'. Report of the Global Call Centre Network (US format). Available online at: http://www.ilr.cornell.edu/globalcallcenter/upload/GCC-Intl-Rept-US-Version.pdf (downloaded on 2 January 2008).

Holtgrewe, U., C. Kerst, and K. Shire (eds). 2002. *Re-Organising Service Work: Call Centres in Germany and Britain*. Aldershot, UK: Ashgate.

Richardson, R., V. Belt, and N. Marshall. 2000. 'Taking Calls to Newcastle: The Regional Implications of the Growth in Call Centers', *Regional Studies*, 4: 357–69.

Richardson, R. and V. Belt. 2001. 'Saved by the Bell? Call Centres and Economic Development in Less Favoured Regions', *Economic and Industrial Democracy*, 22(1): 67–98.

Russell, B. 2008. 'Call Centres: A Decade of Research', *International Journal of Management Reviews*, 10(3): 195–219.

Zeithaml, V.A., L.L. Berry, and A. Parasuraman. 1990. *Delivering Quality Service: Balancing Customer Perceptions and Expectations*. New York: Free Press.

SECTION ONE

INDIAN PERSPECTIVES

2

An Overview of the Indian Contact Centre Industry

Catriona Wallace

INTRODUCTION

In January 2007, we touched down at Bangalore Airport. As a regional analyst for the contact centre and BPO industries, this was my third trip to India in the past six months. This time, however, I was accompanied by three executives from the Unites States (US), visiting India for the first time to conduct the regional launch of their voice and data recording software for contact centres. As my guests emerged from the airport, they were first hit by the hot and humid night air, then the constant sound of car horns honking, and finally stood staring unbelievingly into the swarming sea of brown faces and cars. Their look of incredulity persisted as we drove into the heart of Bangalore, the business process outsourcing (BPO) capital of the world, dodging cattle and swerving cars. We passed midrise new corporate buildings, ramshackle Indian houses, Hindu temples, and finally arrived at a five-star hotel. The chief marketing officer said to me, 'I don't believe this place, it's so challenging.' I laughed and said, 'Welcome to India.'

This chapter will provide an overview of the Indian contact centre industry from the perspective of the Asia-Pacific region. Where possible, contact centre industry data from other countries will be provided as a means of comparison. The statistics referred to in this chapter are sourced from various reports prepared by researchers at callcentres.net, the central portal for the contact centre industry in the Asia-Pacific region. These reports can be accessed via the web links provided in the reference list. The sample for the primary reference cited in this chapter, the 2007 Asian Contact Centre Benchmarking Report, is 696 in-depth interviews with Asian contact centre executives who manage one or more contact centres in the region, including 107 interviews with contact centre managers based in India. A study of human resource management (HRM) in Asian contact centres is also referenced and includes a sample of 74 case studies of HR performance and practices in contact centres, including seven centres in India. The chapter begins with a broad profiling of the Indian contact centre industry and proceeds to examine some of the critical HRM challenges faced by the industry, such as recruitment and employee turnover.

PROFILE OF THE INDIAN CONTACT CENTRE INDUSTRY

Indian Contact Centre Market Parameters

In a country of 1,130,000,000 people, the Indian call or contact centre industry is estimated to be approximately 500,000 'organised' seats with a further half million 'disorganised seats'. This distinction between organised and disorganised is a terminology the Indians themselves use to differentiate between legitimate centres and the many fly-by-night call centres and BPOs that are set-up and dismantled shortly thereafter. The key contact centre cities in India are Delhi, Mumbai, Chennai, Hyderabad and Bangalore. As a point of size comparison, the Korean contact centre industry has over 300,000 seats, China has 230,000, Australia, 200,000, the Philippines, 140,000, Malaysia, 35,000, Thailand, 30,000, New Zealand, 27,000 and Singapore, 20,000 seats. Thus, India is the largest contact centre market in the region. The Asia-Pacific contact centre industry at a regional level is growing at about 22 per cent per annum in seat size.

Compared to other countries, such as the Philippines where the seat growth rate is about 33 per cent per annum, India's growth rate in seats, 16 per cent per annum, is proportionately lower and has been reducing year on year. Two-thirds of the Indian contact centre industry is outsourced or provided by third-party organisations and about one-third constitute captive or in-house contact centres. About 68 per cent of organisations with contact centres have only one contact centre in India, about 14 per cent have two centres and 18 per cent have three centres or more. The mean number of seats per organisation in India is 522 and this number is predicted to grow to 728 seats by the beginning of 2008.

About one-third of contact centres in India currently service international markets, with 22 per cent of contact centres servicing the United States of America (USA), 18 per cent service the United Kingdom (UK), 7 per cent service Australia, 3 per cent service Singapore, 2 per cent service a global customer base, 1 per cent service Hong Kong, 1 per cent service Japan and 1 per cent service New Zealand. About three-quarters of all Indian contact centres also service the domestic economy.

On average, one-quarter of calls into an Indian contact centre require agents to speak in a language other than the national language and eight in 10 centres require a proportion of agents to speak English to customers. About eight in 10 centres also require a proportion of agents to speak Hindi to customers. Other languages required in the Indian market are Kannada, Telugu, Spanish, Tamil, French, German, Italian and Malay.

In India, six in 10 contact centres operate seven days per week and one-third operate 24 hours a day, seven days per week (Wallace and Organ 2007a).

Transaction Handling

In India, of all contacts made by customers, potential customers or parties external to an organisation, 89 per cent are handled by the contact centre (including 81 per cent over the phone and 8 per cent on the web). Less significant channels include the sales force which handles only 6 per cent of all external interactions and the branch or retail networks which handle only 5 per cent of external contacts.

Across the Asia-Pacific region, the percentage of the total market constituting dedicated outbound contact centres is about 10 per cent. However, in India, the primary activity, at 39 per cent of contact centres, is providing outbound sales, which is a statistically significantly higher proportion than any other country in the region. The next most common Indian contact centre type is customer service at 29 per cent, inbound sales at 16 per cent, technical support at 11 per cent and collections at 4 per cent of contact centres.

An average contact centre in India handles 131,036 transactions per week. The larger centres (100+ seats) handle over 300,000 contacts per week. The share of transactions through each contact centre channel shows a considerable reliance on agents. Agents handle 45 per cent of all transactions that come through the contact centre with no automation, plus an additional 39 per cent of transactions after some functions have been handled by the interactive voice response (IVR) technologies. Email constitutes about 5 per cent of all transactions, speech recognition constitutes about 2 per cent and web channels handle about 2 per cent of total transactions.

Indian agents dedicated to inbound calls handle an average of 78 calls per shift per day. This compares to an Asia-Pacific regional average of 80 calls per day, but more than the Australian average of 70 inbound calls per day and less than the Chinese average which is 96 inbound calls per day.

Agents dedicated to outbound calls handle an average of 82 calls per shift per day, which is comparable to the regional average of 80 calls. As a point of comparison, Australian agents make 72 calls per day and Chinese agents make 94 calls per day (Wallace and Organ 2007a).

Contact Centre Budgets and Costs

On average, 50 per cent of the total contact centre budget in India is allocated to labour-related expenses including salaries, recruitment and training costs; 20 per cent of the budget is allocated to telecommunications and 18 per cent is allocated to technology expenses. This compares to 69 per cent of total contact centre budget dedicated to labour-related expenses in a country such as Australia.

The average operating cost per seat per annum in each key market in the region is set out in Table 2.1. These calculations are based on one seat, operating for a 12 hour shift, six days per week, and include all labour, telecommunications, technology and other expenses that enable a contact centre seat to operate.

These operating costs per seat across the region show that India has the second lowest operating cost at US$ 15,872, second only to China which has the lowest operating cost per seat of US$ 13,543. India also has the second lowest cost per transaction at US$ 0.30 per contact. This cost differential is why India remains a compelling location for outsourced contact centre work, and also why the Indian market is looking carefully at the role that the potentially massive Chinese market might play (Wallace and Organ 2007a).

Table 2.1:   Operating Costs per Seat per Annum

	Mean Costs (US$*)		
Country	Annual Cost per Seat	Hourly Cost per Seat	Cost per Transaction
Australia (N = 140)	124,248	33.19	2.76
New Zealand (N = 55)	104,648	27.95	2.33
India (N = 107)	15,872	4.24	0.35
China (N = 105)	13,543	3.62	0.30
Malaysia (N = 98)	34,779	9.29	0.77
The Philippines (N = 67)	18,086	4.83	0.40
Thailand (N = 65)	18,527	4.95	0.41
Singapore (N = 59)	66,998	18.46	1.54

Source: Wallace and Organ (2007a).
Note: *Exchange rate calculated as in January 2007.

Performance in Indian Contact Centres

Based on key performance metrics for contact centres, as set out in Table 2.2, India has a higher average speed of answer (ASA) (total time in queue divided by the total number of calls answered and includes both technology-handled calls as well as live agent calls) of 30 seconds compared to the regional average of 20 seconds; a marginally higher abandonment rate (percentage of calls abandoned before answering) of 9 per cent compared to the regional average of 8 per cent and a lower first call resolution (percentage of calls closed in the first call) rate of 67 per cent compared to the 77 per cent regional average and lower occupancy rate (talk time plus hold plus wrap time divided by log in time) of 74 per cent compared to the regional average of 78 per cent (Wallace and Organ 2007a).

Thus, from a regional comparative level, it may be argued that India is not performing as well against these key performance indicators, as other countries. However, it is interesting to note that the results in India compare closely with the two other outsourcing focused countries, the Philippines and Malaysia. Also, to be taken into account is that these are key inbound

Table 2.2: Asia-Pacific Contact Centre Performance Metrics, 2007

Country	Average Speed of Answer (Seconds)	Average Abandonment Rate (%)	First Call Resolution (%)	Occupancy Rate (%)
	Mean Scores			
Overall (N = 696)	20	8	77	78
Australia (N = 140)	34	4	77	78
New Zealand (N = 55)	22	6	78	72
India (N = 107)	30	9	67	74
China (N = 105)	7	12	83	84
Malaysia (N = 98)	19	10	73	74
The Philippines (N = 67)	26	10	73	75
Thailand (N = 65)	12	9	75	79
Singapore (N = 59)	29	6	81	74

Source: Wallace and Organ (2007a).

call metrics, and given that the Indian market has a sizable percentage of outbound centres, these metrics may be more difficult for the Indian industry to perform against than for the inbound focused industries such as in Australia or Singapore.

Thus, the Indian contact centre industry, as measured by seat size, is the largest in the Asia-Pacific region. The growth rate per annum, although lower than other countries in the region, is measured off a much higher base number of seats, which in raw seat numbers is still very significant growth. The Indian industry is distinguished from all other countries in the region, with the exception of the Philippines, due to its high percentage of outsourced contact centres as well as its high percentage of outbound contact centres. These two key differences make managing contact centres in India very difficult as there is a much greater HRM challenge experienced in outsourced and outbound centres, compared to captive and inbound or blended centres. The next section of this chapter will explore the HRM challenge in Indian contact centres.

HRM IN INDIAN CONTACT CENTRES

The challenge of managing HR in contact centres is a global issue. Indeed, across Asia-Pacific, excluding Thailand, all contact centre industries cite the number one management challenge as HRM (see Table 2.3) (Wallace and Organ 2007a). So, it is important to note that India is not alone in this regard, and that HRM is a critical regional problem.

Profile of Human Resources

At a regional level, 88 per cent of the contact centre industry comprises full-time employees and 12 per cent part-time employees. India has a similar ratio of 87 per cent full-time and 13 per cent part-time contact centre employees. Also, at a global

Table 2.3:   Asia-Pacific Contact Centre Industry Challenges

Country	Top Four Challenges in the Next 12 Months
Overall (N = 696)	HR (76%), Technology (59%), Customer service (52%), Sales (46%)
Australia (N = 140)	HR (84%), Technology (60%), Organisational change (44%), Sales (38%)
New Zealand (N = 55)	HR (89%), Technology (60%), Customer service (42%), Sales (38%)
India (N = 107)	HR (79%), Technology (65%), Sales (60%), Customer service (52%)
China (N = 105)	HR (66%), Customer service (55%), Technology (49%), Organisational change (47%)
Malaysia (N = 98)	HR (84%), Sales (66%), Customer service (62%), Technology (58%)
The Philippines (N = 67)	HR (82%), Customer service (67%), Technology (63%), Sales (58%), Finance (58%)
Thailand (N = 65)	Technology (66%), Customer service (65%), HR (34%), Sales (15%)
Singapore (N = 59)	HR (88%), Customer service (49%), Technology (48%), Sales (42%)

Source: Wallace and Organ (2007a).

and regional level, the contact centre industry comprises a majority of female agents (two-thirds of the total workforce). In India, the proportion of male agents is considerably higher, with 47 per cent of male customer service representatives (CSRs) and 53 per cent female agents. The majority of agents in India, 92 per cent, are aged between 18–34 years of age.

Base salary levels (excluding benefits and incentives, commissions, etc.) for contact centre agents, team leaders and managers across the region are set out in Table 2.4. Indian agents on average are paid an annual base salary of US$ 3,334, the second lowest salary level in the region. As a point of comparison, Australian agents are paid about US$ 31,000 and Chinese agents are paid about US$ 2,500 per annum. On average, Indian contact centres add 25 per cent to their agent's salaries for financial incentives and 15 per cent for overtime or shift allowances.

Across the Asian contact centre industry, the outsourced contact centres pay a lower average base salary to agents, at

Table 2.4: Base Annual Salary Levels: Regional Comparison

| | Mean Annual Base Salary (US$*) | | |
Country	Full-Time Agents	Team Leaders/ Supervisors	Contact Centre Managers
Australia (N = 140)	30,997	40,705	60,746
New Zealand (N = 55)	25,661	34,824	55,102
India (N = 107)	3,334	4,794	6,937
China (N = 105)	2,558	3,780	6,106
Malaysia (N = 98)	5,442	8,592	12,786
The Philippines (N = 67)	3,348	5,470	9,665
Thailand (N = 65)	3,656	6,336	11,222
Singapore (N = 59)	13,677	21,476	34,203

Source: Wallace and Organ (2007a).
Note: *Exchange rate calculated as in January 2007.

US$ 4,114 compared to US$ 4,754 for salaries paid to agents by in-house or captive centres (see Table 2.5) (Wallace and Organ 2007a).

The fact that outsourced centres pay lower salaries adds to the tensions of managing human resources in these centres. For many years management commentators have argued that money or remuneration is not a driver of employee satisfaction or commitment. We see now that this is an outdated argument. In particular, the Generation Y employees, those under 30 years of age (born between 1977 and 1990), are particularly driven by remuneration. In a contact centre employee study conducted by

Table 2.5: Base Annual Salary Comparisons: Outsourced vs In-house Centres: Asia

| | Mean Annual Base Salary (US$*) | | |
Country	Full-Time Agents	Team Leaders/ Supervisors	Contact Centre Managers
Asia (N = 501)	4,754	7,230	11,417
Asia In-house (N = 371)	4,975	7,637	12,266
Asia Outsourced (N = 130)	4,114	6,099	8,992

Source: Wallace and Organ (2007a).
Note: *Exchange rate calculated as in January 2007.

Wallace and Organ (2007b), 718 contact centre employees in Australia and New Zealand were surveyed and asked to nominate the key attributes of their job that would increase their happiness and commitment to the contact centre they worked in. The results were as follows: 70 per cent nominated 'increase in remuneration'; 36 per cent nominated 'career development'; 17 per cent nominated 'job variety'; 16 per cent nominated 'flexible work conditions'; 15 per cent nominated 'communication' and 14 per cent nominated 'recognition'. The study also shows that male contact centre workers are more highly motivated by remuneration than female workers, and given that the Indian industry has the highest proportion of Generation Y and male workers in the region, the remuneration attribute of their job becomes a critical factor.

On average, in India the ratio of contact centre manager or supervisor to agent, or span of control, is 1:8. This ratio is very similar to Australia's ratio of one manager or supervisor to seven agents and it is far lower than the Chinese ratio of one manager or supervisor to 29 agents.

New recruits in India receive on average 16 days training before starting work in the contact centre and experienced agents (who have more than 12 months tenure) receive on average 11 days of external or internal classroom training per year. Experienced agents also receive on average 19 days on the job training and seven days of e-learning training per year.

Only 3 per cent of contact centres in India allow their agents to telework (home-based agents), a trend which is becoming prevalent in mature contact centre industries such as in Australia which has close to 20 per cent of contact centres that have some home-based work.

Indian contact centre agents have a statistically significantly higher level of sick leave or unplanned absences, at 15 days per agent per annum, than any other country in the region. As a point of comparison, Australian agents take eight days unplanned or sick leave and Chinese agents take 11 days unplanned leave.

Recruitment Challenges

The Indian contact centre industry is facing significant recruitment challenges, as with other countries in the Asia-Pacific region. The predominant recruitment challenges in the region in order of magnitude are: (a) shortage of candidates with the right skill sets (85 per cent contact centre managers cite this difficulty); (b) shortage of candidates in the marketplace (57 per cent cite difficulties); (c) uncompetitive salaries (35 per cent cite difficulties); (d) unable to offer flexible work conditions (24 per cent cite difficulties); (e) unable to offer career paths (15 per cent cite difficulties) and (f) location of the contact centre (13 per cent cite difficulties) (Wallace and Organ 2007c).

In fact, this situation is so pressing currently that 86 per cent of contact centre managers in the Asia-Pacific region, including India, cited that they had candidates for contact centre agent positions refuse job offers and overall about 20 per cent of agent contact centre jobs that are offered to potential recruits in the region are declined.

Employee Turnover

In India, the mean attrition or turnover rate of full-time agents is 38 per cent and the mean attrition rate of part-time agents is 32 per cent. This rate is calculated at a centre level (not weighted for size of centre) rather than at a raw agent number level (the actual number of agents who left a contact centre as a percentage of the total base of agents), a calculation which results in a higher rate of turnover, over 50 per cent per annum. Comparative agent attrition levels, measured at the centre level are presented in Figure 2.1.

It is important to distinguish between voluntary and involuntary attrition of agents. In India, 62 per cent of agents who leave contact centres have done so by resigning; 14 per cent of those who leave are dismissed or retrenched; 12 per cent are transferred to other parts of the business and one in 10 agents

Figure 2.1:   Agent Attrition Level Measured at Centre Level (2007)

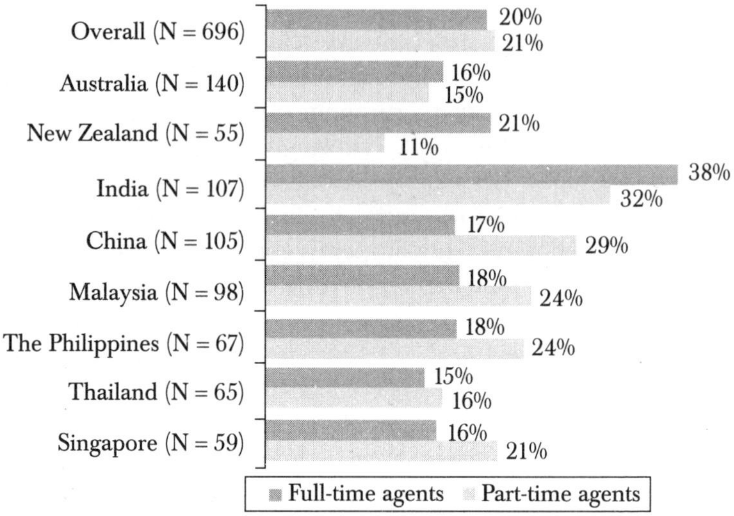

Source: Wallace and Organ (2007a).

did not renew their contract (Wallace and Organ 2007a). There is a statistically significantly higher level of agent turnover in outsourced centres in India and across the Asia-Pacific region with the average agent attrition rate for captive centres being 18 per cent per annum, compared to over 30 per cent in outsourced centres. This higher level of turnover in outsourced centres is tied to several factors including (a) a lower level of salary paid to outsourced contact centre workers, (b) a focus on outbound call types which are thought to be more stressful than most inbound work, (c) a higher percentage of male workers in outbound centres. Male contact centre workers tend to have lower levels of job satisfaction and a higher likelihood to turnover than female workers (Wallace and Organ 2007b).

Reflective of high agent attrition levels, agent tenure in India is also the lowest in the region at 11 months for full-time agents and nine months for part-time agents. Team leader and contact centre manager tenure is also lowest in the region at 14 months and 18 months respectively.

The costs of agent attrition in India are amplified by the replacement costs for agents, which on average in India is US$ 1,892 per agent which includes recruitment fees, training of a new agent and lost productivity. When looking at the statistically significant differences between those contact centres in Asia-Pacific, including Indian centres, with high agent turnover (>30 per cent per annum) and low agent turnover (<30 per cent per annum) some clear patterns emerge (Wallace and Organ 2007c). Centres with high turnover:

1. Are large contact centres with 100 seats or more.
2. Are significantly more likely to be in the outsource sector.
3. Have a significantly higher level of agent absenteeism.
4. Have a significantly higher proportion of younger agents (aged less than 25 years).
5. Have a higher proportion of male agents.
6. Pay agents a lower salary.

HRM Challenges

HRM in Indian contact centres is made perhaps more challenging than other countries because of several notable factors: (*a*) the industry is characterised by having a higher proportion of outsourced centres, (*b*) it also has a higher proportion of outbound centres where the work type is regarded as often being more difficult and perhaps less interesting than in inbound or captive centres, (*c*) the industry also pays comparatively low levels of remuneration, (*d*) it has a higher percentage of male workers and (*e*) it has a high proportion of young workers, or Generation Y employees. There is a statistically significantly higher level of agent absenteeism and attrition associated with each of these five factors (Wallace and Organ 2007a, 2007b).

To illustrate the difficult nature of managing human resources in an Indian contact centre, three Indian contact centres are profiled in the Appendix (Wallace and Organ 2007c). These case studies highlight the arguments made here that Indian contact centres are experiencing significant HR challenges, particularly the outsourced centres which are experiencing particularly high levels of agent turnover. The primary reasons why agents leave are a lack of remuneration and the most successful recruitment strategies also focus on offering higher salaries to potential recruits.

Future Trends

Despite this being the current state of affairs in Indian contact centres, the future, however, looks more positive. Changes to the Indian contact centre industry are likely to be driven by (*a*) advanced technology, (*b*) Generation Y consumer demands, (*c*) internet protocol (IP) enabled contact centres and (*d*) an increased move towards contact centres becoming profit centres. As such, the following predictions are made:

Advanced Technology

The continued advancement of contact centre technologies, such as workforce planning, quality monitoring, customer analytics and self-service technologies such as speech and web channels will assist in reducing operating costs, handle mundane and routine tasks and provide self-service options for customers. This should allow for better HRM, more interesting work and better service levels.

The Coming of the Generation Y Consumer

The Generation Y consumer, currently 16–30 years of age, are to date, history's most powerful consumers. Generation Y value connectivity through technology, are permanently connected to mobile devices, like to spend money and do not like to expend emotional or mental energy interacting with organisations.

Generation Y are happy to use self-service technology for routine and medium complexity transactions, they want mobile access, 24×7, and will change their preference to speak to an agent and choose to interact with technology if they are required to wait on hold (Wallace and Organ 2007d). Thus, service strategies will become more technology enabled to cater for this influential customer group, and hence less dependent on human resources, taking some pressure off of HRM.

The Virtual Contact Centre: Session Initiated Protocol (SIP)/Presence and Home-based Agents

The current pressure to continually differentiate service, reduce costs and manage human resources challenges will drive contact centres towards being virtual. Already a number of advanced IP enabled contact centres have dissolved the four walls of the standard contact centre and have virtual agents, either through: (*a*) session initiated protocol (SIP) and presence, where subject matter experts in the organisation can log on and register that they are 'present' to take calls, or (*b*) by routing overflow calls to other parts of the organisation, or (*c*) by having home-based agents. Companies with home-based agents, such as Unity 4 in Australia, which is an entirely virtual contact centre with many hundreds of agents, cite increased levels of agent satisfaction, low agent attrition, reduced operating costs and increased performance.

This trend is already evident in mature contact centre industries. By 2008, 20 per cent of Australian contact centres will allow home-based work and by 2010 it is predicted that about 30 per cent of contact centres globally will be working with some virtual capacity. IP enablement will be essential.

Contact Centres as Profit Centres

Many chief-level executives now realise the most cost-effective method of selling to customers is via the contact centre.

Currently in Australia 85 per cent of all revenue generated by the contact centre industry is from up-selling and cross-selling to inbound customers. In order to effectively generate revenue from a contact centre, the industry will need to focus on (a) increasing agent sales skills, (b) establishing a sales culture and (c) implementing technology which supports the sales process (Wallace and Organ 2007a). Although, today, two-thirds of all contact centres globally are still measured as cost centres, one-third already operate as profit centres and by 2010 this is expected to increase to 50 per cent being profit centres. Contact centres operating as profit centres rather than cost centres and functioning as the primary sales channel will result in resources being invested back into the contact centre, in particular into HRM.

If these four predictions eventuate, it is likely the HRM challenge in India will ease, and the contact centre industry's potential in this extraordinary country may be realised.

CONCLUSION

Echoing the remark of the US chief marketing officer visiting India for the first time, there is perhaps no more challenging industry anywhere than the Indian contact centre sector, particularly the outsourced centres, as they experience the most difficult tensions and contradictions.

In a country of over one billion people, the industry is challenged with finding suitable resources to staff its growing contact centres. Those people who come to work in an Indian contact centre will not stay for long, which affects service levels, knowledge management and general morale. Issues of remuneration, career and work variety are cited as the key reasons Indian agents leave. Why is this so acute in India?

Unlike almost every other country, India has a higher percentage of outsourced and outbound centres. In an industry that was originally created as an in-house service centre, India has had to pioneer the way in outsourcing and outbound calling. This has been very difficult. The outsource providers are under constant pressure by their client companies to reduce operating costs and increase service levels, and to remain competitive they must do so. In addition, client companies are demanding increased service levels and more recently, greater levels of up-selling and cross selling by agents. Thus the industry is caught in a critical management tension of reducing costs, increasing service and selling, and this tension is felt at the front line, at the expense of its HR. This tension has been previously described as the sacrificial HR strategy, whereby the employee's well-being and job satisfaction are sacrificed in order to achieve company objectives (Wallace et al. 2000). The concept of a sacrificial HR strategy would seem to be particularly apropos in regards to the Indian call centre industry.

Our analysis shows that the Indian contact centre industry, particularly the outsourced sector, appears to have significant competitive advantage compared to other nations in the region. India is able to attract outsourced business due to its low cost structures, largely driven by its low cost human resources, reasonably high skill levels, advanced technologies and a mostly reliable telecommunications infrastructure. However, the component of this equation now under threat is its human resources. India is inflicted with significant human resource issues, the most acute in the region. Upward pressure on wages and high employee attrition which has processional effects on customer service and knowledge retention, are eroding the existing competitive advantage India has. Thus, India is at risk of losing its dominant position as the preferred outsourcing location for contact centre work in the region. Indeed the Philippines has already won outsourced work from India and China is gearing up to play a significant role in the outsourcing sector. Subsequently, further opportunities and continued growth in the contact centre and BPO sectors will only be fully realised if India immediately addresses its HRM challenges.

The statistics presented in this chapter provide an insight into the Indian contact centre and outsourcing sector. Given the depth and complexity of this industry, in this rapidly developing nation, such an analysis only provides a high-level assessment of the current situation. To fully understand this challenging industry, further in-depth research to identify the economic, cultural, social and business influences on these industries is required.

APPENDIX: INDIAN CONTACT CENTRE CASE STUDIES

Case Study 1: Indian Contact Centre—IT Industry

This centre in India is in the IT industry and has about 133 agents. The centre takes blended calls, that is, both inbound and outbound calls. Agent attrition is well over 20 per cent per annum, but the contact centre manager regarded this as good practice in comparison to other centres. The manager stated that the length of tenure for those who have left the contact centre recently is about four months. The primary reason the contact centre manager cites for agent turnover is a lack of re-muneration. The most successful method used to retain agents has been to offer financial incentives and reward programmes for the agents. The contact centre manager also stated that the primary recruitment challenges were (*a*) a general shortage of candidates in the marketplace and (*b*) a shortage of candidates with the right skill set. This contact centre intends to recruit another 200 agents in the ensuing six months and regards the most effective recruitment practices to be offering higher salaries, offering incentives and career development.

Case Study 2: Indian Contact Centre—Outsourcer A

This Indian contact centre was a small outsourced centre, of 30 agent positions, who handled blended calls. Turnover for both full-time and part-time agents was over 30 per cent per annum. Full-time tenure for those agents who had recently resigned was three months for full-time agents and two months for part-time agents. The primary reason the contact centre manager cited for agents leaving this centre was that the employees did not intend to pursue a career in the contact centre industry. The key methods cited that had been successful in this centre for retaining agents included financial incentives and paying above market rates. The contact centre manager stated that they were experiencing difficulty in recruiting agents due to (a) a general shortage of candidates in the marketplace and (b) a shortage of candidates with the right skill set. This centre intended to double its size within six months and regarded the most successful recruitment strategies as bringing the recruitment process in-house, offering higher salaries and offering incentives.

Case Study 3: Indian Contact Centre—Outsourcer B

The third case study is a large outsourced contact centre with 9,500 agents who handle blended calls. Agent attrition was about 45 per cent per annum and the length of tenure was about nine months for full-time agents. Lack of remuneration was regarded as the primary reason agents were leaving this centre and the key methods to retain agents were offering financial incentives and flexible working conditions. The contact centre manager stated that they intended to recruit another 700 agents over the next six months and currently were suffering the recruitment challenges of (a) a general shortage of candidates in the marketplace, (b) a shortage of candidates with the right skill set and (c) offering uncompetitive salaries. The most successful recruitment initiatives to date have been bringing the recruitment process in-house, offering higher salaries and offering career development options.

REFERENCES

Wallace, C.M., G. Eagleson, and R. Waldersee. 2000. 'The Sacrificial Human Resource Strategy in Call Centres', *International Journal of Service Industry Management*, 11 (2): 174–85.

Wallace, C.M. and J.M. Organ. 2007a. 'callcentres.net 2007 Contact Centre Industry Benchmarking Report: Asia-Pacific'. Available online at: http://www.callcentres.net/CALLCENTRES/LIVE/Resources/Documents/callcentresnetAPACReport.pdf

Wallace, C.M. and J.M. Organ. 2007b. 'callcentres.net & Kelly Services 2007 Contact Centre Industry Employee Satisfaction Report'. Available online at: http://www.callcentres.net/CALLCENTRES/LIVE/Resources/Documents/callcentresnetEMPSAT.pdf

——. 2007c. 'callcentres.net 2007 Asian Contact Centre Industry Human Resource Management, Turnover and Recruitment Report'. Available online at: http://www.callcentres.net/CALLCENTRES/LIVE/Resources/Documents/callcentresnetAsianHRMReport.pdf

——. 2007d. 'callcentres.net and Nuance 2007 Speech Recognition Customer Satisfaction Report'. Available online at: http://www.callcentres.net

3

Human Resource Management in Indian Call Centres/Business Process Outsourcing

Mohan Thite and Bob Russell

INTRODUCTION

Customer contact/call centre services are now the most used form of customer interface and present the 'personality of the firm to the customer over the phone' (Belt et al. 1999). They are one of the fastest growing parts of the information/service economy with employment constituting anywhere from 1–3 per cent of total employment in the United States (US) and Europe (Batt and Moynihan 2002). Contact centre service settings differ from conventional manufacturing work in important ways. The relative non-tangibility of output, lower levels of inter-dependence among workers, consumers as co-producers and the simultaneity of production and consumption (no re-work) (Batt and Moynihan 2006; Lovelock 2005) add complexity to the concept of quality in info-service work. To this list we can also add the phenomena of globalisation, that is, the outsourcing and offshoring of interactive service work.

There has been considerable debate as to the nature of the employment that is being created in call centres, or conversely the type of employment that is required for this form of service delivery (Russell 2004). For some, call centre service delivery represents the arrival of mass production techniques to the realm of service provision. Automated delivery of work, short job cycles, consisting of highly repetitive work activity and new capacities for electronic monitoring create new 'assembly lines in the head' (Bain et al. 2002; Callaghan and Thompson 2001; Taylor and Bain 1999). Others argue that mass production models are inappropriate for the production and distribution of information. Consequently, a new paradigm of mass customisation is being created, which demands a more skilled workforce, with analytical problem solving, communication and computer skills (Frenkel et al. 1998, 1999; Korczynski 2001, 2002). In particular, call centres are viewed as appropriate sites for the development of high performance work systems, where the exercise of skill and commitment are rewarded with better jobs and performance related forms of remuneration (Batt 1999, 2000, 2002; Kinnie et al. 2000). Such work systems dovetail with market segmentation strategies and in particular with relational as opposed to transactional work with an organisation's clients (Hutchinson et al. 2000).

While these debates continue, an even more recent phenomenon has been the business process outsourcing (BPO) of call centre services to countries such as India. This represents a true globalisation of info-service work, where transnational companies outsource customer service work to agents in third countries. BPO is a direct result of business process re-engineering whereby firms decide on what activities to undertake themselves based on their core competencies and outsource the rest, either by setting up their own 'captive' centres offshore or enter into strategic agreements with third-party business partners around the world to lower their transaction costs or improve synergies (Thite 2008). The third-party service providers in turn may set up onshore, near-shore or offshore centres depending on where they can maximise synergies (Srivastava and Theodore 2006). In the Indian info-service context, these services come under the umbrella of information technology enabled services (ITES) and include call centres, BPO and, recently, knowledge process outsourcing (KPO) that combines IT with knowledge embedded in software. This chapter relates to Indian call centres within the context of offshored ITES/BPO. In 2006–2007, the Indian ITES/BPO industry yielded an export revenue of US$ 8.4 billion at an annual growth rate of 33.5 per cent and an employment base of nearly half a million (NASSCOM 2008).

Human resources (HR) are regarded as the key, sustainable and difficult to imitate competitive advantage in any service sector. Therefore, attracting, developing, retaining and engaging talent are crucial to the survival and growth of any service-oriented firm. This chapter focuses on the strategic and operational aspects of human resource management (HRM) in the Indian call centre/BPO sector. We begin with the macro analysis of key HR issues, challenges and strategies followed by an operational overview. We then introduce our research methodology that taps into both managerial and employee perspectives on certain key aspects of HR delivery, namely, recruitment, training, remuneration, career management and occupational health and safety. We then focus on two crucial outcomes of HRM, namely, employee relations and engagement. The chapter concludes with a discussion of research findings and their implications for HR theory and practice.

STRATEGIC HR ISSUES IN INDIAN CALL CENTRES

Many call centres focus on cost minimisation, measured by efficiency metrics, such as call handling time and number of customers handled per employee. When this focus translates to HR systems with low levels of employee training, employee discretion and incentives, the likely result is high absenteeism and turnover (Deery et al. 2002). The global call centre industry is, therefore, often plagued by high employee turnover and customer dissatisfaction (Batt and Moynihan 2006). This is more so with outsourced or offshore call centres where subcontractors are under intense pressure to contain costs and are, therefore, less likely to invest in employees (Batt et al., in this volume).

The most widely accepted dimensions of service quality in call centres are: tangibles, reliability, assurance that the customer has about the service, responsiveness to customer demands and empathy towards the customer (Zeithaml et al. 1990). The latter three dimensions account for almost 60 per cent of customer satisfaction scores and are primarily driven by the ability of employees to respond to customers. In a survey of 64 US-based call centres, Batt and Moynihan (2006) concluded that investment in HR systems, including training, employee discretion-oriented work designs and incentives lead to higher service quality and higher net revenues per call. Another study of UK call centres indicated that affective organisational commitment followed by job satisfaction had a significant impact on service quality delivered (Malhotra and Mukherjee 2004).

Many writers have characterised call centre work with dramatic labels such as 'electronic panopticons' and 'dark satanic mills of the 21st century' (Fernie and Metcalf 1998; Garson 1988). However, contrary to such stereotyped images, employee well-being in call centres is found to be similar to that in other comparable forms of work and is associated with effective job design, less intense and development-oriented performance monitoring and supportive team leadership (Holman 2002, 2003). Similarly, Zapf et al. (2003) found that call centre jobs, particularly, outbound activities, were less stressful with regard to job stressors, thanks to better organisation and investment in information technologies.

Against this global backdrop, India provides a unique mix of strategic and operational HR issues and challenges. In relation to its competitors (such as China, Israel, Ireland and east European countries), India enjoys an excellent climate for BPO offshoring, underpinned by an educated and English-speaking labour pool, cheap labour costs and government support (Mehta et al. 2006). BPO in India is a youthful industry in more ways than one. The workforce is composed almost entirely of young university graduates with an annual national supply of around 3 million per year. This scenario has been a major selling feature for the industry. Young, highly educated and ambitious cohorts are said to make for dedicated, committed professionals (D'Cruz and Noronha 2006; Noronha and D'Cruz 2006), exactly the kinds of workers that interactive customer service requires.

Yet, in spite of what could be taken as highly favourable conditions for selection, recruitment and the further development of BPO, employee turnover, has quickly become the number one challenge facing the burgeoning industry (Budhwar et al. 2006a). According to a global call centre report, Indian call centres have the highest employee turnover of 40 per cent against a global average of 20 per cent and almost 60 per cent of employees have less than one year of tenure at work (Holman et al. 2007). Similarly, Wallace reports in her chapter in this book that a comparative analysis of call centres in the Asia-Pacific region including China, India, the Philippines, Australia, Malaysia and Singapore reveals that while India had the second lowest average full-time customer service agent annual salary (US$ 3,334) behind China, it had the greatest level of agent attrition (38 per cent) and lowest average employee tenure (11 months).

Clearly, human resources are both the greatest strength and challenge to Indian BPO firms. At the strategic level, India will continue to reap the benefits of growth in the outsourcing phenomenon, that now includes KPO, but will continue to struggle with rising costs, operational problems and intense competition, squeezing its profit margins (Mehta et al. 2006; Thite and Russell 2007).

Operational HR Issues in Indian Call Centres

The trends noted here have a number of implications for the delivery of HRM in the call centre/BPO industry. First, it means that a great deal of HR activity is occupied with the recruitment and selection function. This may have implications for resourcing other elements of HR such as ongoing training and career development. Second, high turnover rates impact productivity and production costs. When a significant proportion of the workforce is in learning mode, it is difficult for an organisation to optimise productivity. Moreover, as workers become more experienced, the costs of providing a unit of service should diminish. Although service level agreements (SLAs) may reflect these assumptions, they are much more difficult to attain when attrition rates are high. The current situation in BPO poses an intriguing paradox. The competitive advantage that Indian BPO is thought to leverage is premised upon low cost, but dedicated professional labour. But as we have seen, turnover rates are not only high, but considerably above estimates of call centre attrition in the West as well in the rest of the Asia-Pacific region.

There is a distinct dichotomy in the way Indian call centre employees are portrayed in the business and the HRM literature. The business press heaps praises on the service quality, productivity, professionalism and high skills of Indian call centre agents (Taylor and Bain 2003), whereas researchers point to the difficulties and bitter experiences these agents often face in servicing overseas clients, such as working on mostly graveyard shifts, locational masking and having to assume Westernised pseudonyms (Mirchandani, in this volume), which entails organisational control over employee identity (D'Cruz and Noronha 2006). The ill-effects of an extreme version of the mass production model (Taylor and Bain 2005) and physiological and psychological ill-health (Ramesh 2004) are also frequently cited outcomes. In service jobs that involve emotional labour, work-related factors, such as lack of autonomy, length of tenure, working hours, workload and lack of variety can lead to emotional exhaustion and absenteeism (Deery et al. 2002; Wharton, 1993). The inherent negative characteristics of offshored call centre work with high performance monitoring and low job discretion are said to contribute to employee dissatisfaction and therefore, turnover (Batt et al. 2005).

Indian BPOs exhibit formal, structured and rationalised HRM systems that include tightly controlled structures with a customer focus, a strategic role played by the HRM function and several employee involvement and commitment work practices (Budhwar et al. 2006a and Budhwar et al. in this volume). More broadly, some researchers have suggested that call centres use HRM in ways that combine job satisfaction with high levels of control in a 'fun and surveillance' complex (Kinnie et al. 2000). Other aspects of call centre HRM such as strategic recruitment and selection (Callaghan and Thompson 2002), comprehensive training programmes and secure employment may have the same effect of merging low discretion work processes with high commitment HR practices, although success (higher commitment, lower turnover) is not necessarily guaranteed (Houlihan 2002; Mulholland 2002). In the domain of call centres, desirable HR practices are said to consist of teamwork, relatively skilled work and incentivised remuneration systems (Batt 2000). Shah and Bandi (2003) report upon a similar culture amongst the help desk call centre workers they studied. Training, continuous learning and progression to more challenging responsibilities at this case study site lent an aura of true professional work to the activities undertaken at this BPO provider. Another study among software professionals in India revealed that 'HRM practices such as an employee-friendly work environment, career development, development-oriented appraisal, and comprehensive training show a significant positive relationship with organisational commitment' (Paul and Anantharaman 2004: 77).

Employee engagement is a recent addition to the battery of HR outcome measures in contemporary organisations, underpinned by a resource-based view of competitive advantage within and between firms (Frank et al. 2004). It is defined as 'employees' willingness and ability to help their company succeed, largely by providing discretionary effort on a sustained basis' (Towers Perrin 2005: 9). It involves various aspects of employee contribution in not just meeting but exceeding the goals by 'going the extra mile' through emotional and psychological engagement. A global workforce study revealed that in India, only 7 per cent of employees were highly engaged, 37 per cent were moderately engaged and 56 per cent were disengaged (Towers Perrin 2006). A study of employee engagement in Indian ITES employees found that employees showed low levels of engagement at the beginning and at completion of 16 months with the organisation but showed high engagement levels during the intermediate stages, indicating limited retention potential of a good level of employee engagement (Bhatnagar 2007). In the light of high employee turnover in Indian call centres, it would be worthwhile to ascertain employee perceptions of engagement measures, such as knowledge sharing, concern for co-workers and attitudes to demands over and above the normal workload.

METHODOLOGY

As aptly described by Batt et al. (in this volume), studies on Indian call centres are guided more by 'heated debate than systematic em-pirical investigation'. Many of these initial studies were based on interviews with managers (Batt et al. 2005; Taylor and Bain 2005); however, some studies have emerged recently involving surveys/interviews with field agents or customer service representatives (CSRs) (Budhwar et al. 2006a, 2006b; D'Cruz and Noronha 2006). In the study reported here, we adopt a holistic approach to our research on Indian call centres, first, by considering a wide range of work and employment aspects both at macro and micro levels and second, by covering both managers and employees. By capturing the 'employee voice', we are able to better evaluate the effectiveness of HR measures, rather than relying on the managerial rhetoric, as is often the case with studies mostly based on managerial interviews.

We began our research in mid-2005 by conducting preliminary interviews of Indian call centre managers to better understand the realities of offshored call centre work and to build a case for their participation. Based on this feedback, we fine-tuned our interview protocols and employee survey questionnaire to better reflect the unique aspects of call centre employment. The Indian BPO industry is very reluctant to provide access for data collection, particularly from employees, for a variety of reasons, including political sensitivity surrounding outsourcing in Western countries, confidentiality agreements with overseas clients and negative reports in the Indian media about the ill-effects of call centre employment. Therefore, we adopted a case study approach and managed to convince four large Indian BPO firms to participate in the study by tapping into our personal, academic and industry networks. A total of 15 HR and operations managers participated in the interview sessions and 638 CSRs took part in the survey.

The managerial interviews entailed the use of two protocols, one for the HR management team and the other for the operations management side of the business. These sessions sought to elicit more detailed data on employee costs, work design, recruitment challenges and general business profiles and relations with clients. The interview sessions were held sometimes with one manager and sometimes with the manager and other members of his/her team. Interview notes were taken at these meetings and observer triangulation was employed for each session.

The employee survey contains five sections, composed of both Likert scale questions and other close-ended queries that were developed by the authors specifically for the Indian call centre/BPO sector. The sections include a general biographical section, training (both initial and ongoing), career intentions, work organisation (pace and intensity of work, performance monitoring, job discretion, work skill requirements), workplace relations (work teams, social activities, discretionary behaviours) and occupational health and safety (OHS). For the purpose of this chapter, we cover selected aspects of our data, namely, recruitment, training, career aspects, OHS, employee relations and engagement.

Case Study Organisation and Employee Profile

All four case study organisations in our study are indi-genous third-party providers and 100 per cent subsidiaries of some of the largest Indian IT companies. They provide front- and back-office services to the customers of overseas' clients. As BPO providers they offer whatever ITES the principle client needs. If these capabilities are not ready at hand, they will be developed in very short order through strategic recruitment and hiring. This business logic dictates amongst other things: the size of Indian customer contact operations; the internal structure of operations and the design of work flows and jobs. By comparative standards, Indian BPO providers can only be classified as large companies in their own right. Employment at the time of our study at the four centres ranged from 1,700 to 12,500 CSRs. Workers are employed across multiple sites, located in different cities, with the largest provider occupying seven different facilities in five major cities.

Following on from their raison d'etre and their size is the multi-functional character of operations. In the literature on call centres it is common to distinguish between inbound customer service and outbound centres, as well as between front office customer care and back-office processing. The Indian operations include all of these within the notion of BPO. For example, amongst the companies included here, one divided its workforce on a 40:40:20 basis between inbound, outbound and back-office work respectively. In another, the workforce was split exactly in half between voice services and back-office work, while the largest company in the study classified 60 per cent of its employees as call centre CSRs. In the remaining company, only 20 per cent of its 5,300-strong workforce was involved in voice-based call centre work. Once again, the idea is to supply whatever services the foreign business client desires and in the mix that is required.

Each of the companies examined here had numerous overseas clients and this adds to the complexity of understanding the business model and how it works as compared to the in-house contact centres that predominate in the West. Overseas business clients cover a broad array of undertakings, including financial services (banking and insurance), healthcare, telecommunications, internet service and IT service/support. Some companies try to leverage off of their parent companies' expertise by offering IT servicing as a speciality, while others do not privilege any particular sector and take on business as it becomes available.

The business profiles associated with BPO activity also determine the internal organisation of work. Teams are associated with specific clients and services. Although team size is similar to in-house call centres in the West (that is, around 15 CSRs per team), the overall size of the centres and number of business principles served makes for huge numbers of teams. For example, one of the companies included here was organised around between 200 and 220 CSR process teams spread across three sites. Clients and teams are equated to business processes and each process has its own targets/key performance indicators (KPIs) as agreed to with the principle in SLAs. This means that there are no common metrics in Indian contact centres; each process/contract contains its own quantitative and qualitative targets as agreed to by the principal and the BPO provider.

Our study covered 638 CSRs, also known as process executives. Seventy-two per cent did not have previous experience as a CSR. On an average, these employees had put in 11 months of service with the employer they worked for at the time of the survey. Only 28 per cent of them had previous call centre experience. Sixty-four per cent of them worked in an inbound call area, 16 per cent in an outbound area and 20 per cent in both. Ninety-eight per cent were full-time employees. In terms of gender, 61 per cent were males. Ninety-two per cent were under 30 years of age and only 7 per cent were in the age group of 30–40. Eighty-three per cent were singles and never married. Ninety per cent of the CSRs had a graduate qualification, of which 23 per cent were postgraduates.

RESULTS

Recruitment

In the managerial interviews, talent attraction was frequently quoted as one of the key HR challenges facing the Indian call centre/BPO industry. The BPO industry took off in India in 2002 and has been growing at double the rate of the IT industry since then and, therefore, has had less time to mature and manage scalability. During its initial growth period, the recession in the IT industry augured well to attract talent for BPO firms, but since then not only has the IT industry recovered but other sectors in the Indian economy, such as leisure and recreation, aviation and infrastructure, started showing strong growth resulting in a strong demand for talent and lower standards applied during recruitment.

The managers stated that the main recruitment challenges for the call centre/BPO industry include employability/trainability of prospective employees as well as the negative employment image and social stigma associated with the industry, in terms of night shift working, work stress and monotonous and routinised work. For instance, one of the firms covered in our study needed to recruit 300 CSRs every month but found only six out of every 100 interviewees employable and 25 per cent of its employee turnover was involuntary arising out of employment terminations based on poor performance. Moreover, 50 per cent of voluntary turnover at this firm occurred in the first 90 days.[1] In all of the firms in our study, marriage was one of the main reasons for employee turnover as married employees, particularly women, found it difficult to continue to work on night shifts. Call centre employment is not seen as a stable, long-term, socially prestigious employment; rather it is viewed as an ad hoc, low esteem job.

In our study, 32 per cent of the CSRs had obtained employment via an employment agency, 26 per cent through newspaper/internet advertisements, 19 per cent via employee referrals and 18 per cent had approached the employer on their own. Campus recruitment is growing as a key means of recruitment (refer to Nandita Gurjar's chapter in this volume). In terms of the typical recruitment process, the initial screening is done based on resumes. Graduates in any discipline are preferred. Final selection is based on an aptitude test, group discussion and personal interviews conducted by team leaders and the HR department. The process normally takes one week. Once a candidate is rejected, he/she may be put on hold and not allowed to appear for another test for six months. In the light of recent cases of employee fraud, some firms conduct reference checks for integrity and criminal record.[2]

Training

The induction training is very important to the Indian call centre/BPO firms as most employees have no prior experience. Typically, it varies from four to six weeks. In one firm, the induction training lasts for eight weeks and is divided into pre-process, process and nesting phases. The pre-process training involves communication and cultural training for two to three weeks, followed by a product based process training for four to six weeks and concludes with on-the-job training (nesting phase) for three weeks.[3] In another firm, the initial training lasts one month and comprises voice, language and process training.[4]

According to the employee survey, 51 per cent of respondents believed that the induction training was equally divided between classroom and on-the-job instruction and mainly conducted by in-house trainers (69 per cent) asked to nominate the importance of various training topics by the amount of time devoted to them, 42 per cent indicated that product knowledge acquisition was most important, 16 per cent cited software/systems training, 12 per cent customer service, 10 per cent quality process and 8 per cent social skills adeptness. Contrary to media reports, language training and inter-cultural preparation were rated as the most important aspects of BPO training by comparatively samll proportions of the sample (8 per cent and 3 per cent, respectively). Nearly 50 per cent of employees stated that they received additional ongoing training and that they could nominate themselves to receive additional training.

In terms of employee satisfaction with training, the response was very positive with regard to the adequacy of training, efficiency of trainers, split between classroom and on-the-job training and accessibility for additional training when required (see Table 3.1).

Table 3.1: Employee Satisfaction with Training

Item	Agree (%)	Disagree (%)	Neutral (%)
The trainer(s) at this company do a good job.	85	6	9
The split between classroom and on-the-job training was about right.	69	12	17
The initial training that I received at this company was adequate for me to meet the expectations of my job.	74	13	13
I am given adequate training when new products and services are introduced.	74	10	13
I can access additional training if I don't think I am adequately responding to customer questions.	63	10	17

Remuneration/Employee Costs

Managerial interviews revealed that the employment costs in the four firms covered in our study varied between 60–70 per cent of total costs. The typical breakdown of employment costs was: 30 per cent fixed salary, 15 per cent incentive payments, 15 per cent transportation costs to and from home, 6–8 per cent food vouchers and the remaining for full or partially subsidised dormitory accommodation, recruitment and training costs and technology expenses.

The employee survey contained limited items on remuneration and rewards. Employees indicated that satisfaction with wages was the 'most important reason' for them to stay in the job and conversely, to leave the job (see the next section). This clearly indicates the importance of remuneration in motivating employees. Further, 78 per cent of employees in our survey indicated that 'any performance bonuses that I receive at this call centre are important to me' and also 54 per cent of them wished that they had more performance competitions.

Career Management

Our research questions under this section included performance management processes, career pathing and progression. In one of the firms covered in our study, performance appraisal is conducted every six months while job-level feedback is given every month. 360-degree feedback is obtained for senior people. Bell curve is applied to the evaluation process and each employee is provided with individual rating as well as comparative rating. Appraisal feeds into identification of training needs drawing up a training plan. Appraisal is used for promotions, variable pay and increments. Balanced scorecard methodology is followed by incorpor-ating team goals.[5]

According to HR managers, career pathing is a very important challenge in terms of employee retention. Most companies in the industry promote from within but obviously there is a limit to the number of employees who could be promoted to team leader positions and above. The managers found it frustrating that many employees expected promotion based on tenure and believed that promotion meant no more telephone handling and only supervision. In the words of one manager, 'the BPO industry lacks the flexibility of IT industry in providing job enrichment, job enlargement, job rotation and task variety as motivational measures'.[6] In one firm, horizontal movement across processes and clients was one way to address monotony on the job.[7] From the managerial point of view, the main problem with employee retention is that call centre employment is not seen as a career. Going up the value chain is seen as one way to engage and retain employees. However, specialist call centre services in data mining, accountancy, equity research and other specialised services require special domain knowledge and expertise and are out of bounds for generalists which most CSRs are.[8]

When asked 'whether you see yourself staying in your current job for the next three years', 38 per cent of employees said yes; 26 per cent said no and 36 per cent were unsure. Combining no and unsure responses, the potential employee turnover amounts to 62 per cent over three years. When asked to nominate the 'most important factor in your decision to stay in your job', 27 per cent of employees nominated satisfaction with wages, 20 per cent enjoyment of the work and 17 per cent chances for advancement. These were followed by workers who suggested employment security (13 per cent), lack of other career opportunities (8 per cent), flexible working hours (7 per cent), fair treatment from management (5 per cent) and friendships at work (4 per cent) as the most important reason for staying. Similarly, when asked 'what is the most important factor that might motivate you to look for other career options', not surprisingly, dissatisfaction with wages topped the list (39 per cent) followed by lack of chances for advancement (22 per cent) and the routine/boring nature of job (7 per cent).

Occupational Health and Safety

According to our employee survey, at the end of a working day, 34 per cent of employees felt 'quite tired or drained', 41 per cent felt 'moderately tired' and 25 per cent felt 'not particularly tired'. Workers characterised this tiredness equally between physical fatigue and mental/emotional tiredness. When asked 'whether you ever suffer from stress or symptoms of stress that are induced by your work situation', 45 per cent said yes, 38 per cent said no and 18 per cent were unsure. In terms of the 'three most important sources of stress', employees nominated performance targets (29 per cent), working during odd hours (21 per cent) and call volumes (16 per cent). The only other notable stressor was 'repetitive work' (13 per cent).

As illustrated in Table 3.2, in regard to the various aspects of emotional labour attached with their jobs, only a minority felt depressed (19 per cent), had no desire to talk to others at the end of the shift (25 per cent) and considered their job as important to their emotional well-being (41 per cent). On the physical aspects of their work environments, employees were happy with the noise levels and the standard of equipment used but only 46 per cent felt that management considered OHS as a priority.

Table 3.2: OHS

Item	Agree (%)	Disagree (%)	Neutral (%)
This job leaves me feeling depressed.	19	46	30
My work area is very noisy making it hard to listen to callers.	17	41.5	23
My workstation and the equipment I use is of a high standard.	61	16	20
At the end of my shift, I don't feel like talking to anyone.	25	51	22
This job is important to my emotional well-being.	41	17	34
Occupational health and safety takes priority with management at this call centre.	46	20	30

Employee Relations

In this section, we probed employees about the quality of their relationship with their employer in terms of trust and recognition and representation of employee voice. Normally trade unions are a potent symbol of employee voice in the workplace, as is generally the case with the call centres in the West; however, when asked whether there was a trade union representation in their workplace, 74 per cent of employees said no and only 30 per cent believed that there 'should be one'. However, as can be seen from Table 3.3, employees do not necessarily trust the organisation and believe that there tends to be an 'us' and 'them' relationship between labour and management.

Table 3.3: Employee Relations

Item	Agree (%)	Disagree (%)	Neutral (%)
This organisation recognises and rewards employee loyalty.	48	20	28
Management has problems trusting its employees at this call centre.	23	41	31
There tends to be an 'us' and 'them' relationship between employees and managers at this organisation.	35	26	33
Employees can trust this organisation to do what is right by them.	49	17	31
The likelihood of lay off or retrenchment at this call centre is high.	32	22	36

In the absence of a union, a majority of employees rely more on taking their work-related problems to their team leader for consultation. Further, in the face of acute employee retention problems, employers try various means to identify and address employee grievances, including frequent town hall style meetings. One of the firms covered in our study setup an 'Employee Advocate Group' run by operations personnel in close collaboration with the HR department.[9] The purpose is to flesh out floor-level issues by people who have risen from the ranks. This also facilitates career enrichment for CSRs with aptitude for people management.

Employee Engagement

On various measures of employee engagement, including concern for co-workers, sharing of knowledge, working extra hours and staying late at work without additional payment as well as in terms of commitment to organisational goals and looking forward to coming to work, employee responses are quite positive, as can be seen from Table 3.4.

Table 3.4:   Employee Engagement

Item	Agree (%)	Disagree (%)	Neutral (%)
If I am absent from work, I become concerned about the effects this will have on other members of my team.	64	12	22
If you see a way in which your job could be done more efficiently, would you (*Circle only one response*)	• Keep that knowledge to yourself : 4 • Share it with a co-worker: 59 • Show your supervisor: 36		
If I was asked to work extra hours after my normal shift at my usual rate of pay in order to help out the organisation, I would generally agree to do so.	50	28	21
I don't mind staying late at work after the end of my shift in order to complete a call or post-call work.	57	19	15
I strongly identify with the mission and values of this organisation.	75	5	18
Working for this organisation provides me with an important sense of who I am.	63	12	22
I usually look forward to coming into work.	61	13	24

DISCUSSION

An evaluation of the HRM function within Indian call centres/ BPO needs to be grounded in the global realities of call centres in general. The global call centre industry is hardly 10 years old, whereas the BPO part of the industry is half that age. The business landscape in terms of service offerings, information and communication technologies, competitive strategies and synergies are constantly changing, throwing new challenges to researchers struggling to get a grip on the industry. The nature of work in this industry is often characterised by routinised work flows and monotony within a stressful work environment leading to relatively high employment turnover.

Against this global backdrop, the results of our study show several positives in the way HRM is conducted and delivered in the Indian call centre/BPO industry. For example, the quality of training, the standard of technologies and the adoption of several progressive HR practices are world class in the large info-service providers. However, despite the supply of a large, educated labour force with a proven core competency in IT, the 'employability' of people wanting to enter the industry is a major challenge. In the context of the Indian BPO industry, the opportunities for gainful employment provided by the industry for fresh graduates leads to a strong work and organisational commitment in the short term. However, a perceived lack of career advancement in the call centre industry coupled with routine, monotonous, graveyard shift jobs motivates employees to jump from one job to another looking for short-term gains, such as higher salaries, despite general working conditions and career prospects remaining almost the same. Even though our study reports arguably high levels of employee engagement, the same employees are leaving in big numbers, thus eroding the value of HR's contribution. Improving employment branding and facilitating career advancement are major challenges faced by HR professionals.

Just as the nature and extent of India's role in the global information services sector is often underestimated, the competency, capability and motivation of human resources in India are also often exaggerated. While our study identifies the existence and extent of many elements of strategic HRM, it also highlights that these positive aspects of HRM have little effect on the very high employee turnover. Our findings have a number of implications for both the management of contact services especially in an offshore environment and for the broader connections that are made between employee commitment and turnover in the HR literature.

Coupled with escalating wage costs, the competitive advantage enjoyed by the Indian info-service providers takes a beating with the emergence of other low-cost countries, such as China and the Philippines. By moving up the value chain and entering into KPO, many of the large BPO firms that have been set up by the IT majors in India have managed to retain their competitive positioning, at least in the short to medium term; however, this seems to have had limited impact on the long-term career prospects of employees. To move up the career ladder, BPO employees need specialist domain knowledge and, therefore, several progressive employers offer tuition reimbursement and flexible work arrangements. These career development measures need to be broadened and strengthened. Where workers are satisfied with the opportunities to use their qualifications and with the prospects for further professional advancement, they are less likely to consider leaving their employment. This holds true even in the context of favourable labour market conditions.

With regard to the operational aspects of HRM, where HR is preoccupied with high maintenance and administrative activities (such as, constant and large-scale recruitment, training and performance appraisal), there is little time for strategic thinking, planning and implementation. For example, rather than addressing employee attrition solely by additional recruitment, HR professionals need to pay close attention to the nature, types and causes of attrition at various levels, by drilling down data from exit interviews and employee satisfaction surveys, to see where excess bleeding is occurring and why, so that proactive HR measures can be taken to prevent the problem.

One of the major limitations of our study is that it did not cover the captives set up by Western multinational corporations where the employee turnover is reported to be lower; however, it has been recently reported in the business press that many of the captives are being sold to indigenous providers as they face increasing wage costs and decreasing core competency. Other limitations of our study include lack of breadth across various types and sizes of the BPO industry and an inability to conduct on-site field research that could have unearthed broader and deeper employment issues.

The main contribution of our study lies in the capturing of employee voice in understanding and evaluating HR practices and outcomes on a scale and canvas not covered in previous studies. However, the fast changing business scenario in the global info-services sector means that we are chasing a moving target, limiting the contextual applicability of any critical analysis to the time period, location, size and type of organisations.

ACKNOWLEDGEMENTS

The authors are grateful to the Service Industry Research Centre, Griffith University, for providing seed funding to conduct the research project in India.

NOTES

1. Interview with chief people officer of a Bangalore-based BPO firm dated 13 October 2005.
2. Interview with senior manager, HRD, of a Bangalore-based BPO firm dated 17 October 2005.
3. Interview with general manager, HR, of a Bangalore-based BPO firm dated 13 October 2005.
4. Interview with HR manager of a Hyderabad-based firm dated 18 October 2005.
5. Interview with senior manager, HRD, of a Bangalore-based BPO firm dated 17 October 2005.
6. Interview with senior manager, talent engagement and development, Pune branch, dated 27 June 2005.
7. Interview with HR manager of a Hyderabad-based firm dated 18 October 2005.
8. Interview with senior vice president, HR, of a Bangalore-based BPO firm dated 22 July 2005.
9. Interview with manager, Talent Engagement and Development, Delhi branch, dated 21 October 2005.

REFERENCES

Bain, P., A. Watson, G. Mulvey, P. Taylor, and G. Gall. 2002. 'Taylorism, Targets and the Pursuit of Quantity and Quality by Call Centre Management', *New Technology, Work and Employment,* 17: 170–85.

Batt, R. 1999. 'Work Organization, Technology and Performance in Customer Service and Sales', *Industrial and Labor Relations Review,* 52: 539–64.

———. 2000. 'Strategic Segmentation in Front Line Services: Matching Customers, Employees and Human Resource Management Systems', *International Journal of Human Resource Management,* 11: 540–61.

———. 2002. 'Managing Customer Services: Human Resource Practices, Quit Rates and Sales Growth', *Academy of Management Journal,* 45: 587–97.

Batt, R. and L. Moynihan. 2002. 'The Viability of Alternate Call Centre Production Models', *Human Resource Management Journal,* 12(4): 14–34.

———. 2006. 'Human Resource Management, Service Quality, and Economic Performance in Call Centres', Working paper series number 06-01. Ithaca, NY, Cornell University, School of Industrial and Labor Relations, Center for Advanced Human Resource Studies.

Batt, R., V. Doellgast, and H. Kwon. 2008. 'Employment Systems in Call Centres in the United States and India', in Mohan Thite and Bob Russell (eds), *The Next Available Operator: Managing Human Resources in Indian Business Process Outsourcing Industry,* pp. 217–52. New Delhi: Sage.

Batt, R., V. Doellgast, H. Kwon, M. Nopany, and P. Nopany. 2005. *The Indian Call Centre Industry: National Benchmarking Report. Strategy, HR Practices and Performance.* Ithaca, NY: Cornell University.

Belt, V. and R. Richardson, and J. Webster. 1999. 'Smiling Down the Phone: Women's Work in Telephone Call Centres', Workshop on Telephone call centres, London School of Economics, March.

Bhatnagar, J. 2007. 'Talent Management Strategy of Employee Engagement in Indian ITES Employees: Key to Retention', *Employee Relations,* 29(6): 640–63.

Budhwar, P., H.K. Luthar, and J. Bhatnagar. 2006a. 'The Dynamics of HRM Systems in Indian BPO Firms', *Journal of Labor Research,* 27(3): 339–60.

Budhwar, P., A. Varma, V. Singh, and R. Dhar. 2006b. 'HRM Systems of Indian Call Centres: An Exploratory Study', *International Journal of Human Resource Management,* 17(5): 881–97.

Callaghan, G. and P. Thompson. 2001. 'Edwards Revisited: Technical Control and Call Centres', *Economic and Industrial Democracy,* 22: 13–37.

———. 2002. '"We Recruit Attitude": The Selections and Shaping of Routine Call Centre Labour', *Journal of Management Studies,* 39(2): 233–54.

D'Cruz, P. and E. Noronha. 2006. 'Being Professional: Organisational Control in Indian Call Centres', *Social Science Computer Review*, 24(3): 342–61.

Deery, S., R. Iverson, and J. Walsh. 2002. 'Work Relations in Telephone Call Centres: Understanding Emotional Exhaustion and Employee Withdrawal', *Journal of Management Studies*, 39(4): 471–96.

Fernie, S. and D. Metcalf. 1998. '(Not) Hanging on the Telephone: Payment Systems in the New Sweatshops', *Centrepiece*, 3: 7–11.

Frank, F.D., R.P. Finnegan, and C.R. Taylor. 2004. 'The Race for Talent: Retaining and Engaging Workers in the 21st Century', *Human Resource Planning*, 27(3): 12–25.

Frenkel, S., M. Korczynski, K. Shire, and M. Tam. 1999. *On the Front Line: Organization of Work in the Information Economy*. Ithaca, NY: Cornell University IRL Press.

Frenkel, S., M. Tam, M. Korczynski, and K. Shire. 1998. 'Beyond Bureaucracy? Work Organization in Call Centres', *International Journal of Human Resource Management*, 9: 957–79.

Garson, B. 1988. *The Electronic Sweatshops: How Computers are Transforming the Office of the Future into the Factory of the Past*. New York: Simon and Schuster.

Holman, D. 2002. 'Employee Wellbeing in Call Centres', *Human Resource Management Journal*, 12(4): 35–50.

———. 2003. 'Phoning in Sick? An Overview of Employee Stress in Call Centres', *Leadership and Organization Development Journal*, 24(3): 123–30.

Holman, D., R. Batt, and U. Holtgrewe. 2007. 'The Global Call Centre Report: International Perspectives on Management and Employment', Report of the Global Call Centre Network (US format). Available online at: http://www.ilr.cornell.edu/globalcallcenter/upload/GCC-Intl-Rept-US-Version.pdf (accessed on 2 January 2008).

Houlihan, M. 2002. 'Tensions and Variations in Call Centre Management Strategies', *Human Resource Management Journal*, 12(4): 67–85.

Hutchinson, S., J. Purcell, and N. Kinnie. 2000. 'Evolving High Commitment Management and the Experience of the RAC Call Centre', *Human Resource Management Journal*, 10(1): 63–78.

Kinnie, N., S. Hutchinson, and J. Purcell. 2000. '"Fun and Surveillance": The Paradox of High Commitment Management in Call Centres', *International Journal of Human Resource Management*, 11(5): 967–85.

Korczynski, M. 2001. 'The Contradiction of Service Work: Call Centre as Customer-oriented Bureaucracy', in A. Sturdy, I. Grugulis, and H. Willmott (eds), *Customer Service: Empowerment and Entrapment*, pp. 79–101. Houndmills: Palgrave.

———. 2002. *Human Resource Management in Service Work*. Houndmills: Palgrave.

Lovelock, C. 2005. *Services Marketing: People, Technology, Strategy*. New Jersey: Prentice Hall.

Malhotra, N. and A. Mukherjee. 2004. 'The Relative Influence of Organisational Commitment and Job Satisfaction on Service Quality of Customer-
contact Employees in Banking call centres', *The Journal of Services
Marketing*, 18(2/3): 162–74.

Mehta, A., A. Armenakis, N. Mehta, and F. Irani. 2006. 'Challenges and Opportunities of Business Process Outsourcing in India', *Journal of Labor
Research*, 27(3): 323–38.

Mirchandani, K. 2008. 'Transnationalism in Indian Call Centres'; in Mohan
Thite and Bob Russell (eds), *The Next Available Operator: Managing Human
Resources in Indian Business Process Outsourcing Industry*, pp. 83–111. New
Delhi: Sage.

Mulholland, K. 2002. 'Gender, Emotional Labour and Teamworking in a
Call Centre', *Personnel Review*, 31(3): 283–303.

NASSCOM. 2008. *Indian ITES-BPO Industry–Fact Sheet*. New Delhi: National
Association of Software and Service Companies.

Noronha, E. and P. D'Cruz. 2006. 'Organising Call Centre Agents: Emerging
Issues', *Economic and Political Weekly* (21–27 May): 2115–121.

Paul, A.K. and R.N. Anantharaman. 2004. 'Influence of HRM Practices on
Organisational Commitment: A Study Among Software Professionals
in India', *Human Resource Development Quarterly*, 15(1): 77–88.

Ramesh, B.P. 2004. '"Cyber Coolies" in BPO: Insecurities and Vulnerabilities of Non-standard Work', *Economic and Political Weekly* (31 January):
492–97.

Russell, B. 2004. 'Are All Call Centres the Same?', *Labour and Industry*,
14: 91–109.

Shah, V. and R. Bandi. 2003. 'Capability Development in Knowledge Intensive IT Enabled Services', *European Journal of Work and Organizational
Psychology*, 12(4): 418–27.

Srivastava, S. and N. Theodore. 2006. 'Offshoring Call Centres: The View
from the Wall Street', in J. Burgess and J. Connell (eds), *Developments in
the Call Centre Industry*, pp. 19–35. Abingdon, OX: Routledge.

Taylor, P. and P. Bain. 1999. 'An Assembly Line in the Head: Work and
Employee Relations in the Call Centre', *Industrial Relations Journal*,
30: 101–117.

———. 2003. *Call Centre Outsourcing to India: The Revenge of History?* Call centre
research. New Castle, Australia, University of New Castle.

———. 2004. 'Call Centre Outsourcing to India: The Revenge of History?',
Labour and Industry, 14(3): 15–38.

———. 2005. '"India Calling to the Far Away Towns": The Call Centre
Labour Process and Globalisation', *Work, Employment and Society*, 19(2):
261–82.

———. 2006. 'Work Organisation and Employee Relations in Indian Call
Centres', in J. Burgess and J. Connell (eds), *Developments in the Call Centre
Industry*, pp. 36–57. Abingdon, Oxfordshire: Routledge.

Thite, M. 2008. 'Business Process Outsourcing Management Issues', in C. Wankel (ed.), *The Handbook of 21st Century Management*, pp. 443–450. Thousand Oaks, CA: Sage.

Thite, M. and B. Russell. 2007. 'India and Business Process Outsourcing', in J. Burgess and J. Connell (eds), *Globalisation and Work in Asia*. Oxford: Chandos Publishing.

Towers Perrin. 2006. 'Winning Strategies for a Global Workforce', *Towers Perrin Global Workforce Study*. Available online at: http://www.towersperrin.com/tp/getwebcachedoc?webc=HRS/USA/2006/200602/GWS.pdf (accessed on 15 February 2008).

Wharton, A.S. 1993. 'The Affective Consequences of Service Work', *Work and Occupations*, 20: 205–32.

Zapf, D., A. Isic, M. Bechtoldt, and P. Blau. 2003. 'What is Typical for Call Centre Jobs? Job Characteristics and Service Interactions in Different Call Centres', *European Journal of Work and Organizational Psychology*, 12(4): 311–40.

Zeithaml, V., L.L. Berry, and A. Parasuraman. 1990. *Delivering Quality Service: Balancing Customer Perceptions and Expectations*. New York: Free Press.

4

Work Processes and Emerging Problems in Indian Call Centres

Pawan Budhwar, Neeru Malhotra and Virender Singh

INTRODUCTION

Over the last decade or so, the services sector has witnessed significant changes in the context of service delivery. Call centres (CCs), providing the benefits of cost savings and customer service efficiency have now become an integral aspect of the services sector. The existing literature highlights the existence of a number of studies related to work organisation and management of human resources in CCs operating in different parts of the world (for example, see special issue of *Human Resources Management Journal*, 2002; The Global Call Centre Report by Holman et al. 2007). However, most of these studies have been conducted in CCs operating in developed countries (for example, Deery and Kinnie 2004; Holtgrewe et al. 2002).

Over the last eight years or so, India, due to the availability of a large number of skilled and cheap human resources (HR) along with developed software and information technology industry and established infrastructure has been successful in developing a strong business process outsourcing (BPO)/CC sector and attracting a significant amount of work from Western countries [mainly from the United Kingdom (UK) and the

United States (US)]. For example, over 400 of the Fortune 500 and more than 70 of Financial Times Stock Exchange (FTSE) 100 companies are now outsourcing businesses to Indian CCs. At present, US and UK together account for nearly 80 per cent of the existing outsourced work to centres in India (see Das et al. 2007; Ravichandaran 2005). Due to economic reasons (for example, UK firms can save around £10 million for every 1,000 offshored jobs to India), the interest of foreign companies in outsourcing work to Indian CCs is expected to continue (see Willmott 2006; *The Hindu* 2005).

At present, there are around 500 BPOs/CCs operating in India (NASSCOM 2007). In a short space of time, the exports from this sector have grown from US$ 565 million in 2000 to about US$ 7.3 billion in 2005. They were projected to increase to US$ 20 billion by the end of 2007 and employment in the sector is expected to rise from its current level of 300,000 to over 1.2 million by 2008 (NASSCOM 2007). Further, Morgan Stanley reports that outsourcing to India is expected to earn export revenues of US$ 62 billion by 2010 (Punch 2004; Ravichandran 2005). Given the current forecast of 40–50 per cent annual growth for the next five years, clearly the Indian outsourcing industry seems to have a tremendous future.

With this rapid growth there have also been emerging issues related to management of HR in the sector, such as high attrition rates, motivation, efficiency and the well-being of employees (Budhwar et al. 2006b; Punch 2004). If not addressed, these could adversely affect the growth of Indian CCs and also impact the UK and US businesses that are outsourcing work to India (Taylor and Bain 2005; Willmott 2006). In the absence of reliable research evidence it is not clear how serious these issues are and accordingly it would be difficult to propose any cure for the same. The existing literature does provide information about the nature of work systems and issues related to HR for CCs operating in developed countries (for example, Deery and Kinnie 2004; Holtgrewe et al. 2002). However, there is little empirically reliable research available for the Indian context. Considering the unique Indian business context (such as management systems that do not converge either with the West or East, see Sparrow and Budhwar 1997), one should not be surprised if the pattern of work practices of CCs in India and the logic surrounding the same turn out be different to CCs operating in the West. In the absence of reliable information such assumptions cannot be tested. Considering the strong growth of this sector and the interest of many in the same, it is important to conduct robust research and highlight the work systems relevant for CCs operating in India. This should contribute to both better theory and practice development.

Lately, some research has been pursued in the Indian CC context (see Batt et al., in this volume; Budhwar et al. 2006a, 2006b; Das et al. 2007; D'Cruz and Noronha 2006; Noronha and D'Cruz 2006; Raman et al. 2007; Taylor and Bain 2005). Still, given the scarcity of research regarding the patterns of work systems, human resources management (HRM) processes and, perhaps more important, about the emerging problems in Indian CCs, there is a clear need for more research analysis. This study makes an attempt to contribute in this regard. Based on the analysis of the existing literature and the emerging gaps in the same, the aims of this research are twofold. First we highlight the emerging patterns of work processes in Indian CCs. Second, we report on the emerging problems experienced by Indian CCs and their employees and the steps taken by CCs to tackle these challenges.

WORK ORGANISATION AND HRM IN CCS

Frenkel et al. (1998) debate about two contrasting perspectives on work processes in CCs–first emphasising the bureaucratic and constraining nature of the work settings; and second highlighting the positive and empowering work set-up (also see Batt 1999; Batt and Appelbaum 1995). The first stance seems to be dominating in CCs the world over, especially those in which the nature of work is known to be routine, monotonous, deskilling and similar to a traditional assembly line. Such work is characterised as 'dead-end' and one offering few career prospects (Deery and Kinnie 2004: 3). On the other hand, there are operations which offer freedom and encourage an empowering environment in the belief that empowered employees work to the needs of customers and are more productive than the routine workers. Frenkel et al. (1998) believe that the truth lies somewhere in between as elements of both views coexist and propose the existence of a hybrid model and call it the 'mass customised bureaucracy' which remains bureaucratic but has elements associated with professional or knowledge-intensive settings appropriate to the customisation of products and services (also see Knights and McCabe 1998).

Taylor and Bain (1999) point out that due to the shift in the role of CCs from 'simple enquiry' to customer relationship management, the importance is now attached to quality of service, hence, the management has to keep in mind that de-motivated staff cannot provide quality service. Along with quality, the issue of quantity still remains a priority and this creates a dilemma to the management of quality and quantity at the same time. Understanding such complications of CC work, Batt and Moynihan (2002) summarise it into three categories, namely, mass-production, professional services and hybrid mass-customisation. In an ideal world, the management would like to go for a win–win situation where the emphasis should be both on cost-efficiency and customer satisfaction. To achieve this, CCs seem to adopt a formal, rationalised and structured approach to HRM. Emerging information suggests that perhaps this is also happening in the Indian set-up (see Budhwar et al. 2006a, 2006b), but the available information is scanty and not conclusive as the CC sector is still evolving in India.

It is observed that front-line employees in CCs are often underpaid, under-trained and highly stressed (for example, Deery and Kinnie 2004). This has serious implications for their service performance and turnover (Batt and Moynihan 2002). Employee turnover rates are noted at times as more than 40 per cent in many CCs in the UK and are rapidly growing in India

(Budhwar et al. 2006a; Taylor and Bain 2005). Research indicates that monotonous and repetitive work in CCs is positively associated with emotional exhaustion (Deery and Kinnie 2004), leading to high attrition rates. There is then an increasing need to redesign these jobs by adding more variety, and thereby reducing monotony in the work of front-line employees (Holman 2002). This has serious implications for quality performance.

EMERGING PROBLEMS IN INDIAN CCS

As highlighted here, the Indian outsourcing industry seems to have a tremendous future. Nonetheless, all is not well with its phenomenal success story. Some of the barriers for this growth reported in the media and National Association of Software and Service Companies (NASSCOM) reports include (*a*) relatively poor infrastructure and electricity, (*b*) the lack of a customer service culture, (*c*) cultural differences between employees and clients, (*d*) under-trained representatives speaking English with a heavy accent, (*e*) scarcity of language skills other than English, (*f*) employees with relatively little work experience in the outsourcing sector, (*g*) increasing automation of customer interaction technologies, (*h*) regional political instabilities (*i*) lengthy periods required to acquire government clearance to allow foreign firms to start operations, (*j*) increasing competition from other low-cost providers in the Philippines, China, eastern Europe, South Africa and (*k*) increasing costs (for details see Budhwar et al. 2006a, 2006b; Christopher 2005; Das et al. 2007; NASSCOM 2007; Pande 2005; Prashad and Rai 2005). The impact of such constraints is clearly demonstrated by the fact that a number of operators in the business have gone bust in the past (*Businessline* 2003).

There have also been several emerging media reports that highlight a number of health, social and psychological problems which can seriously affect the predicted high growth rate for this sector (Cacanas 2004; Singh 2005; Walletwatch 2003; Witt et al. 2004). For example, many CC employees are asked to assume multiple identities by expecting them to change their names, acquire foreign accent(s) and develop new interests and hobbies to better converse and satisfy the clients. This often causes psychological problems such as 'multiple personality disorder' while at present a lot of outsourcing firms do not seem to be concerned about the long-term effects of such issues. Things are further complicated by the use of 'graveyard shifts' to match working hours in Western countries. These erratic long working hours make normal socialisation difficult, leading to alienation, withdrawal and increased irritability. Psychologists note that many young individuals employed in CCs are susceptible to burn-out stress syndrome (BOSS), symptoms of which include chronic fatigue, insomnia and alteration of the body's 24-hour biological rhythm (George 2005). In addition to this, disturbed sleep and prolonged working hours may lead to gastric ulcers, high blood pressure, diabetes or clinical depression. Other aliments ranging from hypertension and asthma to spondylitis are also reported as an outcome of working in CCs.

Other factors contributing towards stress especially in international CCs is the problem of racial abuse from irate customers. Many Indian CC front-line workers face an array of problems from rudeness to sexual harassment to fury at unsolicited sales calls, to open racism (Baliga 2005; *The Hindu* 2005). One of the main pre-requisites of the Indian CC industry is to work at odd hours especially night shifts, which often leads to family and social problems, including problems with traditional 'arranged' marriages.

To summarise, the problems faced by employees within the Indian CC industry range from stressful work environments, adverse working conditions and a lack of control, to the absence of career development opportunities, physical confinement, over-regimentation, unsociable working hours and abusive clients. However, it is important to note that the very nature of the CC industry (for example, its emphasis on speed and quality) is such that some of these problems are inevitable and might still continue. But it also raises the serious issue regarding the extent to which organisations are pursuing different initiatives to tackle these emerging problems. If they are not handled properly then they may be disastrous for the sector.

METHODOLOGY

Given the exploratory nature of this research, an in-depth interview-based research design was adopted for this investigation. Research discussions were held with 64 employees (representing different levels) in 14 CCs during March–April 2007. Sixty per cent of the research firms are India based and the remaining are foreign firms. In each firm, interviews were conducted with one senior HR manager and up to two team leaders and two–three shop-floor employees. Apart from interviews, other sources such as mission statements, annual reports, letters, memoranda and other communiqués, proposals, progress reports and other internal documents were used to collect relevant data. The interviews were tape-recorded at most of the firms (with the exception of few which did not allow for this), and the qualitative data was content analysed. On average the interviews with the HR managers lasted for up to two hours and with others around one hour. The main issues examined during the in-depth interviews are: the organisation–its activities, strategies and composition of employees; the structuring of work; the nature of the HR department and HR practices including recruitment, training and development, compensation, performance appraisal, attrition and retention.

FINDINGS

Factors Contributing to Growth of CCs in India

An analysis of the existing literature and the interview data highlight a number of factors responsible for the growth of the CC/BPO sector within India. These include the existence of a number of good quality academic institutions producing a large number of quality graduates every year and the liberalisation of the Indian economy in 1991, which attracted lots of foreign direct investment including funds directed to the establishment of a BPO sector. Along with these, several other factors have led to the emergence and success of this sector in India. These include:

1. The availability of good talent.
2. A strong base of blue chip companies.
3. Significant government support to the sector including a number of tax incentives such as tax exemption for export services.
4. Competition among state governments to attract outsourcing investments.
5. Powerful venture capital interest in investing in growth opportunity.
6. Developing track records of proven systems/process delivery.
7. Improved international bandwidth.
8. The time difference between India and main clients (based in UK and US), along with comparative national cost advantages (also see Budhwar et al. 2006a, 2006b; Chengappa and Goyal 2002; Punch 2004; Raman et al. 2007; Ramchandran and Voleti 2004; *The Economist* 2004).

Structuring of Work at Shop-floor Level in Indian CCs

Based on the analysis of our data, a clear pattern is emerging regarding the structuring of the work at the shop-floor level in Indian CCs. A mixture of both inbound and outbound and voice and data-driven operations are organised by the research firms. They provide a whole range of services from basic customer services, transcription, billing, coding, telemarketing to financial reporting, asset management, legal and portfolio management, content development, that is, digital content, research and development (R&D), local area network (LAN) and application maintenance, pay and HR administration, R&D and imaging and internet support.

All the centres organise their shop-floor level work into teams consisting of 12–25 associates/executives/agents/front-line employees or customer service representatives (CSRs) led by a team leader. The team leaders report to an assistant manager, who in turn reports to a manager. The span of control of a team leader is small in the case of voice-based operations and large for data-driven projects. The workplace is generally in the form of open plan offices with chest-high partitions. The work of agents in the case of both inbound and outbound voice-based operations in comparison to data-driven, project-based centres seems to be more structured, tightly controlled and involves repetitive activities. Employees work in shifts of around nine hours with up to one hour of breaks (tea, comfort and dinner). Generally, a team meets 15 minutes before the start of the shift with a pre-shift *'team-huddle'* where the team leader shares with the team member's concerns about their well-being, what happened at their last shift, new process information and any project-based information such as targets and challenges. The shift finishes with a post-shift team-huddle to see how things went during the shift and to report/share on any significant occurrences. The associates are not generally allowed to swap teams or projects and work in the same team and shift for many months. The following comments by a CSR summarises the pattern of most call centre work:

> The flow of work is clearly structured. We have to work for eight and a half hours with a half hour break, generally for at least a month on the same task. Things are very much time oriented, like you have to finish your work in a specified period. At times relaxation is provided if we need to stretch but that happens only on limited occasions. We receive clear guidelines; know what is expected from us, what we need to perform and what we are supposed to deliver to the customer. We have some freedom of expression to propose things for improvement and many a times they are accepted. (CSR of a French non-voice based CC in Pune)

During the work shift, the team leader can be approached by the associates either via email, or by raising their hand in case of need. The team leaders provide support to associates on a variety of matters such as technical aspects of the task, personal matters, acting as a trouble-shooter, motivator and instant messenger. Team leaders also provide information on 'internal job postings/promotions' and guide associates on HR matters (for example, leave, change of shift, etc.). Team leaders are expected to act as mentors and regularly provide feedback to associates on their performance while ensuring their well-being. Further, the team leader puts the output of each associate on a board while also feeding it into a dataset. This system is very objective (as it is data driven) and also transparent as the board is updated on a regular basis along with individual associates' datasets. This information is used to assess the team performance and to later decide about both individual and team rewards. The following comments of an associate give a good overview about the supervision system existing in Indian CCs:

> We find the supervisors very useful as they have practical knowledge, know the procedures and have undergone relevant training. The format of communication with the immediate supervisor is not very defined because they are easily accessible to us. They sit along with our team and most of the times they are working with us. We can go to their desk for a one-to-one discussion if something needs urgent attention or they can come to us. The benefit of this kind of supervision system is that somebody is easily accessible to help and support you. It is a system which is good for the company. (Associate of a voice-based American CC)

Most of the associates describe their work environment as supportive, with structured information available that encourages performance. Management is viewed as transparent and data-driven resulting in objectivity. Jobs are viewed as secure, work loads well distributed and infrastructure is seen to be good, while top management is approachable. Such a set-up leads to better levels of growth, attachment to teams, trust, better bonding and a balance between professional and personal life as reflected in the following remarks made by an agent working in a non-voice based centre:

> I can summarise the work environment here by saying that it is very enjoyable. If it is any occasion then it is very indulging, we have got all the privileges on the occasion and people know how much they are expected to work, to get a particular task done or to get evaluated positively. So we know where we stand at a particular point of time and how to get on a higher level. This is a very transparent organisation and all the managers and everybody is very accessible. (Agent working in an Indian data-driven, non-voice based centre)

While a majority of the associates seem to project a number of positive aspects of their work and supervision system, a few highlight drawbacks as well. These include at times a long wait to approach a team leader (due to large span of the team leader), lack of trust between the team leader and associate, feedback from clients is not always shared with individual associates and a lack of transparency with internal promotion matters. Further, associates report issues related to leave, moving of shifts, graveyard shifts, pressure from team leaders to meet targets, impacts on social life, lack of growth opportunities, not being paid for extra working time, health and hygiene (for example, unsociable working hours, monotonous jobs, dirty washrooms, etc.).

> Perhaps, the drawback of this kind of supervision system is that people don't want to be supervised all the time; they don't want to be checked and monitored by someone all the time. Also, the team leaders can be subjective in their evaluation at times, but largely due to the data-driven nature of the system they are fine. (Associate of an Indian voice-based centre)

All such factors directly or indirectly contribute to high attrition rate in the Indian CC industry, which perhaps is the most serious problem. Realising these emerging problems, CCs have initiated a number of provisions for employees and also a number of avenues to involve them in order to listen to their grievances, improve the systems and make the work more enjoyable and less stressful.

FACILITIES AND EMPLOYEE INVOLVEMENT PRACTICES IN INDIAN CCS

CCs in India seem to be providing extra facilities in comparison to other sectors in order to attract, motivate and retain their employees. In the last few years, the number of such facilities/ incentives/benefits has significantly increased. Broadly, they include provision of free transport (from home and back), canteen, free tea/coffee, 24×7 medical room, desk facilities (to provide support for banking, travel, cinema tickets, mortgage, insurance, utility bill payments and insurance), 24×7 television in canteens and other leisure amenities (gym, yoga classes), extra pay during holidays, sick leave, customer satisfaction bonuses and funding to support higher education.

Along with these, most organisations organise a number of recreation and fun activities such as regular cricket, chess and other matches, dance parties, family day outings, picnics, quiz, dance and song competitions and celebrations of all major festivals. In certain cases, where CCs were found to be operating in cities like Mumbai, which is well known for housing and transportation problems, the associates are also provided with accommodation facilities at subsidised rates near the call centres.

Realising the importance of involving employees in various activities and regularly getting their feedback to improve the work systems, most organisations are adopting a number of mechanisms. Some of the prominent ones are: 'town-hall' gatherings [where the chief executive officer (CEO) along with the top managers meets the employees in open sessions)], esatisfaction committees (which regularly looks at the satisfaction of employees at the workplace both formally and informally), different committees (such as for canteen, transportation, sports), 'skip meetings' (where a manager sits with a team leader and an associate on a one-to-one basis to discuss any issue) and 'all hands meet' (on a quarterly basis, the senior management communicates company goals and objectives, future plans, performance and profitability, new processes, budgets, etc., to all the employees of the organisation). Promotion of different clubs (for example, trekking, nature visits), 'touch-time' (in case of any urgent updates the managers come to the floor to share it), 'open-house' and 'open hands' meetings, workshops on stress, motivation capsules, business games (to make the employees aware about the developments in the sector), free voice online (to raise any concerns), quarterly R&R (reward and recognition) functions, 'fun-do-Friday' (parties, celebrations of key events such as an employee's birthday or festivals), scope surveys (on a yearly basis to find out about the company, employees and jobs) and 'post an idea' (to encourage creative suggestions from associates regarding how to improve work systems) are also common initiatives. The following comments of two associates from different CCs give an indication about the various mechanisms adopted to involve them to make the workplace more interesting.

> We have people from different teams who form part of our cultural community—we have skits, drama, some people sing and we entertain ourselves. We do have outdoor games tournaments and at times we go to parties along with the team members. This helps people to mix with one another and enjoy working in teams. (Agent of an Indian voice-based centre)

> We have different committees organised and run by employees such as committees for transport, food, IT, satisfaction and recreation. These are voluntary but very functional and helpful for employees. Similarly, the management has a number of mechanisms in place for involving employees in improving systems. Such initiatives result in innovation, team spirit, professionalism and integrity. (Associate of a British voice-based centre)

Despite so many innovative initiatives, the CC industry is facing serious problems of attrition, employee morale and retention. Perhaps an analysis of the associates' dislikes about their jobs can aid in understanding the main causes of dissatisfaction. The majority of associates comment about the status of the CC industry being seen by the general public as bad, that is, 'it is not seen as a good place to work', one which cannot provide a

solid career, where the work is stressful and has serious implications on social life. Perhaps the strongest drawback of the CC
industry is the lack of promotion opportunities for the associates
which results in huge discontentment and high attrition. Such
feelings are clearly evidenced by the following comments of
an associate.

> Sometimes there are problems as an outcome of CC work or if you
> look at the CC industry as such in India which is not very acceptable
> in society. The moment you say that you work in a CC, you know that
> is not considered as a good job. So we need to really work and create
> a good impression in society so that it is taken as a very good industry
> to work in. Perhaps, because of this, people are a bit conservative in
> this regard. Thus, it leads to attrition. The sector needs to have a better
> image in society. To be very honest, I like the work I am doing because
> I always wanted to do something different, so whatever I was looking
> for I have got here, but it feels bad when people label CC work as less
> prestigious. (Associate of a voice-based Indian CC)

MANAGING EMPLOYEE ATTRITION

Most of the attrition in the Indian CCs is at the associate level
(the shop-floor level) and happens in the initial three months
of the job. The attrition rate varies significantly as per different sources (for example, NASSCOM and other media reports,
managers and associates). It is reported at anywhere from 20
per cent to over 100 per cent. It also varies depending on the
kind of operations the associates are working on, for example,
it is higher in voice-based centres. Broadly speaking, the main
reasons provided by the associates for leaving jobs include
better opportunities in the market, money (either less paid at
their work or better offered by others) and lack of promotions.
Job-hopping can occur because of very trivial reasons such as
dissatisfaction with the canteen or other facilities to more serious
ones like not liking one's boss, night shifts, better comparative
benefits offered by other firms, or personal reasons such as pursuit of higher education or marriage.

A number of suggestions have been made by HR managers, team leaders and associates regarding how the increasing problem of attrition can be tackled. HR managers in particular suggest selecting candidates who fit well with the company's culture. Raising the image of the industry and changing the psyche of people about the industry in an effort to better sell jobs has also been mentioned as has shifting employment to second and third-tier Indian cities. There is also a need for developing better reward and recognition programmes, to work with vocational institutes to develop relevant courses and modules in order to inculcate specific skills in graduates, reducing shift timings and developing anti-employee-poaching policies for competing firms. The comments of an HR manager of a French CC based in Gurgaon nicely summarises the attrition scenario in Indian CCs:

The attrition problem, I believe, will continue for some time because the industry is still maturing but the people it is hiring are still immature. It needs to be checked at the time of recruitment by taking in the right kind of people who have right expectations. If I target a group from 20–25 years of age who lack maturity, unless and until we can show them that they have a good career ahead, which I expect in this organisation is the case, we will not be able to retain them. We need to have a system in the sector that restricts people from job-hopping. We need most of the organisations to follow simple things in their policies. For example, they should try to check whether the person has left his previous job for a genuine reason or otherwise. In that case, they should not take that person in as earlier he was an absconding employee. If you start the practice and other organisations also pursue it, it will certainly discourage those people who job hop. This will compel them to look at their job in CCs as a career option. Also, we need to continue developing talent management practices on the pattern that other companies are providing, like giving their employees opportunities to pursue higher education. We are providing them with teachers, class room lectures and also tying up with some institutes. We also have distance learning programmes. We have talked about having a NASSCOM test where anybody across India can take the test. Unfortunately despite being a very promising enterprise, it never happened. We also suggested blacklisting people who breached the rules of leaving without a proper notice, but no tracking data was generated. Such things don't materialise easily and it is disappointing that it only ends in discussions.

Team leaders also propose a number of mechanisms which might help in reducing the attrition problem. These include the need to focus on delivery of programmes to associates such as developing more avenues for promotion, better communication and transparency, work on an industry-wide salary structure, revise salary packages for employees, develop reliable datasets (to keep a track of job-hoppers), make jobs more enriching and further highlight their importance, develop more courses for agents in order for them to grow, provide job security, offer better counselling to employees, ensure a minimum qualification at the entry point, do a more thorough background check and develop better practices to satisfy the employees. Similar views are shared by the associates.

The fact is that the Indian CC industry is still evolving and as a result better systems are being developed and it can be assumed that in the next couple of years it will mature. The following comments of a supervisor in the HR department of one of India's top IT BPO firms summarises the issues involved with growing attrition problems in the sector:

> To reduce the attrition rate, we use a variety of incentives. We are working very hard towards this because it is something which we need to cut off. We are trying to motivate our employees to get their friends and relatives so that they get a referral reward. This is creating a kind of earn and learn environment. As more companies are entering the field, the problem of attrition is increasing. I think in two or three years this problem will be taken care of because by then the sector will have matured. I believe that the BPO companies need to come to a common platform and need to think over the issue very seriously. Perhaps then they can come up with a system of tracking why a person has moved from one company to another, if he has moved to a higher position by job-hopping etc.... What we normally do is that we conduct exit interviews with the HR and then we prepare an attrition dash board listing why the attrition has been high. This helps to identify the main reasons contributing to attrition. And then these are sent to the higher levels. I am not aware whether we are going to have incentives for retention but we should have incentives for this. The HR spends a lot of effort in retaining employees as retention is far more important to the organisation than hiring and training. We try to keep the employees satisfied by different means. We motivate

our employees through training, various incentives and through different activities. The company sponsors outings for them. The kind of environment that we provide here also helps to retain employees. We work towards increasing their salaries in terms of bonuses, etc. Employee commitment is another area where we work. We have meetings to discuss issues that they face. If a person is not satisfied with the transport then we talk to the transport people. That is how we try to make them feel that this is their own company. Service level agreements (SLAs) are shared with every employee and they are aware of it. We have got a quality department which takes care of their quality-related issues. Our clients too offer incentives for our employees like certificates and bonuses. All these things are there. So people are not really leaving due to psychological, socio-psychological or such similar problems. In all the exit interviews I have taken, most employees said they were leaving specifically for money, better opportunities and for higher education.... So we cannot do anything. In that case we try our level best but still they leave.

CONCLUSIONS AND THE WAY FORWARD

The work of associates (especially in voice-based centres) is highly monitored and scripted to a great extent. Most of the work systems are formal and structured and are similar to the ones existing in Western countries. Indian CCs are now experiencing a serious problem of very high labour turnover. All the CCs employ only full-time employees. An emphasis is given to academic achievements and specific attitudes towards work while recruiting new employees. The CCs under study emphasise the training of their employees. A mixed approach to compensation (that is, performance based and experience based) is adopted in all the firms. Moreover, the CCs studied are adopting a formal, structured and professional approach to work organisation and for most HRM functions.

Based on our analyses of interview data, and drawing from various media reports, we have found that organisations are taking a step forward in certain areas to combat attrition. However, there still remains a big gap in other areas which demand immediate attention. In conclusion, we now discuss those key areas which are crucial to curb attrition and where some progress has been made by these organisations, and also propose some interventions that are likely to help reduce high attrition rates in Indian CCs.

1. One of the key issues that need to be addressed by both the government and CC management is protecting employees and women in particular, working in international CCs from sexual and racial abuse received from overseas clients. Several respondents listed this as a key determinant of their intent-to-turnover. Indeed, it is heartening to note that some CCs have started developing 'black-lists' of abusive clients, and putting them on their 'do-not-call-list'. The HR department can play a useful role by training both associates and team leaders regarding how best to handle such clients.

2. The projected growth of call centres and the concurrent shortage of skilled workers in the industry in India suggest the need for training programmes specific to the needs of the industry. For example, media reports estimate a potential demand for over 160,000 foreign language professionals in India by 2010, while only 40,000 qualified individuals are projected to be available. Clearly, this will create a supply-side constraint. As such, both the government and institutions of learning need to step in and create programmes that will help minimize this gap. Nevertheless, in such circumstances, the HR managers will be left with the challenging task of developing appropriate mechanisms to recruit quality candidates from a scarce labour pool.

3. There is also a need for better career planning in Indian CCs. In order for organisations to attract and retain qualified candidates, organisations need to address issues beyond the obvious 'pull' factors such as high pay. With properly developed career progression models, recruiters may be able to convince qualified candidates to consider

CCs as a career option, not just a job. Although most organisations are found to consider the 'IJP' internal job promotion (IJP) scheme very seriously (with more than 70 per cent of 'team leaders' coming from internal promotions within the associates/CSRs working in the organisations), there is a need to pursue this IJP scheme for higher level promotions as well. However, there is now a strong need to develop other more attractive career development paths for associates in order to retain them and also convince them and the general public that one can have a good career in this sector. The HR needs to play a more proactive role in this regard of not only convincing the top decision makers about the need for such developments but also to create a brand image about a good career in the CC sector.

4. The disruption of normal life and business caused by the rains in Mumbai some time ago has prompted many firms to examine establishing CCs in different cities. Also, the increasing travel time (to pick-up and drop associates from home to work and back), shrinking talent pool along with other factors such as rising rents strongly support the case of CCs to be established in second and third-tier Indian cities. Further, given the high attrition rates in big metropolitan cities like Bangalore, smaller cities might be a viable and profitable option. Further, since many students in the big cities migrate from these small towns, they would prefer having access to such work in their home town, as it could offer a better quality of life. This is now already happening on a large scale with the emergence of CCs in tier-two and three cities such as Pune, Vizag, Chandigarh, Jaipur and Hyderabad.

5. CCs also need to move beyond the traditional methods of recruitment (that is, newspaper advertisements) and move to innovative methods that are emerging to be popular in India. They have started to explore new channels of hiring, such as job portals on the internet, walk-ins

and employee referrals. They also need to look into other channels. Job fairs could be a potential source considering the mushrooming CC industry where prospective employees could be given an opportunity to meet representatives of various organisations, so that they can understand each other's needs better. A significant number of CCs are now adopting innovative techniques to recruit new employees such as employing 'college ambassadors' (where they send their existing employees to their respective alma maters to spread word about the attractions of working in their centres). Given the growing difficulties with recruitment in the sector, the HR departments need to continuously develop new ways for attracting and retaining employees.

6. Given that the outsourcing industry has put India on the world economic map, there is a need for governmental assistance to support training, as is done in Singapore and other countries (see Debrah et al. 2000). The Indian government should either reimburse companies for the cost of training, or put into place required training courses either through the private sector or primary, secondary and tertiary education in the country. Such proposals are time and again mooted by NASSCOM and different state governments but nothing solid has emerged so far.

7. Given the high stress environment of CCs and the monotonous nature of work, stress-relieving interventions such as frequent parties, casual dress days and recreational facilities are employed by many CCs under study and the response of associates towards the same has been good. To a great extent, such initiatives are becoming a regular feature of many CCs in India.

8. Perhaps because most employees in the CCs are young, many of the organisations seem to have paid scant attention to welfare and healthcare measures. However, given the stress often caused by the nature of work, organisations need to pay special attention to this need. As an example, in contrast with other countries, Indian

CC employees lay special emphasis on the provision of 'food', 'transport' and other facilities as being the important factors influencing their performance and commitment. The HR departments should ensure that such provisions are delivered properly and should regularly update them.

9. There is a strong need for NASSCOM and the government to develop and seriously implement a 'non-poaching' agreement. It is hoped that such a policy will help alleviate some of the concerns of attrition. In the past such an initiative was pursued by 10 or so organisations, but without support from the government and NASSCOM, it could not be sustained.

10. It is important for the people in India to accept CC jobs as just another 'normal' job that involves working in shifts, as is prevalent in the nursing profession, hospitality industry and factories. It is crucial that the emerging cultural stigma attached with CC jobs is wiped away at the earliest. This is important because one of the key causes of attrition found amongst CC representatives at the associate level was a quest for a more 'acceptable' profession. Given that most employees are college-age individuals, our interview findings indicate that some organisations have found inviting their parents/family and involving them on different occasions such as national festivals or fun-days, helpful in creating a better image of the CC sector.

11. It is crucial that organisations realise the importance of employee-job fit, even at the associate level. Recruitment practices should be geared to achieve this fit as jobs should be 'marketed' to the targeted employees depending upon their knowledge and expertise. This is more important for domestic CCs, as a move from a domestic to an international CC is seen as 'career progression' from the associate's perspective. This was found to be another key cause of attrition in CCs. For example, language skills can be a major factor in employee job-fit. When recruiting employees for domestic CCs, proficiency in

the 'local language' should be the main focus rather than English. As a result, domestic CCs can establish a niche by attracting employees 'not so' proficient in English, but capable of handling calls in the local language. Realising their limitation, these employees will not venture into 'international' CCs just for a mere career move.

Based on this analysis, we believe that this study contributes to the literature relating to organisation studies, HRM and CCs. It also provides useful information to foreign firms operating in India or who are planning to start operations in India regarding the nature of work processes suitable to the Indian context. This discussion also highlights the key role for HR in the sector.

ACKNOWLEDGEMENT

This research is funded by an ESRC grant–RES-000-22-1876. We greatly appreciate this support and also thank the participating firms for all their cooperation with data collection.

REFERENCES

Baliga, H. 2005. 'Should Indian Girls Really take the Sexual and Racial Abuse over Phone in Call Center Jobs? Are these BPO or Virtual Brothels?'. Available online at: http://www.indiadaily.com/editorial/2937.asp (accessed on 5 June 2008).
Batt, R. 1999. 'Work Organization, Technology, and Performance in Customer Service and Sales', *Industrial and Labour Relations Review*, 52(4): 539–64.
Batt, R. and E. Appelbaum. 1995. 'Worker Participation in Diverse Settings: Does the Form Affect the Outcome, if so, who Benefits?', *British Journal of Industrial Relations*, 33(3): 353–78.
Batt, R. and L. Moynihan. 2002. 'The Viability of Alternative Call Centre Production Models', *Human Resource Management Journal*, 12(4): 14–34.
Batt, R., V. Doellgast, and H. Kwon. 2008. 'Employment Systems in Call Centres in the United States and India', in Mohan Thite and Bob Russell (eds), *The Next Available Operator: Managing Human Resources in Indian Business Process Outsourcing Industry*, pp. 217–52. New Delhi: Sage.

Budhwar, P., A. Varma, V. Singh, and R. Dhar. 2006b. 'HRM Systems of Indian Call Centres: An Exploratory Study', *The International Journal of Human Resource Management*, 17(5): 881–97.

Budhwar, P., H. Luthar, and J. Bhatnagar. 2006a. 'Dynamics of HRM Systems in BPOs Operating in India', *Journal of Labor Research*, 27(3): 339–60.

Businessline. 2003. 'HR Department in Call Centres has Its Hands Full', 16 June.

Cacanas, Z. 2004. 'Passage to India', *Human Resources*, March: 46–50.

Chengappa, R. and M. Goyal. 2002. 'House Keepers to the World', *India Today*, November: 18–48.

Christopher, E. 2005. 'Offshoring Goes Complex, But it Pays', *The Economic Times Online* (12 January). Available online at: http://economictimes. indiatimes.com/articleshow/988808.cms (accessed on 25 January 2005).

Das, D., R. Dharwadkar, and P. Brandes. 2007. 'The Importance of Being Something: Identity Centrality and Work Outcomes of Offshored Call Centers in India', *Paper in Best Paper Proceedings of Academy of Management.*

D'Cruz, P. and E. Noronha. 2006. 'Being Professional: Organization Control in India Call Centres', *Social Science Computer Review*, 24(3): 342–61.

Debrah, Y., I. McGovern, and P. Budhwar. 2000. 'Complementarity or Competition: The Development of Human Resources in a Growth Triangle', *The International Journal of Human Resource Management*, 11: 314–35.

Deery, S. and N. Kinnie. 2004. 'Introduction: The Nature and Management of Call Centre Work', in S. Deery and N. Kinnie (eds), *Call Centres and Human Resource Management: A Cross-National Perspective*, pp. 1–22. Basingstoke: Palgrave Macmillan.

Frenkel, S., M. Korczynski, K. Shire, and M. Tam. 1998. 'Beyond Bureaucracy? Work Organization in Call Centres', *International Journal of Human Resource Management*, 9: 957–79.

George, S. 2005. 'Are BPOs the New Age Sweatshops?', *The Economic Times*, 12 May.

Holman, D. 2002. 'Employee Wellbeing in Call Centres', *Human Resource Management Journal*, 12(4): 35–50.

Holman, D., R. Batt, and U. Holtgrewe. 2007. 'Global Call Centre Report'. Available online at: www.globalcallcenter.org (accessed on 24 June 2008).

Holtgrewe, U.C., C. Kerst, and K. Shire (eds). 2002. *Reorganizing Service Work: Call Centres in Germany and Britain*. Burlington: Ashgate.

Knights, D. and D. McCabe. 1998. 'What Happens When the Phones Go Wild? Staff, Stress and Spaces for Escape in a BPR Telephone Banking Work Regime', *Journal of Management Studies*, 35(2): 163–94.

Kochan, T. A., L. Dyer, and R. Batt. 1992. 'International Human Resource Studies: A Framework for Future Research', in D. Lewin, O. S. Mitchell, and P. D. Sherer (eds), *Research Frontiers in Industrial Relations and Human Resources*, pp. 309–37. Wisconsin: IRRA.

NASSCOM. 2007. *NASSCOM IDC Study on Domestic Services Market Opportunities*. New Delhi: NASSCOM.

Noronha, E. and P. D'Cruz. 2006. 'Organising Call Centre Agents: Emerging Issues', *Economic and Political Weekly*, 27 May: 2115–121.

Pande, B. 2005. 'Sun, Survey Can't Deter the Call of Duty', *The Economic Times Online* (29 July). Available online at: http://economictimes. indiatimes.com/articleshow/msid-1185174,prtpage-1.cms (accessed on 5 August 2005).

Punch, L. 2004. 'The Global Back Office: Beyond the Hype', *Credit Card Management*, 16(January): 26–34.

Prashad, S. and A.R. Rai. 2005. 'Are Indian BPOs Losing Their Cutting Edge?', *Business Standard,* Tuesday, 22 March: 1.

Raman, S.R., P. Budhwar, and G. Balasubramanian. 2007. 'People Management Issues in Indian KPOs', *Employee Relations,* 29(6): 696–710.

Ramchandran, K. and S. Voleti. 2004. 'Business Process Outsourcing (BPO): Emerging Scenario and Strategic Options for IT-enabled Serv-ices', *Vikalpa,* 29(1): 49–62.

Ravichandaran, R. 2005. 'BPO, ITES Sectors to Hot Up in 2005, Says NASSCOM Report', *The Financial Express,* 9 March.

Singh, H. 2005. 'Is the BPO Iceberg Melting Under Attrition Heat?', *The Economic Times,* 10 February.

Sparrow, P. R. and P. Budhwar. 1997. 'Competition and Change: Mapping The Indian HRM Recipe Against World Wide Patterns', *Journal of World Business,* 32(3): 224–42.

Taylor, P. and P. Bain 1999. 'An Assembly Line in the Head: The Call Centre Labour Process', *Industrial Relations Journal,* 30(2): 101–17.

——. 2005. 'India Calling to the Far Away Towns: The Call Centre Labour Process and Globalization', *Work, Employment and Society,* 19(2): 261–82.

The Economist. 2004. 'India's Shinning Hopes: A Survey of India', *The Economist,* 21 February.

The Hindu. 2005. 'UK Firms Save 10mn Pounds for Every 1000 Offshored Jobs', *The Hindu,* 25 January: 2.

Walletwatch. 2003. 'Call Centre Attrition puts HR Managers to Test'. Available online at: http://www.samachar.com/biz/fullstory.html (accessed on 8 May 2007).

Willmott, J. 2006. 'Growing Revenue, Not Cutting Costs', in *CRM, Call Centre and Marketing Systems Contents.* September. Available online at: http://www.conspectus.com/2005/september/article19.asp (accessed on 26 October 2007).

Witt, L.A., Martha C. Andrews, and Dawn S. Carlson. 2004. 'When Conscientiousness Isn't Enough: Emotional Exhaustion and Performance among Call Center Customer Service Representatives', *Journal of Management,* 30: 149–60.

5

Transnationalism in Indian Call Centres

Kiran Mirchandani

Globalised work processes have fundamentally altered the ways in which labour markets are organised around the world. While recognising that the globalisation of work is far from a new trend, there has been much focus in the recent literature on the need to highlight the ways in which globalisation is actually 'achieved'. Critiquing the construction of globalisation as an inevitable and irreversible process by which capitalism dominates nations, labour markets and households, Bergeron, for example, focuses on the '"gaps and margins" of the processes of global capitalism' (2001: 999). Sassen, in a similar vein, notes the need to 'shift emphasis to the *practices* that constitute what we call economic globalization and global control' (2001:196, emphasis in the original). Freeman suggests that such an approach would allow for a rethinking of the hegemonic 'masculinist grand theories of globalization that ignore gender as an analytic lens and local empirical studies of globalization in which gender takes centre stage' (2001: 1008). These theorists argue that grand theories which characterise globalisation as a 'meta-myth' (Bradley 2000), a 'rape script' (Bergeron 2001) or a 'narrative of eviction' (Sassen 2001), do not sufficiently allow for an exploration of the incomplete and contested nature of the movements of capital and labour. Instead, the ways in which workforces are neither homogeneous, not passive in relation to globalised work relations needs to be highlighted. Such an approach emphasises, as Sassen (2002) notes, the 'cracks' which exist in the 'wobbly political architecture' of social spaces. This chapter is an attempt to document the practices of globalisation within a newly emerging transnational labour force– call centre workers in New Delhi and Pune, India, who provide voice-to-voice service to clients dialing toll-free numbers in North America. In the past decade, India has installed reliable high capacity telephone lines in most of its major cities and since then has experienced high growth in the call centre services market (Srivastava 2004). Estimates indicate that the industry is likely to employ 1.2 million people by 2008 (Das et al. 2007). Examples of companies which have outsourced their call centres to India include British Airways, TechneCall, Dell Computers, America On-Line, GE Capital, Cap Gemini, Swiss Air and American Express. In fact, three quarters of the call centre industry in India caters to international markets (Das et al. 2007). Operators in these centres make telemarketing calls, or provide service to customers calling about issues such as their insurance claims, credit cards, computer hardware, network connections, banking and financial plans. Through the use of satellites, calls are seamlessly and inexpensively routed across geographical spaces.

I begin with a review of literature on theoretical approaches to globalisation which focus on the practices of transnational economic capitalism. Recent theorists have noted that such analyses demonstrate that capitalism is continually under construction, that labour in the Third World is heterogeneous and that workers play important roles in relation to transnational corporate processes. Accordingly, I trace three practices which constitute transnational call centre work–scripting, synchronicity and location masking–and examine the ways in which these practices are under continual construction and negotiation by Indian workers.

PRACTICES OF GLOBAL CAPITAL:
GAPS, CRACKS AND IRONIES

Sassen notes that understandings of global processes have traditionally been limited to analyses of cross-border processes such as international trade and investment. These analyses have produced a 'rather empirically and theoretically "thin" account' of the ways in which 'the global economy needs to be implemented, reproduced, serviced, financed' (2001: 190, 192). In order to challenge the 'transnational centrism' (Grewal and Kaplan 1994) implicit in assumptions about the inherently powerful nature of multinational corporations and the inevitability of the spread of economic globalisation, theorists have argued for the need to focus on the *practices* through which what is known as 'globalisation' is continually being constituted. These practices refer to the systems, norms and work relations which structure workers' experiences and which constitute 'globalisation'. An exploration of the practices of globalisation reveals the 'intersecting effects and material consequences of so-called globalisation in a particular place' (Katz 2001: 1214). As Sassen notes, 'the global economy cannot be taken simply as given, whether what is given is a set of markets or a function of the power of multinational corporations' (2000: 217). The shift of focus onto the practices that constitute what we refer to as economic globalisation allows for analyses of the ways in which diverse groups of workers play varied and active roles vis-à-vis transnational corporate and financial practices (Sassen 2001: 196).

The focus on the practices of globalisation in this chapter facilitates a heightened awareness of two processes at play. First, it allows for an exploration of the active ways in which workers define and construct their work situations (Mirchandani 2004). As Gibson-Graham notes, 'reading globalization... as a scripted series of steps and signals allows [us] to see the MNC [multinational corporation] attempting to place regions, workforces and governments in positions of passivity and victimization and being met by a range of responses–some of which play into the standard script and others that don't' (1996: 132). Second, the focus on the practices of globalisation highlights what Sassen (2001) refers to as the 'cracks' and inconsistencies in global economic capitalism. Such cracks, which can be sites of the 'hidden transcript' of power, may provide insight on the opportunities for political resistance (Scott 1990). As Scott notes, 'the social sites of the hidden transcript are those locations in which the unspoken, riposte, stifled anger, and bitten tongues created by relations of domination find a vehement, full-throated expression' (1990: 120). Focusing on the gaps between the representation and experience of call centre work, for example, reveals the incomplete and contested nature of transnational corporations in India. Appadurai challenges the view that globalisation brings about a straightforward cultural homogenisation. Rather, he argues that we live in a 'world of flows' characterised by the constant movement of ideas, ideologies, people, goods, images, messages and technologies (2000: 5). Appadurai notes that 'if a global cultural system is emerging, it is filled with ironies and resistances' (1996: 29).

As Brah summarises, 'globalization does not exist in some rarefied stratosphere. It always touches the ground' (2002: 26). Ethnographies of women and men working 'on the ground' reveal the diversity of practices arising from globalised work processes. Carla Freeman, for example, provides a vivid illustration of worker attempts to define their work, and notes that 'informatics workers in Barbados demonstrate through a variety of practices that they are not the passive pawns of multinational capital they have sometimes been depicted to be' (2000: 36). She notes that women's jobs are both a source of pride and pleasure, and simultaneously a source of stress and dissatisfaction. She challenges assumptions that women in the Third World are passive pawns of multinational capital and instead focuses on the agency women enact through their work and their lives. Freeman demonstrates that global capitalism is not monolithic; constructions of the 'ideal Third World worker' are both shifting and context specific. While other studies have revealed, for example, that young, childless and unmarried women constitute ideal Third World women workers, in Barbados family responsibilities are often believed to make women more committed to their jobs. Contrary to the assumption that multinationals seek a predefined flexible female labour force in the Third World, Freeman argues that ideal pools of flexible labour are actively and continuously created. In India, for example, multinational corporations are attracted not only by the large reservoir of cheap labour but also by the abundance of skilled and highly trained workers (Chhachhi 1999; Nanda 2000: 44).

Rather than focusing on trade agreements, state policies and corporate structures, this chapter highlights the practices of globalisation as experienced by workers doing transnational call centre work. The analyses explores 'the intersecting effects and material consequences of so-called globalization in a particular place to reveal a local that is constitutively global...' (Katz 2001: 1214). Following a brief discussion of the interviews I conducted and nature of subcontracted call centre work in India, I describe the relationships and processes which this work fosters.

METHODS

The primary purpose of this project was to explore the nature of call centre work within the context of global economy relations. Indian state policies encourage the subcontracting of information technology (IT) related jobs to India through tax relief, free trade zones and incentives to private training colleges (Kaushalesh 2001; Nayar 2003). Types of IT service jobs now located in India include back office, remote support, medical transcription, call centres, database services and content development (NASSCOM 2001:14).[1] While the call centre sector is not the largest source of subcontracted IT service jobs, it is a sector which has seen considerable growth in the past few years. Datta (2004) notes that the Indian call centre industry has experienced a 60 per cent annual growth rate. The revenues from the sector have grown from around US$ 565 million in 2000 to more than US$ 3 billion by March 2004 and are projected to increase beyond US$ 17 billion by 2008 (Poster 2007). Unlike most other IT service jobs, call centre work involves direct interaction between Indian workers and North American customers. In this sense, call centre work occupies a different place in the global assembly line compared to traditional manufacturing work. Taylor and Bain note that 'the call centre with its distinctive labour process can be offshored less easily than other non-customer facing, routine servicing activities' (2004: 20). As noted in the popular press, 'cultural distance is a bit harder to kill [when] company and customer are talking to each other on the telephone' (*The Economist* 29 April 2000: 87).

Interviews were conducted in 2002 and 2006 with workers in New Delhi and Pune. Although customers were not interviewed, workers provided detailed descriptions of their interactions with customers and these are included in the analysis. All respondents were with organisations serving British or North American clients.

Twenty-five workers (13 men and 12 women) were interviewed from 13 companies. Respondents were, on average, 26 years of age. Only four respondents were married; the remainder were single. All respondents had bachelors' degrees, and several had masters' degrees or additional diplomas as well. Workers interviewed in 2002 earned between Rs 5,500 and Rs 10,000 (US$ 125–225) per month with the exception of one male worker who had seven years of work experience and earned Rs 30,000 (US$ 670). For respondents interviewed in 2006, salaries ranged from Rs 10,000 to Rs 25,000 (US$ 225–560) per month with an average salary of Rs 16,000 (US$ 360). A significant portion of salaries was tied to performance incentives. Although extremely low in comparison to comparable salaries in the West, these salaries are considerably higher than those in local service industries (Van den Broek 2004).

In addition to salaries, call centre jobs are attractive to workers due to the clean work spaces and the fact that these organisations are marketed as fun places to work. Employees also receive perks such as free transportation, free dinners, free gifts for good performance, onsite cafeterias and recreational facilities, all of which are generally not available in other Indian workplaces.

In addition to call centre workers, I also interviewed managers at three call centres, as well as representatives of three agencies which provide training for workers. These interviews with managers and trainers focused on the history of the industry, labour force demographics and work processes.

PRACTICES OF GLOBALISATION IN TRANSNATIONAL CALL CENTRE WORK

Language and Scripted Taylorism: 'Like a Keyed Toy'

One of the central mechanisms through which transnational corporations attempt to control the nature, timing, norms and structure of work in India is through the use of standardised service scripts. As Leidner notes, workers engaged in interactive service work are often required to perform emotional labour as part of their jobs. Part of the work of providing service for a wage is the 'management of feeling to create a publically observable facial and bodily display' (Leidner 1999: 82).[2] Emotional labour is controlled by organisations through the development of detailed specifications of conduct (the scripting of 'feeling rules') and the close monitoring of individuals' work. Call centre workers perform emotional labour over the telephone; given the synchronous ('live') nature of their interactions with customers, considerable resources are expended to develop processes within which the appropriate emotional labour can be facilitated, controlled and monitored. As a result, the work practices in place at call centres in India can be paralleled to those in foreign-owned data processing centres in the Caribbean where 'the open office is, at one and the same time, factory like in terms of its labour process and office like in its muffled quiet ambience' (Freeman 2001: 200).

Scripted service work in call centres is ensured through both monitoring and language training. Workers undergo both generic (such as accent, grammar, customer service) and process-specific (about the products) training before they are allowed to take calls (Mirchandani and Maitra 2007). Some centres provide this training in-house and pay workers while they are being trained, while others outsource the training to adult education sites where individuals themselves pay for the training they receive. Through training programmes, transnational call centres engage in 'language trafficking' which is the spread of particular types of English throughout the world (Swales 1997). As Phillipson (2001) notes, English is a key instrument used by transnational corporations to break down national barriers. One worker describes the training programme she was required to undergo:

> For the accent training we were being taught by cassettes. We had a special trainer–he was singing songs and listening to some conversations. And then we were made to see some movies and stuff. We were actually taught by cassette and we had to repeat all things like they do in nursery standards [schools], repeating the Aa, Puh, Tuh, Duh, and things like that. It was, you know, a bit funny at that time, we all used to laugh our guts out. What nonsense is this! You know at times you feel so frustrated. It's OK the way we speak is the way we speak. Why do we have to learn such stuff? Then we were told, the basic idea is that those people should understand you. (Respondent 13)

Many of the managers and trainers interviewed for this project objected to reports in the media that they were teaching workers to speak in American accents. As one manager notes:

> Voice training is not really developing an accent, it's neutralising it… when you are looking at servicing an American client, you do not really need to sound American, however, you need to have a clarity of speech, and a pace of speech that is understandable by the other side. (Manager)

The justification provided for 'neutralising' accents draws heavily from discourses of human resource development whereby Indian labour is constructed as a flexible commodity which can be trained to meet client needs. As trainers and managers note:

> Many Punjabi guys [sic] are having a Punjabi accent. Other guys are having other types of accents. So we don't need any kind of accent, we need a very neutral accent so that we can train them and get them the accent that our customers ask for. (Trainer)

> We have a phenomenally robust training system, by which even the least common denominator we convert them into a resource, that is, the raw material, we convert them into a resource which can face the customer in any part of the world. (Manager)

Workers, however, experience the training they receive as an Americanisation of their English. The 'neutral' in this sense contains a significant regional bias, reinforcing the 'racist hierarchisation' implicit in identifying American English as legitimate and Indian English as illegitimate (Phillipson 2001: 11). Workers note:

> In India we speak English in a different, and in the States it is in a different way. [Interviewer: So they want you to learn…] A neutral accent. [Interviewer: What does that mean?] Neutral. Means they can understand what we tell. Like [for example] 'schedule'–they say *sked*ule… And the American accent you have more r's rolling, there's a stress on the r's. So it's sem-eye-conductor, it's not se-me- conductor…You're not supposed to speak anything except English, except American English. (Respondent 7)

> They have to tell us about the pronunciation part, about how to use an American accent. They actually make us listen to CDs, and they tell us constantly to watch CNN and all these channels. (Respondent 11)

Nanda argues that while multinational corporations are often said to have strong alliances to their 'home' countries but, in fact, 'MNCs chief alliances is to profits, not to national boundaries' (2000: 44). At the same time, the focus on developing 'neutral' but American accents suggests that there is often a confluence between capitalist and nationalist goals. This is particularly evident in the ways in which regional and south Indian accents are deemed to require much more 'correction' than urban and north Indian accents (Mirchandani 2008).

Language training is accompanied by the emphasis on following predefined scripts. One woman who was undergoing training at the time of our interview noted:

> This is our script, we have to go through this. Thank you for choosing [name of American company]. My name is Tanya [assigned pseudonym]. May I have your first and last name. Thank you. May I call you by your first name? Thank you very much. How are you doing today?... These are the typical statements that we have to say–Great. Thank you. Excellent, wonderful job. These are the power words. We have to use those words in our scripts. (Respondent 6)

While Leidner's (1999) research reveals that such service scripts can, in some situations, help workers to enforce their will over their customers and distance themselves from disagreeable interactions, the call centre workers interviewed for the present project experienced scripts as deskilling, repetitive and tedious:

> It's not that you are using your own words. You have to use these standard scripts. You have to use these same sentences...You're like a keyed toy... We were just told that we had to do the standard scripts. Just stick to your standard scripts. (Respondent 4 and respondent 5 in conversation)

As D'Cruz and Noronha note, 'the emphasis on customer orientation is embedded in the appeal to professionalism in the call centre industry in India... Being professional is at the heart of organizational control' (2006: 344). While training programmes and scripts are used as mechanisms of control through which workers are taught to emulate American culture, as Appadurai (1996) has noted, globalisation seldom brings about a straightforward cultural homogenisation. Bhabha argues, in his often cited essay, 'Of Mimicry and Man', that 'colonial mimicry is the desire for a reformed, recognizable Other as a subject of difference that is almost the same, but not quite'

(1994: 86). Referring to the ways in which the English construct the Anglicised (that is emphatically not English), Bhabha notes that 'the discourse of mimicry contains an ambivalence; in order to be effective mimicry must continually produce its slippage, its excess, its difference' (1994: 86). In this sense, mimicry, in producing a false copy of the original, makes a mockery of the colonial enterprise of engendering post-Enlightment civility. Bhabha focuses on the ambivalence of colonial authority; similarly while Indian workers are taught to mimic American work norms, there is a slippage between the information they are presented about Americans and the ways in which they interpret this information. In this sense, mimicry involves not only the coloniser's construction of the Other, but also the Other's construction of the coloniser. Specifically, through their discussions of their customers, workers construct Americans as rich but stupid.[3] In the context of the fact that workers are told that 'customers are Gods for us' (Respondent 2) and 'you have to be humble to the customer' (Respondent 4), this rhetoric allows workers to pity rather than revere their American customers, thus subverting the ideology of the 'West' as being superior to the rest of the world (Hall 1996).

One of the ways in which workers construct Americans as 'stupid' is by making frequent reference to the lower value placed on higher education in the US:

> Being a graduate in US can be a matter of prestige but being a graduate in India is just below average. Because average, average is even a post-graduation. (Respondent 3)

Workers note that nationality overrides class boundaries which are being crossed with call centre work whereby highly educated Indian workers employed in middle class, white collar occupations are serving often lower class, poorly educated American callers:

> Some Americans, they call [and] say, I want to talk to an American. Oh man, go on! You got an Indian and you are telling an Indian that

you want to talk to an American!... Some of them, they really speak very very fast and that is a bit difficult... In any case we have to handle the calls. We can't say that, you are an American, we can't talk to you. Like they have the freedom to say anything but we can't say anything. (Respondent 2)

The notion of Americans as less educated than Indians is also reinforced through the training which workers are provided. One worker says, for example,

> Our CEO says that an average American is uneducated. (Respondent 3)

Another worker describes scenarios provided during their training to illustrate responses workers should expect from American customers:

> They don't know anything about computers... If you say to them, just go to the start button, they will not be able to find the start button. Where is the start button?... And sometimes people are... talking about the trouble shooting steps and they're not sitting in front of their computers. [They say] I'm not able to see anything. And then we ask, 'Are you sitting in front of your computer?' He said, 'No I'm not sitting in front of my computer.' My God! One time [someone] called up and he said, you sent me a coffee mug tray and it was broken, send me another one... We asked our supervisor, was there any such scheme of sending in a coffee tray along with the thing?... Then [we realised] it was the CD drive! He used to put his coffee mug! We have so many examples like that. My God! (Respondent 6)

Many workers refer to the fact that while customers have little knowledge they have high disposable incomes:

> There are a lot of old people also that are hard to hearing, and you have to talk to them like your explaining to a little child, because a lot of them are not very good with mobile phone, and they don't even know what a SIM card is, and people say GOSH! Are Americans so dumb, they don't even know what a SIM card is, probably when mobile phones came to India, Indians were the same. A lot of people don't understand that they don't have patience to understand that. You have to explain to them like little children how to put the phone, how to put the SIM card together. (Respondent 20)

They don't know anything about computers. They put the [CD] upside down... We ask, OK how are you putting it in? The shiny portion should be down... Previously before we started interacting with Americans I basically had what I might refer to as [pause] it was in my mind, they are really good, they are really very intelligent, they have a lot of knowledge, nobody can beat the Americans. That was what my perception was. When I started handling calls the type of questions they ask, I said, Oh, it's bad. They only have money. They don't have brains. (Respondent 2)

Workers thus draw attention to the uneven development (which privileges national origin rather than education or intelligence) fostered by global capitalism (Wright 2001). In this context, while they are often told that they need to speak in American accents so that Americans can understand them, workers interpret this as evidence of the parochial and erratic nature of Americans:

The basic idea is that people should understand you... So that was the main motive behind learning all accent skills... Many a times people are very happy, and those people [say] how is it possible that staying in India[4] you can speak such good English?... But at times people are so rude–Oh, let me talk to someone who can speak English! I cannot understand you. We get customers like this also. One call, the customer is saying, oh you have fabulous English, you speak so well. And other call you get, oh my god let me talk to someone who can speak English. (Respondent 13)

Work processes and structures in Indian subcontracted call centres privilege the needs and sometimes racist perspectives of American customers. One worker shares an image she drew during her training programme (see Figure 5.1) which captures the ways in which workers are cast as subservient and machine-like. At the same time, workers' description of customers as stupid, uneducated, socially isolated and erratic allow workers to pity rather than revere Americans. In these ways, the focus on the practices of globalised work regimes provides vivid illustrations of workers' attempt to 'live with industrial systems without losing [their] human dignity' (Ong 1991: 296).

Figure 5.1:   Image Drawn by a Call Centre Worker as Part of Her
Notes during Training

Synchronicity and the Myth of Globalised Time

Sassen notes that globalisation involves the conflating of
'national time and capitalist time' (2000: 222); Indian call centres
are at the forefront of such a confluence given the time-sensitive
nature of synchronous customer service work. As Adam notes,
time is a 'quantifiable resource that is open to manipulation,
management and control, and subject to commodification, allocation, use and abuse' (1998: 14). Indian call centres providing
service to American customers are required to operate primarily
during American daytime hours, and with the time difference of
between 12 and 16 hours between the United States (US) and
India, this means that call centres operate primarily in the night.
Adam notes that such an arrangement signifies a 'colonization
with time' (2002: 21) whereby Western clock time is exported
across the globe and used as the standard. Indeed, India is promoted as an ideal location for the outsourcing of call centre
work from North America because of the different time zones
which allow companies to operate in a seamless fashion around
the clock. Adam notes that 'in tune with the globalization of
clock time, all that is local, context-dependent and seasonal
becomes an obstacle to be overcome while particular histories

and personal biographies are rendered irrelevant' (2002:17). Time is cited as a key factor in the literature advertising India's ideal location for IT outsourcing as it has 'a virtual 12-hour time zone difference with USA and other major markets providing 24×7 business service platform' (NASSCOM 2001). Time is a product which has economic value, is produced and exchanged. Such an approach which constructs time as money is based on the assumption that 'capitalism has a built in clock that is always ticking' (Adam 2002: 18). Typical shifts at Indian call centres are from 8 p.m. to 4 a.m., midnight to 8 a.m. and 4 a.m. to noon. Workers are sometimes picked up and dropped off in vans, which many workers greatly appreciate even though the vans operate on schedules which sometimes add between one and three hours to workers' time at the call centre. Workers experiences of shift work, however, highlight the fundamentally 'temporal features of living' (Adam 1998) and the conflicts between local and global timescapes have a significant impact on their health, families and unpaid activities:

> When I went [for this] job, I was very jubilant. I thought, OK, I'll study a lot, daytime is mine, so I'll be able to do anything. That's not possible. You're so tired. You're not able to do anything. Whatever time [you have] you sleep, even if you sleep for ten hours you don't get enough…you can never compensate a night's sleep… It's taxing, it's taxing, it's taxing on your social, it's taxing on your health, it's taxing on everything. (Respondent 1)

Call centres in India also operate seven days a week, through weekends and on Indian holidays. Workers' have two days off per week, but these days only occasionally fall on weekends. Workers often mention feeling cut off from families and friends.

> I don't get time to talk to them [friends and family]. They all complain… If we work in the night shift, at least you get six and a half hours of sleep. You get up in the afternoon. You have three to four hours to do your work. But actually that is not possible. Because you get so damn tired after work. It's difficult to work in the night, that's what I'll say. (Respondent 2)

Worker shifts also change every few months, so they are constantly adjusting to new work times. While they are told that these constant shifts are necessary so that no-one is permanently required to work the most difficult (all night) shift, some workers mentioned that shift changes served only to ensure that they did not moonlight at other jobs. The constant shift changes have a significant impact on workers' health, as one worker notes:

> You need at least three to four hours of sleep in the night. That's what makes the big difference... That is what is making it difficult. I'm losing my appetite, I'm losing my weight... suddenly we were told we would be having our [shift] from twelve [midnight] to eight. It was very difficult to adjust in the first few weeks. Then I got adjusted to that time. Then again we were told that you're having your shifts from 7:30 till 4 a.m. And this shift, I find it very difficult to adjust. That is because I get home around 7 a.m., and it's very difficult to sleep in the morning because people wake up, they go around here and there. (Respondent 4)

Indian call centre workers, in these ways, live and work in India, but are required to organise their lives in terms of American times, celebrations, and communication styles. Workers are expected to speak with American accents, take on American names, adopt American holidays and greetings, and work on American time. However, many workers identify the fact that they have to work at night as the most difficult part of their jobs thus highlighting the fundamental immobility of time and their continued embeddedness within their local social contexts. While Harvey (1989) argues that one of the central features of global capitalism is 'time space compression' whereby space is annihilated by time, the experiences of call centre workers suggest an opposite trend. They experience what Katz has termed 'time space expansion' in her ethnography of the effects of global restructuring in a village called Howa in Sudan, whereby 'from the vantage point of capital, the world may be shrinking, but, on the marooned grounds of places such as Howa, it appeared to be getting bigger every day' (2001: 1224). Similarly, in transnational call centres providing synchronous service, workers are detached from the spaces of social life such as markets, households and transportation links which occur only during the day.

Night work also manifests the gendered nature of call centre employment (Mirchandani 2006). As Patel notes, 'the urban nightscape is primarily a male domain that often represents danger and spaces of exclusion for women... for a woman in India to be out and about in the middle of the night is generally considered improper and unsafe' (2006:11). Women often encounter significant resistance to working at night as noted by the women quoted here:

> I have friends where I live and [they] say that people who work in BPOs are not good girls.... I have people talking of moral ethics, like people who work in BPOs coming late night... have you heard Radio Mirchi? [They say] people should start wearing condoms, people working in BPOs. (Respondent 20)

> In Darjeeling, people don't have a good feeling about BPOs. My mom she calls me everyday and says come back home.

> In Indian society if you tell somebody that you're working in a call centre they look at you like, oh my God, because you're working at nights and everybody knows the kind of people who work there. Nobody really, from the watchman to your neighbour to your parents, nobody would really respect you so much if you're working in a call centre. (Respondent 23)

Higher than usual salary structures, van services and the construction of work as professional allows some women to challenge the resistance they encounter from family and friends. At the same time, as Patel notes, 'although the presence of middle class women in the urban nightscape represents a break in traditional norms, their mobility and spatial access is based on regimes of control and surveillance' (2006:14). Organisations control when and how women leave their homes and leave their workplaces, and women feel they constantly need to justify the nature of their employment.

Locational Masking and Situated Jobs

Part of the protocol workers in Indian call centres are required to follow is a masking of their geographical location which is part of the new managerial strategy which has been termed 'national identity management' (Poster 2007). Workers are given Americanised pseudonyms, and these are used as their names at work. They are also trained to avoid answering questions from customers about their location. Managers note that they often sign non-disclosure agreements with their American clients, which require them to develop protocols through which their location in India is not revealed to the customers. Such requirements exemplify the prevalence of 'production fetishism' in the current economic order, which is, as Appadurai notes, 'an illusion created by contemporary transnational production loci that masks translocal capital, transnational earning flows, global management and faraway workers' (1996: 41). When asked why such locational masking is necessary and the purposes it serves, managers and trainers provide a number of responses:

> Why are we using this name [pseudonym]? Because it's easier to pronounce. That's customer service. (Manager)

> If we could achieve connectivity, nothing better than that. But if the guy sounds alien, you know, then my comfort levels are very low and I'm not going to impart any information. (Trainer)

> Most of the companies want to outsource their services to improve their productivity. There are various, I would say, concerns in [American] people [who may] say that they may lose their jobs. We want to minimise those effects. Because for sure when they're moving their work outside there are people who are losing their jobs there. (Manager)

> Some of the customers are wary about such things, because for example, there was a famous case of a multinational opening shop in India and they were not providing them with the right environment here. It was more of a sweatshop...customers may think [we are] a sweatshop, so that's one thing they want to avoid. It's bad publicity. (Manager)

These explanations and assumptions about American customers who are calling Indian call centres are used to justify the need to train workers in American accents and cultures, and to require them to use pseudonyms. Revealing that service work has been subcontracted to India may give rise to customer dissatisfaction for a wide variety of reasons, ranging from racism and ignorance towards Indians, concern about local jobs, and assumptions about exploitative transnational corporate practices. These concerns are not unfounded; workers report that they frequently face racism in their interactions with customers. Workers said they were continually accused of personally 'stealing' American jobs (Mirchandani 2008).

> Americans are not really happy outsourcing the job to India. Because I still remember a call from a very old guy, and after doing all the things possible to satisfy his needs, he made one statement, 'You know V– you did a great job, however, I hate you as I hate, because I hate all Indians. And my son is unemployed because of you, because the jobs are being outsourced to India. (Respondent 4)

The racism faced by immigrants to the US is extended to Indians handling calls in India:

> One day a person went, you know, I don't want to speak to you. You have broken English. Please give me someone American. (Respondent 7)

> They call up, they say, I want to speak to an American. (Respondent 2)

> They may ask you, I bought a [product] and I should get support from an American, why should I get support from an Indian? (Respondent 5)

The experiences of call centre workers suggests that Indians in India and Asian immigrants in America are named as equally 'non-American'. Locational masking, which as the quotes here suggest is only partially successful, serves to protect the interests of American corporations in light of the racism of their local customers. In fact, in attempting to reveal little about themselves, workers often reinforce negative stereotypes about Indians. One worker recounts the following incident where an US customer of Indian origin knew that he was likely talking to someone in India:

> [He asked] how is your relationship with Pakistan going? And things like, has Kashmir improved? You can't say anything. I told the ... person, I'm not much involved in the politics. I don't read newspapers. (Respondent 4)

Workers are taught such strategies to minimise customer knowledge about the location of their work. In being asked to follow scripts, and not reveal anything about themselves, however, workers are forced to reinforce notions of themselves as 'keyed toys'. At the same time, as Ong argues, worker resistances extend beyond direct confrontations with employers; 'in manipulating, contesting, or rejecting claims [about their status] working women reassess and remake their identities and communities in important ways for social life' (1991:296). The dominant rhetoric adopted by government, trade organisations and media reports on call centre work in India is that this industry provides highly desirable jobs. Workers evaluate these claims, and in doing so develop and share common understandings of the place of their work in the global order. The following argument about call centre work is made in a recent report by the National Association of Software and Service Companies (NASSCOM) in India:

> Let's go back to the basics. A customer calls with a complaint or query specific to the product or service of the client company. The customer may get impressed with the speed or manner of response, but what he really wants is a satisfactory answer. That does not come from technology–it comes from *knowing*, not just the product, but the customer need, the market scenario, the real end benefit that the customer is looking for, and a familiarity with the marketplace... A call centre handling a tourism product must be manned by people familiar with the tourism industry, and in the same way, one handling process control instrumentation systems must be manned almost exclusively by qualified electronics engineers. (NASSCOM 2001: C28, emphasis in the original)

In this way, call centre work is promoted as a desirable and highly skilled occupation. Transnational centres are housed in clean, well organised structures which often have entrances decorated with glass and marble. Van services for workers adds to the prestige of the work. Workers employed to serve multinational corporations are paid up to twice the salary they would receive in local organisations. Accordingly, media and government outlets have identified call and back-office centres as

'India's new sunshine sector' (*India Today* 18 November 2002). In particular, the notion that call centre work as a privileged occupation is created through the extensive screening process in place at the recruitment stage. Workers (all university graduates) describe being selected from hundreds of applicants and interviewed for hours before being offered the job. Workers reported:

I was interviewed for six rounds with [the career consultant], then with [the call centre] I interviewed for three rounds. Then I cleared the final interview, then I got the call. (Respondent 6)

Around 200 people were shortlisted. And out of that 17 people were selected. (Respondent 11)

[The interview took] seven or eight hours... one was the TOEFL test, and then they gave me a small objective type technical test, after that I was also given a one to one round, and then she gave me something to read out, maybe to see my accent, to see how I speak. Then I have a detailed questionnaire...I had again a one to one round with the technical people. Once I cleared that one, then I had a HR interview. After that HR interview in our company we get to be interviewed by a vice-president or the CEO of the company... maybe a hundred people apply and only seven or eight or maximum 10 are accepted. (Respondent 1)

Managers reinforce the rhetoric the call centre jobs are highly skilled jobs by referring to the higher status of call centre work in India compared to the West:

One thing is there, in India, people take this job very seriously. I was abroad, so I know how seriously people take this job in the West [not very seriously, suggested by facial expression]. [Here] people take this job very, very seriously. They see a career path in this job, because it is a new industry, and in a new industry people move very fast. (Manager)

Despite having undergone a long process to obtain their jobs, call centre workers are unanimously unconvinced by the arguments about the quality of call centre jobs. Most of the workers interviewed in 2002 said that they do not anticipate remaining

in the call centre sector but had taken their jobs due to the lack
of other job opportunities. Workers note,

> What happened with IT was that the balloon burst one day...Now if
> you just pick up yesterday's paper... observe the four page ads, around
> 85 per cent are for call centres...[People] tend to think it's a very glam-
> orous job. In fact, in my hometown [they say], OK you're working for
> a call centre? Great! That's great! You're talking to American clients.
> But they actually don't know how tedious it is. (Respondent 10)

> I know that call centre is not going to last for long. It's very short term. I
> don't have any future plans with this call centre. Not more than a year.
> Because there's no future. You can't sustain the taking calls through-
> out your life. It's just not possible. And this is no career. It's just a
> short-term kind of job. (Respondent 13)

Interviews conducted in 2006 revealed that workers were
more likely to construct the industry as more stable and recognise its growth potential. At the same time, however, workers
stressed the largely deskilled nature of their work:

> I don't think that the graduate person is required for that particular job,
> especially after he gets a training. So I think it would be more better
> if only a person of 12th standard would be. Because I have nothing to
> type, I have nothing to talk because everything is ready made. For this
> particular thing I don't think a graduate is required. (Respondent 22)

While they are paid high salaries in comparison to other service sector jobs, workers note that call centre salaries are far
lower than professional ones:

> I have a buddy of mine, he is having four years of experience as a
> software developer and because of this slack he [had to leave]. He was
> earning around Rs 25,000. And at this point in time [at the call centre]
> he might be earning maximum Rs 8,000. (Respondents 11 and 12 in
> conversation)

Despite the fact that workers were repeatedly told that they
were fortunate to hold clean, white-collar, professional jobs with
a multinational corporation, and that they are paid high salaries, the women and men interviewed for the present study
drew attention to the benefits which both American companies

and Indian subcontractors extract from their labour. As one worker notes:

> If you think about the jobs there [in the US], call centre jobs, they would be paying at least 10 or 15 dollars per hour for a fresh person. So per hour means if you work eight hours you calculate, it would be around like a 150 dollars per day they have to pay. That's ... like legislated minimum wage, not for people with any experience.... It's not that they pay us very less. But they should have paid us more. (Respondent 4)

Many of the workers interviewed talked about the results of their mathematical calculation of the differences between their salaries and the amounts companies would need to pay if customer service was provided within the US. A common set of figures was mentioned by various respondents, suggesting that this information was exchanged and discussed amongst workers. It was noted that the American company allocates US$ 30 for each call handled in the US, the Indian subcontractor receives US$ 18 per call and workers take an average of 20 calls a day. As one worker calculates:

> Each call which lands up to India, they're giving 18 dollars or something like that.... If you count yourself, whthin a single day you give your whole salary.... So this is the call centre industry—they're earning a lot. Exploiting, I can say, 95 per cent of the labour from the people. (Respondent 5)

Others drew attention to their lack of protection. None of the workers interviewed were unionised, and several noted that they encountered employment practices where the calculation of their incentive structures were masked, or they were made to sign 'contracts' which bonded them to their organisations for a period of time after the completion of their training. One worker notes,

> When you do on the floor, when you start taking calls, your salary is much more than what you are supposed to get in training because you have a lot of incentives. They don't explain why they are deducting so much money. They'll make up some or the other excuse. Oh, there is some problem with our headquarters... I'm just HR, I don't know

what is happening. Why don't you contact the other person in the HR department who is never available basically. And if you create a lot of uproar...you get blacklisted. (Respondent 23)

Appadurai notes that we are living in a 'world of flows' characterised by 'objects in motion'; these objects include ideas, people, goods, images, and technologies (2000: 5). Indeed, while call centre workers in India are trained to take on American persona, learn about American society and live on American time, they also gain an awareness of their connection to American labour markets and the global economic relations within which their jobs are situated. Workers situate their jobs in call centres within the wider political economy within which cost-reduction rather than customer service drive the imperatives of capital accumulation and profit maximisation (Taylor and Bain 2004). Such an awareness allows workers to challenge employer definitions of their work as privileged, skilled and desirable. Instead, they note that even experienced, skilled workers earn far less than their American counterparts, thus naming geographical location as the prime determinant of the value of labour in the global economy. Rather than becoming the 'ideal Indian workers' promoted in the state literature in the face of the constant threat of capital flight, workers see their work in call centres as transient and are in constant search of opportunities for more fulfilling work.

CONCLUSIONS

This chapter highlights transnational corporate practices in globalised call centres. These practices are continually under construction, suggesting that global capitalism is neither inevitable, nor predictable. In focusing on the practices of globalisation, this chapter contributes to the work of a number of theorists who have stressed the importance of situating analysis of the 'gaps' and 'cracks' within broader understandings of the political economy of globalisation. As Grewal and Kaplan (1994) argue, it is important to move away from the 'transnational centrism' in analyses of global capitalism which assume that transnational corporations have invincible organisational structures and possess inevitable hegemonic control. As Gibson-Graham notes, 'if we create a hegemonic globalization script with the MNC, the financial sector, the market, and commodification all set-up in relations of mutual reinforcement, and we then proclaim this formation as a "reality", we invite particular outcomes... By querying globalization... we may open up the space for many different scripts' (1996: 145). For example, in drawing parallels between their jobs and call centre jobs in North America, and between service and professional work, Indian workers defy their construction as a passive and grateful workforce, thus 'crafting' themselves in light of the 'shifting fields of power' (Kondo 1990: 260).

In recent years, there has been considerable media coverage on transnational call centres in India. Many reports celebrate the new growth in subcontracting with euphoric enthusiasm and claim, as in a recent article in *The Statesman,* that it proves that the 'Age of India Commeth'. The author of this article notes that 'Money for wages will flow into India in significant amounts, much of it directed into the pockets of India's growing middle class. A whole stratum of the population will earn salaries which, by US or British standards, are low and therefore competitive, but which by Indian standards are, if not princely, more than comfortable...This inflow of money into wages has positive implications for the Indian economy as a whole' (*The Statesman* 24 March 2004). In other reports, such as one based on the views of Praful Bidwai, who argues that transnational call centres reduce young, highly educated Indian workers to 'cyber-coolies', the subcontracting trend is characterised as 'a perfect sweatshop scenario, except that you're working with computers and electronic equipment rather than looms' (BBC News, 11 November 2003).

The analysis in this chapter suggests that these dichotomous perspectives largely fail to capture the experiences of Indian call centre workers. Neither are workers grateful and satisfied with the so-called 'comfortable' jobs which allow them to escape the perils of joblessness or work, nor do they want the subcontracting trend to end despite their recognition of the many negative professional, social and physical effects of their jobs. Rather, for call centre workers, as Sarker and Niyogi De argue, 'resistance and social change arise... from an entanglement with regimes of dominant knowledge/power, not outside them' (2002: 2). Workers object strongly to the routinised and deskilled nature of scripted service work and their resistance is an expression of their continual attempts to improve the quality of their jobs.

Acknowledgements

This project was funded by the Shastri Indo-Canadian Institute and the Social Sciences and Humanities Research Council of Canada. I would like to thank the interview participants for their enthusiastic and generous involvement with the project. This is a revised version of an article entitled 'Practices of Global Capital: Gaps, Cracks and Ironies in Transnational Call Centres in India' published in *Global Networks*, 4(4): 355–74, 2004.

Notes

1. There has been considerable research on call centre jobs in a variety of countries. Examples include Bain and Taylor (2002) (comparing British, Dutch and US call centres); Mitter (2000) (Malaysia); Barnes (2004) (Australia); Larner (2002) (Canada and New Zealand).
2. Although Leidner does not refer to phone-based interactive service work, voice displays, too, can be assumed to involve the management of feeling.
3. A few workers noted positive perceptions of Americans (such as that they were more patient, more willing to solve issues via the telephone) but these were by far the exception.
4. Locational masking is not always successful and customers sometimes guess the location of work.

REFERENCES

Adam, B. 1998. *Timescapes of Modernity: The Environment and Invisible Hands.* London: Routledge.

———. 2002. 'The Gendered Time Politics of Globalization: Of Shadowlands and Elusive Justice', *Feminist Review*, 70: 2–29.

Appadurai, A. 1990. 'Disjuncture and Difference in the Global Cultural Economy', *Theory, Culture and Society*, 7: 295–310.

———. 1996. *Modernity at Large: Cultural Dimensions of Globalization.* Minneapolis: University Minnesota Press.

———. 2000. 'Grassroots Globalization and the Research Imagination', *Public Culture*, 12(1):1–19.

Bain, P. and P. Taylor. 2002. 'Consolidation, "Cowboys" and the Developing Employment Relationship in British, Dutch and US Call Centres', in U. Holtgrewe, C. Kerst, and K. Shire (eds), *Re-organizing Service Work: Call Centers in Germany and Britain*, pp. 42–62. Burlington: Ashgate.

Barnes, A. 2004. 'The Construction of Control: The Impact of the Physical Environment on the Development of Resistance and Accommodation within Call Centers', 22nd International Labour Process Conference, 5–7 April 2004, University of Amsterdam.

Bergeron, S. 2001. 'Political Economy Discourses of Globalization and Feminist Politics', *Signs: Journal of Women in Culture and Society*, Special Issue on Globalization and Gender, 26(44): 983–1006.

Bhabha, H.K. 1994. *The Location of Culture.* Routledge: London and New York.

Brah, A. 2001. 'Feminist Theory and Women of Colour', *International Encyclopaedia of the Social and Behavioural Sciences*, 8: 5491–495.

———. 2002. 'Global Mobilities, Local Predicaments: Globalization and the Critical Imagination', *Feminist Review*, 70: 30–45.

Bradley, H. 2000. *Myths at Work.* Cambridge: Polity Press; Malden Mass: Blackwell.

Chhachhi, A. 1999. 'Gender, Flexibility, Skill and Industrial Restructuring: The Electronics Industry in India', *Gender, Technology and Development*, 3(3): 329–60.

Das, D., R. Dharwadkar, and P. Brandes. 2007. 'The Importance of Being "Something": Indian Centrality and Work Outcomes in Off-shored Call Centres in India'. Academy of Management Best Paper Proceedings. Washington, DC: Academy of Management.

Datta, R.C. 2004. 'Worker and Work–A Case Study of an International Call Centre in India', 22nd International Labour Process Conference, 5–7 April 2004, University of Amsterdam.

D'Cruz, P. and E. Noronha. 2006. 'Being Professional: Organizational Control in Indian Call Centres', *Social Science Computer Review*, 24(3): 342–61.

Gibson-Graham, J. K. 1996. *The End of Capitalism as We Know It.* Cambridge: Blackwell Press.

Grewal, I. and C. Kaplan (eds). 1994. 'Introduction: Transnational Feminist Practices and Questions of Postmodernity', in I. Grewal and C. Kaplan (eds), *Scattered Hegemonies: Postmodernity and Transnational Feminist Practices,* pp. 1–36. Minneapolis: University of Minnesota Press.

Freeman, C. 2000. *High Tech and High Heels in the Global Economy: Women, Work and Pink Collar Identities in the Caribbean.* Durham: Duke University Press.

———. 2001. 'Is Local: Global as Feminine: Masculine? Rethinking the Gender of Globalization', *Signs: Journal of Women in Culture and Society,* Special Issue on Globalization and Gender, 26(4): 1007–1038.

Hall, S. 1996. 'The West and the Rest: Discourse and Power.' in S. Hall, D. Held, D. Hubert and K. Thompson (eds), *Modernity: An Introduction to Modern Societies,* pp. 184–228. Oxford: Blackwell.

Harvey, D. 1989. *The Condition of Postmodernity: An Enquiry into the Origins of Cultural Change.* Oxford: Blackwell.

Kaushalesh, L. 2001. 'Institutional Environment and Development of Information and Communication Technology in India', *The Information Society,* 17: 105–17.

Katz, C. 2001. 'On the Grounds of Globalization: A Topography for Feminist Political Engagement', *Signs: Journal of Women in Culture and Society,* Special Issue on Globalization and Gender, 26(4): 1213–34.

Kondo, D. K. 1990. *Crafting Selves: Power, Gender, and Discourses of Identity in a Japanese Workplace.* Chicago: University of Chicago Press.

Larner, W. 2002. 'Calling Capital: Call Centre Strategies in New Brunswick and New Zealand', *Global Networks,* 2(2): 1470–2266.

Leidner, L. 1999. 'Emotion Labour in Service Work', *Annals of the American Academy of Political and Social Science,* 56(1): 81–95.

Mitter, S. 2000. 'Telework, Teletrade and Sustainable Development: The Indian Experience in a Global Context', *Economic and Political Weekly,* 24–30 June: 35 (26): 2241–52.

Mirchandani, K. 2004. 'Webs of Resistance in Transnational Call Centres: Strategic Agents, Service Providers and Customers', In R. Thomas, A. J. Mills and J. H. Mills (eds), *Identity Politics at Work: Resisting Gender, Gendering Resistance,* pp. 179–95. London: Routledge.

———. 2006. 'Gender Eclipsed?: Racial Hierarchies in Transnational Call Centre Work', *Social Justice,* 32(4): 105–19.

———. 2008. 'Enactments of Class and Nationality in Transnational Call Centres', in S. Fineman (ed.), *The Emotional Organizations: Passions and Power,* pp. 88–101. Oxford: Blackwell.

Mirchandani, K. and S. Maitra. 2007. 'Learning Imperialism through Training in Transnational Call Centers', in L. Farrell and T. Fenwick (eds), *Educating the Global Workplace: Knowledge, Knowledge Work, and Knowledge Workers,* pp. 154–64. Edmonton: Kogan Page.

Nanda, M. 2000. 'Post-Fordist Technology and the Changing Patterns of Women's Employment in the Third World', *Gender, Technology and Development*, 4(1): 25–56.

NASSCOM. 2001. *Nasscom's Handbook: IT Enabled Service Background and Reference Resource*. New Delhi: NASSCOM. Available online at www. nasscom.org

Nayar, B. R. 2003. 'Globalization and India's National Autonomy', *Commonwealth and Comparative Politics*, 41(2): 1–34.

Ong, A. 1991. *Flexible Citizenship: The Cultural Logics of Transnationality*. Durham: Duke University Press.

Patel, R. 2006. 'Working the Night Shift: Gender and the Global Economy', *ACME: An International E Journal for Critical Geographers*, 5(1): 9–27.

Phillipson, R. 2001. 'Global English and Local Language Policies What Denmark Needs', *Language Problems and Language Planning*, 25(1): 1–24.

Poster, W. R. 2007. 'Who's on the Line? Indian Call Centre Agents Post as Americans for U.S Outsourced Firms', *Industrial Relations*, 46(2): 271–304.

Sarker, S. and E. Niyogi De. 2002. *Trans-status Subjects: Gender and the Globalization of South and South East Asia*. Durham: Duke University Press.

Sassen, S. 2000. 'Spatialities and Temporalities of the Global: Elements for a Theorization', *Public Culture*, 12(1): 215–32.

———. 2001. 'Cracked Casings Notes towards an Analytics for Studying Transnational Processes', in L. Pries (ed.), *Transnational Social Spaces International Migration and Transnational Companies in the Early 21st Century*, pp. 187–208. Routledge: New York.

———. 2002. 'The Formation of New Political Subjects under Globalization', Public Lecture at the Institute for Women's Studies and Gender Studies, 29 November 2002, University of Toronto.

Scott, J. C. 1990. *Domination and the Arts of Resistance: Hidden Transcripts*. New Haven: Yale University Press.

Srivastava, S. 2004. 'If Only Indians Would Talk like Americans', *Asia Times*, 8 January 2004. Available online at: http://www.atimes.com/atimes/South Asia/FA08Df04.html (accesed on 30 August 2008).

Swales, J. M. 1997. 'English as Tyrannosaurus Rex', *World English*, 16(3): 373–82.

Taylor, P. and P. Bain. 2004. 'India Calling to the Far Away Towns: The Call Centre Labour Process and Globalization', 22nd International Labour Process Conference, 5–7 April 2004, University of Amsterdam.

The Economist. 2000. 'It's Barbara Calling', *The Economist*, 29 April, 355 (8168): 87.

Van den Broek, D. 2004. 'We Have Values: Customers, Control and Corporate Ideology in Call Centre Operations', *New Technology, Work and Employment*, 19(1): 2–13.

Wright, M. 2001. 'Asian Spies, American Motors, and Speculations on the Space–Time of Value', *Environment and Planning*, A. 33: 2175–88.

SECTION TWO

STAKEHOLDER PERSPECTIVES

6

A Practitioner's Perspective on the Indian Info-services Industry

Nandita Gurjar

INTRODUCTION

The purpose of this chapter is to closely examine the evolving role of human resources (HR) at Infosys BPO in light of the emerging needs of the Indian information technology enabled services–business process outsourcing (ITES-BPO) industry. The chapter also describes the innovative HR practices taken up by Infosys BPO over the period of six years since its inception in 2002, to effectively manage its people-related challenges and enable business growth.

The last six years have witnessed the Indian ITES-BPO sector growing at a phenomenal rate of 40 per cent year on year. The early entrants were the multinational corporation (MNC) subsidiaries, popularly known as the 'captives'. What followed as the next wave was the entry of Indian IT companies. Leveraging their experience of having successfully handled IT outsourcing, they took it to the next level—business process outsourcing—at a much faster pace than what IT had experienced. Evidence of this growth is the fact that the exports of the 6-year-old ITES-BPO industry are more than a third of the exports of the 20-year-old IT industry.[1] Along with the growth and spread of the BPO industry across different domains came the business challenges of managing scale, execution, culture, risk, diversity and cost. These business challenges were coupled with a few people-related challenges, which were similar to those faced by their parent IT companies, namely, challenges in the realm of culture, workforce demographics and time zones of operations. However, the impact of these challenges was much higher for the ITES-BPO industry due to the profile of the workforce and the nature of work which involves real-time interaction with the end customers. This chapter examines the response of Infosys BPO's HR function to business challenges of managing scale, execution, culture, risk, diversity and cost. The chapter also captures the changing landscape of HR in light of emerging needs of business. As Infosys BPO moved from its start-up stage to the growth stage, the HR landscape changed from talent sourcing to talent creation, from people management to people engagement and from people administration to being business partners.

With Infosys BPO expanding its business footprint, the role of HR at Infosys BPO requires its transformation from a support function to a line function. This translates into two opportunities for the HR function. First, HR professionals have to acquire sound business knowledge, align human capital with business needs and translate their work into quantifiable business performance. Second, HR professionals have to influence line managers towards becoming 'human resource' managers. This chapter concludes with some emerging steps of HR towards aligning to line functions.

THE GROWTH STORY OF INFOSYS BPO

In 1981, led by N.R. Narayana Murthy, seven young IT professionals started a small company in Pune, India. Infosys began with just US$ 250 as seed capital, zero infrastructure and a dream to create quality software. Along the way, it rewrote the rules of the industry, inspired a generation and redefined India's image in the world. In 1983, Infosys shifted its base from Pune to Bangalore. In 1987, it opened its first international centre in

Boston, United States. During its early stage of development, Infosys faced several challenges similar to those faced by many start-up organisations, like refining business models, gaining market acceptance and establishing business sustainability. Moreover, the Indian economy was then governed by the 'command and control' rule, high taxes, underdeveloped capital markets, capital shortage for infrastructure investment and poor telecom infrastructure.[2] In 1991, India witnessed major economic reforms and the liberalisation of the Indian economy increased the free and open market by removing several licensing requirements and facilitating access to the capital markets. The new, vibrant and more competitive Indian economy well supported the uphill struggle of Infosys. In 1994, Infosys went public and got listed in the Bombay Stock Exchange (BSE) and was later listed in the National Stock Exchange of India Limited (NSE). Pioneering the global delivery model, Infosys became the first IT company from India to be listed on the National Association of Securities Dealers Automated Quotation System (NASDAQ) in 1999. Infosys also made its debut at number six on the *BusinessWorld*-India poll of India's most respected companies in 1991. The period from 1999–2002 and onwards was the big leap for Infosys. Leveraging a successful business model and its relationship with clients, business trends drove the demand for Infosys expanding its portfolio of services to business process and knowledge process outsourcing.

In 2002, Infosys forayed into business process management in a joint venture set-up with Citicorp International Finance Corporation's 23 per cent stake in its BPO subsidiary Progeon. What drove a successful IT company to venture into business process management was the growth potential associated with the fastest growing ITES-BPO sector in the Indian economy. Soon after it set up Progeon, Infosys realised that BPO was a long-term game and held tremendous opportunity if it could be effectively integrated with its core IT services. In 2006, Infosys bought out Citicorp International Finance Corporation's 23 per cent stake in Progeon and added BPO services to its 'One Infy' offering and renamed it as Infosys BPO.

Infosys BPO Ltd (formerly, Progeon) holds the same vision as the parent company—'To be a globally respected corporation that provides best-of-breed business solutions, leveraging technology, delivered by best-in-class people'. This can be best explained in the words of its chief executive officer (CEO), Amitabh Chaudhry: 'To be the "Infosys" of ITES-BPO industry'. In the six years since its inception, Infosys BPO's revenues have grown from US$ 4 million in 2003 to US$ 147 million in the year ending March 2007. This achievement prompted CNBC to recognise the organisation as the fifth most respected company in the country's BPO sector. Today, Infosys BPO is ranked among the leading BPO companies in India by reputed industry bodies, such as the National Association of Software and Service Companies (NASSCOM) and industry analysts, such as *Dataquest.*

Infosys BPO operates in India, the Czech Republic, China, the Philippines, Poland, Bangkok and Mexico. It employs approximately 16,000 people with an average age of 26 years of whom 38 per cent are women. The education profile of its workforce is 72 per cent graduates (in commerce, science and arts), 5 per cent IT graduates, 18 per cent postgraduates (MBAs, commerce), 5 per cent professionals in chartered accountancy and law.

HR CHALLENGES AT INFOSYS BPO

The ITES-BPO industry is highly volatile in terms of impact of foreign exchange, workforce attrition and increasing number of service providers in the market. Therefore, competing in this industry is not an easy task for any organisation. Infosys BPO, too, faced a set of challenges from competitors, clients, new entrants in the industry and other external (social, economic, government related) factors. These have been profiled and explained in brief in Table 6.1.

Table 6.1: Profiling Business Challenges at Infosys BPO

Forces	Challenges	Infosys BPO Landscape
		Infosys BPO's Response to these Challenges
Competitors	• To succeed amidst strong competition from captives, pure BPO players and other ITES players in the market.	• Operational excellence–through a unique transition methodology which is periodically reviewed and refined to capture the learning from ongoing and completed engagements. • Acquisitions–inorganic growth to expand into new territories and acquire domain expertise to move up the value chain.
Clients/end customers	• To meet the high expectations of clients in terms of better management of operational challenges, expectations of cost savings and productivity gains.	• Managed complexities of scale and scope through efficient staffing and training and development. • Quality of work–by establishing and embedding quality checks into the operations from day one of transition. • Process re-engineering by developing workflow management tools to improve process efficiency.
New entrants	• Countries like China, Mexico and the Philippines were also emerging as the other preferred destinations for outsourcing.	• Nearshoring–Infosys BPO has set-up its centres in China, the Philippines and recently in Mexico. • Expanded global footprints through acquisitions in Poland and Bangkok.

(Table 6.1 continued)

(Table 6.1 continued)

Infosys BPO Landscape

Forces	Challenges	Infosys BPO's Response to these Challenges
Economic, social and government-related factors	• Increasing wage levels—with salary cost forming more than 50 per cent of the total costs, increase in wage levels impacts the bottom line. • Foreign exchange impact—declining cost advantage in face of a stronger rupee value. • Manpower supply—employment statistics show that 40 per cent of available talent pool is not suited to careers in BPO. Therefore, there is a shortfall in terms of 'job ready' talent pool. • Corporate social responsibility—organisations voluntarily taking further steps to improve the quality of life for employees and their families as well as for the local community and society at large.	• Strategy of de-skilling of processes using automation and workflow designs to get better productivity gains. • Strategy of near-shoring and thereby being closer to the customer as well as taking advantage of the low cost talent pool in China/Mexico/the Philippines. • Building industry–academia partnership—introduction of industry-specific curriculum in the education system to expand the 'job ready' talent pool. • Infosys BPO's social responsibility initiatives fall under the purview of the Infosys Affirmative Action Programme. The programme aims at enhancing employment opportunities through strategic partnerships that are in line with its business.

Implications for HR

Be it ensuring cultural fit during mergers and acquisitions, or managing complexities of scale and scope through employees' capabilities, HR has a very critical role in facilitating smooth execution. The key HR challenges for Infosys BPO can therefore be categorised as managing execution in the face of scale, culture, risk, diversity and cost. Infosys BPO has successfully exploited these as opportunities to be a market differentiator by leveraging on its most important asset—its people.

1. Managing execution in the face of scale: Infosys BPO is growing at a rate of 70 per cent year on year. Whether it was obtaining a new client or growing the existing client, seamless execution by managing performance through efficient staffing, training and talent management was the key responsibility of HR. The HR processes have been standardised or automated to meet the complexities of scale, both of the domestic and international centres, without compromising on the commitments of service delivery.

2. Managing risk: From the HR's perspective, there were risks from two areas. First, with expanding global footprints, there was a risk of being non-compliant with the changing labour laws at the various international centres, especially as the organisation started reaching out to the local talent pool for hiring. Second, there is a risk of losing out on knowledge and expertise due to high attrition.

3. Managing diversity: With the organisation expanding its wings to reach out, on one hand, to new geographies and, on the other hand, to second and third tier cities in the home country, Infosys BPO has a diverse workforce. Therefore, building a diverse, truly 'inclusive' and positive work environment has been one of the key responsibilities of HR.

4. Managing costs: Being in a people-intensive industry, people-related costs form 70 per cent of the total cost of the organisation. So, in order to make an impact on the bottom line, HR must focus on costs. The three major

people-related costs are salary, recruitment and training cost. Impacting any of these costs makes a real bottom line impact. Realising this, the HR function has taken up several initiatives to effectively manage its financial performance.

5. Managing culture: An organisation's culture is the common thread that binds its employees together and reflects in the organisation's outlook to the external world. Infosys BPO strongly lives by its values. During mergers and acquisitions, it is very critical for HR to enable smooth collaboration of different cultures into the organisation culture. This means, employees from different cultures, speaking diverse languages and holding diverse beliefs across boundaries understand and interpret Infosys BPO's organisational values in its true sense. Therefore, making mergers and acquisitions 'work' is dependant on the HR's capability of being able to cater to diverse nationalities and making them feel included.

EVOLUTION OF HR PHILOSOPHY AND PRACTICES

The HR philosophy at Infosys BPO is 'Become the employer of choice by attracting right talent; retaining best talent; engaging talent and demonstrating thought leadership'. The cornerstone elements of this philosophy are:

1. BPO to be seen as an attractive long-term career option at all levels of the company for the business to be successful.
2. Developing people plays a major role in attracting and retaining the right talent. Only when people believe that their time in Infosys is adding to their professional resume will they stay. Paradoxically, the more marketable Infosys can make them, the longer they will remain with the company.
3. People leave managers and not companies. Therefore, the first line supervisor is the most important layer in the

organisation. The company needs to invest in building, training and developing this cadre of people.

4. Most people joining BPOs are working for the first time and it is the company's responsibility to ensure that they imbibe good work ethics.

5. Despite inflation, people cost is something that can and must be managed. Infosys BPO has developed sophisticated techniques to do this over the last few years.

Translating the HR philosophy into strategic initiatives evolved as the organisation matured in its processes, businesses and outlook. To understand this change better, let us look at the Infosys BPO life cycle as an organisation.[3]

The first two years (2002–2004) was the start-up phase. With a workforce of 1,878 employees and 14 clients, HR practices were formulated keeping in mind the hygiene needs of the organisation and employees like staffing, training, compensation and benefits, performance management and recognition and rewards. The period 2004–2007 was a stage of rapid growth when the number of clients increased by 40 per cent and employees increased by 450 per cent. HR practices and policies underwent a tremendous change in line with the complexities of scale (see Figure 6.1).

Figure 6.1: The Growth Chart of Infosys BPO

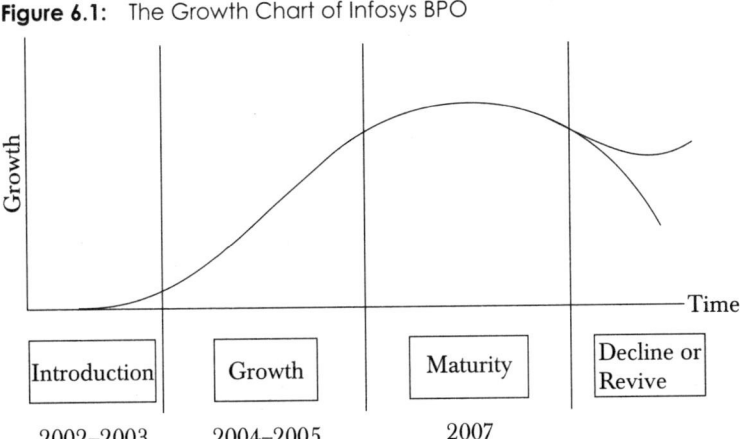

Table 6.2 describes the evolution of HR practices from the start-up stage to the growth stage at Infosys BPO.

Table 6.2: Evolution of HRM Practices at Infosys BPO

Start-up Stage (2002–2004) ⟶	*Growth Stage (2004–2007)*
Hiring	*Talent creation*
The focus was on creating a strong foundation of the hiring function which could stand the complexities associated with hiring huge volumes in future efficiently. Since the hiring targets were not high during the start-up stage, it was managed through the primary sources like consultants, direct applications and employee referrals.	With job demand outpacing workforce growth, there was a need to transform the context from hiring to creating a talent pool proactively and ahead of time. The aim was to keep the gap between the job demand and the available talent as narrow as possible. Several innovative practices were introduced to meet the growing demand for 'job ready' talent.
People management ⟶	*People engagement*
The focus was on carrying out hygiene people management responsibilities of hiring, compensating, training, safety, wellness, benefits, employee motivation, communication and administration effectively.	Employee expectations evolved to develop value proposition through excellent career and increased employability. If career and employability was the primary need for employees, Infosys BPO realised that the means to meet this need was through continuous learning. To facilitate the same, initiatives were introduced to ensure • Better job–person fit through optimum match of employees' skills to that required for the job. 'Optimum' is defined as a notch below the ideal. This gives an employee the motivation to learn and upgrade his skills to the next level.

Start-up Stage (2002–2004)	⟶	Growth Stage (2004–2007)
		• Customising training: (a) finishing school as a comprehensive training curriculum for the entry level to get them started with business, process and people skills and (b) middle management leadership development curriculum to enable individuals to make their career turns successfully. 'Turns' is defined as the upward movement from individual contributor to (i) first time manager to (ii) manager's manager and (iii) the business manager.
HR administration	⟶	*The business partner*
The focus was on HR operations for providing basic HR services to the employee like payroll processing, routine employee query management, employee grievances and employee database management.		With organisation growing at a rate of 70 per cent year on year, HR had two important deliverables. First, partner with business to effectively align the human capital with the business needs. Second, taking HR processes to the next level to manage scale effectively. • Business partner HR for effective people management as (*a*) a friend to the employees, (*b*) collaborator to line managers and (*c*) consultant to the client. • An internal HR consulting partner who would be the quality custodians of HR processes and enhance HR productivity through effective systems and processes.

Evolution of HRM Practices: From Hiring to Talent Creation

Infosys BPO realised that there are certain imperatives that should govern the hiring strategy in order to support the growing business:

1. Sourcing strategies should not be designed to meet just the immediate business needs but should be long-term oriented as well. This implies that the focus of talent sourcing should be on talent acquisition as well as increasing the overall supply of talent in the labour market.
2. Acquiring people with a strong value system who would become the building blocks in the organisation's growth and thus grow with the organisation.
3. In a relatively new industry, the challenge for HR was to make BPO seem as an attractive long-term career option at all levels of the company. Thus employer branding became an integral part of HR responsibility—both building employer brand at campus, credibility with academia and family community needed to be worked on continuously.

Also, industry reports project that 3 million students will graduate in 2010 and requirement in IT/BPO will be 2.3 million.[4] Overall, this seems like an ideal balance. However, almost 40 per cent of this available pool is not suited to careers in BPO. Another 20–25 per cent drop out of the pool for various reasons like higher education, marriage and re-location. This leaves us with just 35 per cent of the available pool. Keeping the hiring imperatives in mind, this gap between the job demand and talent availability can be bridged ahead of time by (a) creating the skills in the potential talent market; (b) enlarging the talent pool; (c) creating awareness about the industry amongst youth, parents and teachers.

Creating the Skills in the Potential Talent Market

The industry requires niche skills in oral and written communication, domain and industry knowledge that are not abundantly available in the country. This limited talent pool is further stretched by the number of BPO companies across the country, thus increasing the demand and supply gap. Therefore, to address the issue of diminishing talent pool, Infosys BPO launched Project Genesis.

Project Genesis

Project Genesis focuses on creating the necessary talent pipeline not only for Infosys BPO but also for other BPO companies with a two-fold objective:

1. Reducing the turnover rate among BPO companies and stabilising salary costs. With the creation of a talent pipeline there would be no need to attract skilled resources from existing players at a salary premium.
2. Increasing the employment opportunities and the employability index especially in second and third tier cities in India.

Design of Genesis—A Four-pronged Strategy

The project was designed to align the educational curriculum of institutes with the skills requirements of the industry and to invest in training for employees even before they joined the organisation. It was important to design this initiative effectively to get the intended outcome. Therefore, it was divided into four phases where each phase was a building block for the next phase. And each stage reaped substantial benefits to the organisation like the creation of a talent pipeline, branding of the organisation and savings in training costs.

Phase 1: Skill Level Assessment and Design of the New Curriculum

The first phase comprised:

1. A skills assessment of the graduate pool in select colleges across the state to understand the competency baseline that existed and to identify the gaps.
2. Curriculum creation: After multiple discussions with lecturers across colleges to understand current gaps and therefore 'must have' skills for a BPO career, the 'Global Skills Enhancement Curriculum' (GSE) was created. It contains modules on communication and analytical skills, corporate etiquette, basic computer skills and ways of building self-confidence.

The benefit from Phase 1 was associated with the assessments conducted in this phase, where the skills available in the different regions across the country were identified. Internally for the organisation, these skills are mapped to the skill clusters as required in different client processes. The manpower planning team along with the recruitment team then draws out a sourcing plan to clearly identify where the client processes can be staffed from. This helps Infosys BPO ensure that it fits the 'right person' for the 'right job'.

Phase 2: Training the Lecturers to Deliver the Programme

A train the trainer workshop was conducted to equip lecturers to deliver the programme. At the end of this rigorous training, lecturers were certified on the GSE curriculum so that they could not only train their students but also work towards enhancing the awareness of opportunities available in the BPO industry among them.

The benefit from this phase was associated with employee turnover which is a key performance indicator for the organisation. Infosys BPO constantly strives to reduce the turnover rates among different groups of employees. During the trainer programme in Phase 2 of Project Genesis, Infosys BPO educates the participating professors on the BPO industry itself also creating awareness of not just the exciting opportunities of growth but also the challenges of such a career. Infosys BPO emphasises the need for employees to grow and build a long-term career in the industry. This information is transferred to the students throughout the duration of the programme and we have found that turnover among Genesis hires currently stands at 0 per cent.

Phase 3: Review and Assessment

The certified lecturers train their students on the curriculum. A follow-up plan provides the identified academia representatives with a forum for real-time support in the form of periodic reviews, assessment, feedback on training methodologies, etc. Periodic refresher training programmes are organised to modify and change the curriculum as maybe required as well as share new developments in the industry and employment scenario in general.

The benefit from this phase is associated with entry-level training costs. Till last year, Infosys BPO followed a long and short training cycle methodology. This meant that all employees would go through the same training irrespective of the skills displayed or the scores gained during the recruitment tests. It was found that employees from first and second tier cities already possessed most of the required skills (fluent verbal communication, written communication and computer skills) and hence went through a short cycle training programme. Employees who joined Infosys BPO from smaller towns had to go through a long cycle training programme so that they could be taught all the skills mentioned earlier from scratch. The long cycle training batch cost the organisation three times as much as the short cycle one. But with the advent of Project Genesis, the training cycle for hires from all places has been brought to a uniform level completely based on skills required for the client process. This has not only resulted in lower costs of training but has helped in ensuring that all employees irrespective of where they are hired from, undergo standardised skill-based training and are ready to hit the floor at a faster rate.

Phase 4: Regional Job Fairs

This phase involves organising job fairs for all those students who have successfully completed and have been GSE certified. The job fair aims at inviting a number of BPO companies to recruit from the newly available skilled talent pool.

The benefit from this phase is associated with salary costs. The largest portion of HR costs is the salary of the employee and it was found that with a shrinking talent pool, BPO companies were waging a war for existing talent purely based on increasing salary packages. This lead to spiraling salary costs for all organisations. Today, Project Genesis, through its job fairs makes a steady source of new talent available to all interested BPO companies. This has resulted in companies mutually agreeing to an unwritten policy of 'no poaching' which has helped stabilise if not bring down the spiraling salary costs.

Benefits of Project Genesis

Project Genesis evolved to be a win–win situation for all stakeholders. It not only benefited Infosys BPO to meet the set objectives but also provided significant benefits to the employees, society and government.

Employees

Project Genesis has helped create employment opportunities in third tier towns by imparting and enhancing BPO requisite skills in graduate students in order to make them employable. Once they join the organisation, they are treated at par with other employees and are extended the same kind of opportunities in learning and development, career growth, cross functional exposure, etc. It has been seen that when such opportunities are provided, such employees are just as good if not better than other employees.

Participating Colleges

The colleges participating in the Project Genesis initiative benefit on many counts. The primary ones being:

1. The curriculum of the colleges gets constantly reviewed and aligned giving it a more practical approach towards skill building.
2. The professors get trained by Infosys BPO's in-house trainers as well as its training partners. This interaction not only helps in enhancing the facilitation skills of the students, but it also gives them a broader understanding of the BPO industry. This awareness is transferred to the students through the programme.
3. The colleges are also able to provide job opportunities for most of their students.
4. Colleges are able to invest in required infrastructure through the investments made by either their corporate or government partners.

Government

The philosophy of the initiative is based on the premise that Infosys BPO would partner and endeavour with academia and government to create industry-ready talent by providing them with the requisite training and opportunities. The government by contributing to this project helps in achieving the goals of the uplift of society, providing employment opportunities to educated and deserving youth, increasing the standard of living of people of these towns, etc.

Society

The initiative has also brought many advantages to society:

1. Employability index: The employability index in the states where Project Genesis has been initiated has seen a definite increase. In some cases, it has increased by as high as 28 per cent. This is because these trained resources are not only hired by Infosys BPO but by other BPO companies as well. Looking at the benefits of Project Genesis, more and more students are applying each year for the GSE programme.

2. Level playing field for urban and rural youth: The training imparted by Project Genesis bridges the gap of skills and potential between the rural and urban youth. Project Genesis has tackled the problem of potential–skill difference at the grass-root level by introducing the Global Skills Curriculum in the educational system that helps students enhance and build requisite skills that are necessarily required in such an industry. The two predominant requirements for this industry are language enhancement and numerical skills which is what the curriculum aims to improve.

3. Standard of living: This initiative resulted in increased opportunities for employment for the youth. Today many of the small and large BPO players are rushing to these towns to get the resources and fulfill their talent pool requirements.

Infosys BPO's endeavours do not stop at Project Genesis. It has launched another initiative, 'Adopt a University', which aims at providing opportunities to the less advantaged class of people. This initiative focuses on extending Project Genesis to all the colleges under the purview of Karnataka University–the identified university for the current year. Infosys BPO has signed memorandums of understanding (MOUs) with two universities to align their curriculum to suit the industry requirements and help them produce employable graduates. The initiative also includes working with educational bodies to align existing course curriculum with industry requirements, provide sabbatical industry assignments to select lecturers to enhance industry awareness and needs, provide summer internships for students and, finally, employ them based on their performance at work and in the programme. Providing career counselling forums in the different colleges, designing joint certification courses, etc., are some other aspects under the initiative. The project is aimed at creating employment opportunities for people in such areas where employment otherwise proves to be quite difficult.

Enlarging the Talent Pool

As the nation's labour pool is limited, organisations which are diversity-elite would win in the war of talent. Diversity and inclusiveness will become the key factors for the growth of the BPO industry and will provide us with a competitive advantage. Realising this, Infosys BPO has launched certain initiatives that are discussed next.

Diversity Initiative

Infosys firmly believes in diversity and inclusivity. The aim underlying this initiative is to make Infosys BPO an equal opportunity employer and creating an inclusive environment for people with different abilities. Hence, it launched two initiatives under the umbrella of diversity:

The Disability Initiative

This focuses on the hiring of differently-abled candidates and ensuring that the working environment is suited for these employees. This initiative required a lot of preparation by the organisation before these differently-abled candidates were hired. This included modification of existing infrastructure, enhancing awareness about differently-abled people, educating managers and team members who would be working with these employees, adapting processes for these employees, etc. Infosys BPO hired 138 differently-abled people in the financial year (FY) 2006–2007 and all of these employees have performed their jobs up to expectation. The supportive and inclusive environment inculcated by this initiative encouraged managers to proactively request for more people with disabilities in their teams. Now, Infosys BPO is aiming at having 6–7 per cent of its workforce comprising persons with disabilities and to open up new opportunities through research and assistive technologies. To meet this aim, it has even made modifications in the structure and facilities so as to make it accessible to the differently-abled employees. All the new buildings in its campuses have been constructed keeping in mind the needs of the differently abled like ramps for easier access to buildings, specially designed washrooms, etc. Infosys BPO has also taken upon itself the task of educating and sensitising its employees about the differently abled. For this purpose, December has been adopted as the 'disability' month. During this time, awareness about this initiative is spread by way of extensive communication campaigns via mails/posters/street plays. A 'disability walk' was organised on 'World Disability Day'. Infosys BPO takes pride in acknowledging that its differently-abled employees deliver at par as compared to its other employees if not more.

Hiring from the Lower Socio-economic Sector

This initiative aimed at providing equal opportunities to people from the lower socio-economic sector. The strategic initiative underlying this programme was to train 50 lecturers from identified government colleges, to train 3,000 graduates in soft skills and enhance their employability in partnership with the state government and to segregate the talent pool and train them based on identified essential skills. Infosys BPO launched the initiative in Karnataka and started by hiring 58 people from such backgrounds and putting them through an intensive three-week training programme in order to make them productive on the processes. Forty-eight of these employees were deployed. Currently, Infosys BPO is working with colleges across Karnataka to hire and deploy over 1,000 such employees.

Creating Awareness about the Industry amongst Youth, Parents and Teachers

The BPO industry is seen as a stop-gap option by graduates. Also, there are myths around the quality of job that the BPO industry offers which is perceived as 'monotonous job at odd working hours'. Such perception prevails amongst parents and even teachers at school/colleges, who have a strong influence on the young minds. Infosys BPO launched two initiatives to increase awareness about the BPO industry in India through industry–academia partnerships. This would expand the pipeline of people willing to join the industry.

1. Campus Ambassador Programme (CAP) (across India, graduate colleges): This is a unique programme which was launched across India to build strategic linkages between the industry and graduate schools. It acts as a forum for shared learning between the students and the industry. CAP is based on a three 'I' concept–information, identification and innovation.

   - Information: The programme is a network of information channels. It is all about enhancing awareness by being able to provide the right information to the right individual at the right time. The programme is a two-way flow of information from industry to students and vice versa. It tells students about the industry and about Infosys BPO and at the same time understands perceptions and expectations that the students may have.
   - Identification: The programme thrives on the identity of the student ambassador. For students on campus,

the ambassador is someone they can identify with and associate with and therefore approach for clarifications and a better understanding of the BPO industry. For the industry, the ambassador is an embodiment of what current talent looks like and how it can be developed for the future.

- Innovation: CAP is truly today's innovation for a brighter tomorrow. In an industry that is fighting to source talent to grow business, Infosys BPO has helped change the context of the available talent pipeline.

As part of this programme, Infosys BPO invites the chosen ambassadors from all over the country to the Infosys BPO campus in Bangalore and gives them real time corporate exposure through senior leadership sessions, a series of assignments and performance appraisals at the end of it. Last year, Infosys BPO had 125 campus ambassadors, from 42 cities covering the geographies of 12 states, who not only spread awareness about careers in the BPO industry but also talked about their own predecessors who had opted to join Infosys BPO and explore the learning opportunities available within the organisation.

2. The Infosys BPO elective: The Infosys BPO elective is a structured programme offered in some of the top business schools across the country. This initiative aims at expanding the middle and senior management talent pipeline. Open to all students, this course aims at educating future young leaders about the BPO industry and helps them interact with the senior management from the organisation in discussions on challenges and opportunities in the industry. It was completely facilitated by the top management of Infosys BPO. Six renowned institutes have been covered under the workshop module and Infosys BPO is currently running a full-fledged Infosys BPO elective in one of the top 10 business schools in India.

Evolution of HRM Practices: From People Management to People Engagement

People management encompasses the tasks of hiring, performance management, compensation, organisation development, employee safety, wellness and benefits, employee motivation, communication, administration and training. These are the basics of HRM. But the essence of effective people management lies in engaging the workforce. Infosys BPO believes that only if the employees are engaged will they stay. This is the reason why the HR landscape of people management at Infosys BPO shifted to people engagement. Employees are best managed when they are fully engaged. Employees often begin to disengage when they feel that their fundamental human needs are not met. One of these needs is to feel competent and have a sense of worth. Employees fail to realise this need when there is a mismatch between the skills required to their job and the ones they possess. According to a Mckinsey survey,[5] employees who are either over skilled or under skilled for the kind of jobs they are anchoring are most dissatisfied with their compensation and career growth which in turn leads to attrition. Therefore, there is a need to develop means to assess the fit of candidates into the jobs they are being offered. Such an assessment tool will ensure hiring the right people who best suit the job description and have the right levels of skill and experience. Considering the issue of job–person misfit and the rapidly depleting talent pool in the industry, Infosys BPO realised that a skill-based approach was pertinent in order to flourish in the market. Hence the initiative of right skilling was developed. This is the first initiative of its kind in the Indian BPO sector.

Right-skilling as the name implies, is the process by which right skills are deployed to the right job. This initiative was taken up by Infosys BPO in October 2006 to develop a method to identify and quantify skills required in the organisation and align people skills to them. Furthermore, these skills will be used as the basis for formulating HR strategy for recruitment, training, deployment, compensation and career development. The objective was to ensure:

1. Optimisation of the internal as well as the external talent pool to the best of its advantage.
2. Training is geared towards developing skills required for the job.
3. Developing an in-house inventory for the talent supply chain.
4. Alignment of compensation with the skills used for the job.
5. All processes become more efficient and deliver the intended outcome.
6. It provides for higher business continuity by positively impacting attrition.

Model Used

The essential skills model has been developed internally by Infosys BPO keeping in view the needs of the BPO industry. Essential skills are the skills people use to carry out a wide variety of everyday life and work tasks. Essential skills are enabling skills that (a) help people perform the tasks required by their occupation and other activities of daily life, (b) provide people with a foundation to learn other skills, (c) enhance people's ability to adapt to change.

The model focuses on essential skills, all or some of which are required for any work in a process. The cornerstone elements of this model are:

1. Some skills are not essential for all employees at all times. Any skill that is required by all in a process at all times is called a 'qualifier'.
2. Levels of complexity are a rating tool by which all skills are measured.

3. Each skill has four or five levels of complexity and is dependent on different factors or dimensions as applicable for a particular job.

Implementation of the Model

The right-skilling exercise was carried out with a two-pronged approach as explained here (see Figure 6.2):

1. Cluster logic–identifying skills required for a particular job: In this, all the processes were bucketised into five clusters on the basis of the essential skills required for these processes. So, the exact skills that were required for a particular process were identified. Accordingly, the candidates were hired for a particular process. The sourcing mix was also worked out accordingly. This served as cost regulator for the organisation and an opportunity of career growth for the employee.

2. Mapping employee skills based on the essential skills model: Each entry-level joinee is tested on a skill profiler tool to identify the skills she/he is best at. All the entry-level training programmes are designed around developing these specific skills to enable them to handle their first job effectively.

This initiative proved to be a win–win situation for all the stakeholders. The benefits of right-skilling as experienced by the employees, clients and the organisation are as follows:

1. The right-skilling advantage to employees: One of the biggest objectives of right-skilling was to enable an employee to explore multiple career opportunities and hone his/her skills through focused training and experience on the right jobs. Advantages offered to an employee were:

    • Skill-based deployment ensuring that his/her skills are fully utilised resulting in high morale.

Figure 6.2:   Diagrammatic Representation of the Implementation
Process

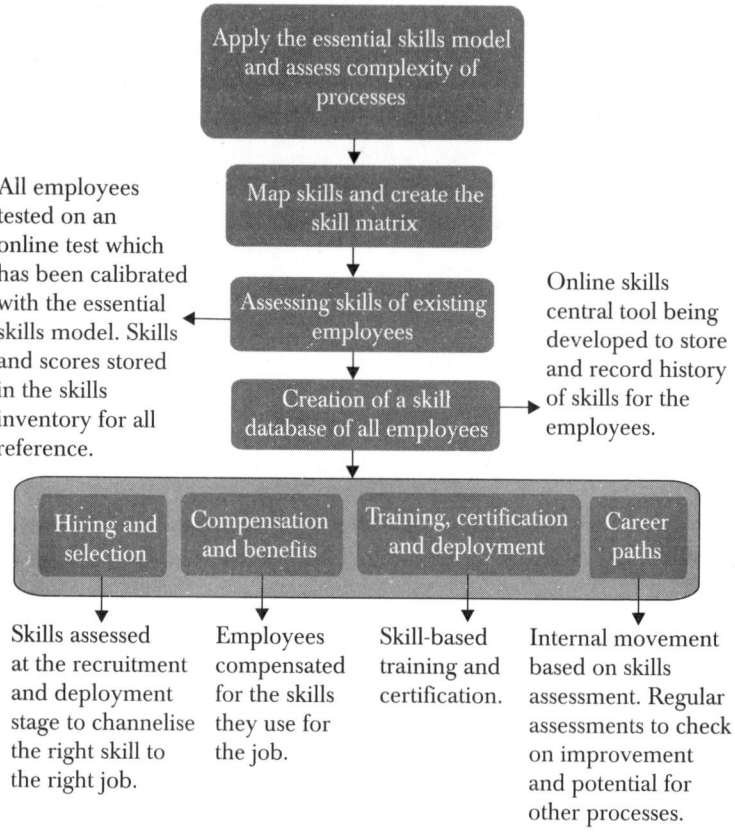

- Skill-based training inputs to ensure that he/She upgrades and hones his/her skills for the next level or complexity of the job.
- More career options to move and acquire more domain/skill expertise.
- Guideline for movement of over-skilled people for higher complexity or transition jobs.
- Increasing his/her employability by giving him/her relevant training based on skills.
- Regular assessments will ensure his/her performance is also tracked by means of a skill inventory which will

capture his skills at various stages of his career with the organisation.

2. The right-skilling advantage to client: Right-skilling allows for a deep understanding of the activities done for each transaction and the skills required to execute them. Hence, it helps operations in making it more objective, process-oriented, less people dependant. From a transition perspective, it also suggests multiple solutions for workflow designing to optimise skill and improve delivery. From a client perspective, the definite takeaways are:

   • Logical and systematic understanding of the processes based on skills.
   • It objectively determines the talent required for different processes in terms of basic and domain skills.
   • Process improvements can be looked at from a de-skilling point of view, which will increase the client's off-shoring ability.

3. The right-skilling advantage to the organisation: The organisation is benefited significantly as a result of this initiative. Some of the advantages are:

   • Less and more focused time spent on training.
   • Multiple workflow solutions can be worked out based on need and availability of skills.
   • Explore flexibility in contracts with regard to (*a*) off campus working; (*b*) part-time workers; and (*c*) fixed pricing/transaction-based pricing.
   • All processes become more efficient and delivered as per the client expectations.
   • Impact on recruitment and training and, therefore, speed of resource deployment.
   • Reduced attrition and higher staff morale due to right-skilling.
   • Supply chain of talent, skills identification ensures a smoother pipeline internally or externally to ensure business continuity.

With right-skilling, Infosys BPO ensured availability of abundant avenues of career growth for the employees within the organisation.

Evolution of HRM Practices: From People Administration to the Business Partner

During the start-up stage of Infosys BPO, the role of HR was highly administrative in nature. It was focused mainly on HR operations, namely, employee database management, time keeping, hiring, payroll and handling exits. Traditionally, the definition of HR 'customer' was 'employees' and, therefore, HR was the custodian of administering all the activities related to employee hygiene. But, with the organisation growing at 70 per cent year on year, the role of HR required transformation from being an administrative function to that of a business partner. This meant creating an HR structure that would deliver the necessary, routine transactional work consistently and efficiently, and at the same time deliver customised solutions to the diverse needs of different organisation/business stakeholders. This necessitated the HR function to align closer to the business. This alignment happened around the three important deliverables of HR function, namely, talent sourcing, talent development and talent engagement:

1. Talent sourcing: It moved closer to being the supply chain management function. The alignment was initiated in the following key elements of the talent sourcing wing:
   - Forecasting needs from the business plan.
   - Ensuring continuous supply of talent through effective pipeline management.
   - Managing buffers to cater to the fluctuating demands of talent.

- Experimenting with different employment models to maintain talent supply.
- Ensuring right-skilling for better job–person fit.
- Hiring at optimum cost.
- Onboarding to ensure effective integration of talent with the organisation.

2. Talent development: It aligned to line by:

- Creating role-based skill development.
- Emphasising on certifications/assessments as the gateway to growth.
- Making line accountable for people development and skill practice.
- Creating a high performance culture where performance drives growth and monetary/non-monetary rewards.

3. Talent engagement: Making employees engaged requires effective integration of an employee with the organisation, his/her job and other employees. This is achieved by:

- Engaging the employees with the organisation by making them understand their stake/role in achieving the business/organisation objectives.
- Engaging the employee to the job by helping them understand how their job contributes to the business/ organisation.
- Engaging the employee with other employees by creating a workplace governed by a sense of camaraderie, respect and values.

THE WAY AHEAD

'The only constant thing in universe is change.' The HR function needs to understand the process of organisational change and what is necessary to implement it. The way ahead for HR is to prepare for the next stage of consolidation proactively and ahead of time. This calls for (*a*) pre-paring the organisation to work in a matrix business structures by delineating roles/responsibilities of verticals/horizontals for effective outcomes; (*b*) tapping on the strengths of emerging HR structures like shared services, outsourcing and centre of excellence; (*c*) investing in analytics as a powerful decision-making tool; (*d*) using technology effectively as a backbone of HR services and (*e*) co-creating employee experience.

These are nothing less than exciting times to come! As Mark Twain said, 'Twenty years from now you will be more disappointed by the things you didn't do than by the ones you did do. So throw off the bowlines. Sail away from the safe harbor. Catch the trade winds in your sails. Explore. Dream. Discover.'[6]

Notes

1. See www.offshoringtimes.com, BPO News; details can be accessed on http://www.offshoringtimes.com/Pages/2006/BPO_news1058.html.
2. See 'Infosys Technologies–An Overview', August 2004, Available online at: www.dravisgroup.com/HTML/documents/Infosys.pdf - P3.
3. See http://sais.aisnet.org/2004/.%5CWynn1.pdf, P2.
4. See statistics published in NASSCOM-Mckinsey Report 2005. Details can be accessed on http://www.mckinsey.com/locations/india/mckinseyonindia/pdf/NASSCOM_McKinsey_Report_2005.pdf.
5. Statistics were published in the NASSCOM-Mckinsey Report (2005). Details can be accessed on http://www.mckinsey.com/locations/india/mckinseyonindia/pdf/NASSCOM_McKinsey_Report_2005.pdf
6. See http://thinkexist.com/quotes/mark_twain/

7

Union Formation in Indian
Call Centres

**Phil Taylor, Premilla D'Cruz, Ernesto Noronha
and Dora Scholarios**

INTRODUCTION

The 'globalisation' of business services facilitated by information and consultation technologies has accelerated at breathtaking pace. The relocation of interactive service work and an expanding range of back-office processes from the so-called developed countries of the global north to the developing countries of the global south increasingly constitutes a core element in corporate strategies. The widespread usage of the term global service delivery reflects the transformative role played by transnational corporations (TNCs) and the intervention of states in extending the reach of capital accumulation and in re-configuring service supply chains to multiple geographies. In this rapidly unfolding global landscape where, amongst others, the Philippines, South Africa, Latin American and east European states are emerging destinations, India remains pre-eminent, accounting for 46 per cent of global business process outsourcing (BPO) (NASSCOM-McKinsey 2005). According to an influential survey, India 'still offers an unbeatable mix of low costs, deep technical and language skills, mature vendors and supportive government policies' (Walker and Gott 2007: 29).

Figures produced by the Indian employers' organisation, the National Association of Software and Service Companies (NASSCOM), are impressive. Excluding the information technology (IT)/software industry, direct employment in information technology enabled services-business process outsourcing (ITES-BPO) was calculated at 553,000 in 2006–2007 compared to 102,000 in 2001–2002 (NASSCOM 2002, 2007a). This five-fold increase in five years is the statistical expression of the creation of a new Indian workforce as part of a new international division of service labour. Centred initially in the tier one locations–National Capital Region (NCR), Bangalore, Hyderabad, Mumbai, Chennai (Taylor and Bain 2005)–cohorts of young, Anglophone, middle-class graduates have been sucked into this 'new economy' by the Indian third-party outsourcers, multinationals, foreign-owned 'captives' and domestic operations that comprise the BPO industry. Yet recently, in conditions of skill shortages, rising labour costs and infrastructural strain, employers have sited facilities in tier two and tier three cities across India. The outcome is a new 'class' of white-collar professionals in the principal cities *and* emergent clusters in lesser cities.

Partly stimulated by the efflorescence of academic interest in call centres, a vigorous literature from contrasting perspectives is now grappling with developments in Indian BPO and the conditions and experiences of its burgeoning workforce. Studies have focused on the transnational, relocated call centre labour process (Remesh 2005; Taylor and Bain 2004, 2005, 2006a), on human resource management (HRM), training and skills (Batt et al. 2005; Budhwar et al. 2006) and on cultural identity (Cohen and El-Sawad 2007; McMillin 2006; Mirchandani, in this volume, 2004; Poster 2007). Salient issues will be discussed next, but this chapter's *specific* focus is on trade union formation in Indian BPO and employees' attitudes to collective organisation. That only a limited commentary exists on trade union developments (Noronha and D'Cruz 2006; Ofresno et al. 2007; Sandhu 2006; Taylor and Bain 2008) is unsurprising given that the first organisation exclusively devoted to organising call centre/BPO employees was only formed in September 2005. The initiative to found the Union of Information Technology Enabled Services Professionals (UNITES Pro) was taken by the Asia-Pacific arm of the International Trade Secretariat, Union Network International (UNI). Notwithstanding this recent history, the academic literature on the potential for union organisation has already laid the basis for meaningful debate. The dominant position stresses the profound difficulties that unions will encounter in organising BPO employees. Most emphatically Sandhu in an article 'Why Unions Fail in Organising India's BPO-ITES Industry' baldly asserts that:

> Call centre employees do not want to be part of trade unions because they associate the latter with 'blue-collar workers' and not with their perceived upward mobility. Also, their work schedules and the highly modernised self-contained work islands they inhabit encourage them to think of unions as unnecessary. (2006: 4319)

Noronha and D'Cruz (2006), following Peetz (2002), highlight employers' exclusivist (that is, explicitly anti-union) and inclusivist strategies as responsible for respectively union avoidance and incorporating employees. It is widely believed that the English-speaking graduates of these virgin workforces embrace their employment opportunity so eagerly that, in identifying uncritically with their company's success, they subordinate themselves entirely to managerial demands. High salaries, professional identity and sophisticated 'substitutionist' HRM strategies 'impede the development of any kind of collective' (Noronha and D'Cruz 2006: 2120) and create a 'productively docile' workforce (Remesh 2005). Strategies of 'corporate culturalism' aimed at winning 'hearts and minds' particularly contribute to keeping unions at bay (D'Cruz and Noronha 2006). More optimistic perspectives emphasise union potential, whilst acknowledging the profound obstacles (Taylor and Bain 2008).

This chapter builds on research conducted over several years by the authors into Indian BPO firms and latterly into working conditions, employee attitudes and embryonic trade union initiatives.[1] We draw upon unique datasets, the first survey of UNITES members and semi-structured interviews, that enable us to drill deep into their experiences and perceptions. A principal aim is to interrogate the categorical claim that organising efforts in Indian BPO will be stillborn. The scope though is broader, given the exploratory nature of this inquiry. Having profiled the UNITES members surveyed, we examine the recruitment process, the reasons for joining and report members' assessment of the obstacles to growth. In addition, we identify the working conditions which members believe are likely to prompt colleagues to join UNITES. Finally, we consider perceptions of management effectiveness, particularly of HRM departments and their ability to substitute for independent employee representation. Before presenting research findings, we provide some essential contextualisation: of offshoring and the Indian BPO industry, of what is already known about working conditions and of embryonic trade union developments. This study's wider significance lies in the fact that little is known of organising workers in the 'offshored' industries of developing economies (Castree et al. 2004: 210; Kelley 2002: 396), a lacuna that reflects actual weaknesses in trade union implantation. The evidence, although specific to India may contain lessons for union organising in BPO in other countries and may have implications beyond this sector.

OFFSHORING OF CALL CENTRES/BPO TO INDIA

Detailed analysis reveals the interplay of political, economic, technological, organisational, geographical, linguistic and cultural factors that have driven and facilitated offshoring (Taylor and Bain 2003, 2006b). Digitalisation and huge increases in optical fibre capacity transformed the ability to store and transmit data (Miozzo and Soete 2001), creating the opportunity for India to become the world's back office. In parallel, the call centre, due to the integration of computer and telephonic technologies and automatic call distribution switches decisively removed the requirement for servicing sites to be located in close proximity to customers (Ellis and Taylor 2006). Manifold consequences followed, not least organisations' ability to centralise previously dispersed activities, to standardise them, to render them transportable and to transform the labour process of interactive service work (Taylor and Bain 2007). Notwithstanding differentiation in call centre type and customer servicing requirements (Batt and Moynihan 2002; Frenkel et al. 1999; Glucksmann 2004), the dominant paradigm was the lean, mass production model in which call-throughput was prioritised.

In the final analysis, driving the near-universal adoption of the call centre as the preferred mode of customer interaction were the imperatives of cost reduction and the maximisation of profits and shareholder value in increasingly competitive markets. The outcome in the developed geographies were distinctive locational patterns of call centres and, to a lesser extent, of data-processing centres. Early call centre analysts (for example, Richardson and Marshall 1996) observed that these clusters in 'peripheral' regions were generated by a combination of lower (particularly labour) costs and the availability of skills, advanced connectivity and infrastructure, and the support of the local and/or national state. From this perspective, the migration of business processes and customer services to India represents essentially an extension, albeit at a transnational scale, of the same cost-saving, profit-maximising spatial, economic and organisational dynamics underlying their location *within* the developed geographies.

Constraints of space prevent a nuanced analysis of the factors driving, facilitating and inhibiting business process migration (Taylor and Bain 2003, 2006a). The promise of cost savings, though, are fundamental with widely-claimed estimates of 40–50 per cent (NASSCOM 2004, 2005, 2006) while more conservative recent figures suggest 25–40 per cent savings (NASSCOM-McKinsey 2005). The most significant element is India's outstanding asset, the low costs of its English-speaking, graduate workforce. However, the wage differential of '70–80

per cent for offshorable processes' (NASSCOM 2003: 65) is
reducing as average labour costs have risen by at least 10–15
per cent per annum (NASSCOM 2006: 74) due to wage inflation in tight labour markets. To these fundamental country advantages may be added economic, political and infrastructural
factors enabling migration; inter alia accessible, reliable and
cheapening telephony and telecommunications; central government de-regulatory policies favourable to foreign direct investment; state governments' support; the facilitatory roles of
NASSCOM and consultants.

Nevertheless, relocation is not necessarily unproblematic.
Multiple inhibiting factors include customer resistance associated with doubts over service quality; regulatory constraints;
cultural and linguistic incompatibility; and infrastructural difficulties. In this abridged analysis of market dynamics emphasis
must be placed upon underlying imbalances in labour supply
and demand, causing a predicted shortfall of half-a-million BPO
employees by 2010 (NASSCOM-McKinsey 2005: 17). Shortages of higher-end linguistic skills are causing severe labour
management challenges in relation to recruitment,[2] training and
attrition. The latter remains the most pressing problem; although
officially running at 30–40 per cent per annum (NASSCOM
2006) the real rate is perhaps 65–75 per cent overall, although
this exceeds 100 per cent in certain companies, locations and
particular processes. Turnover is higher in call centres than on
non-voice processes, higher on night-time working for the
United States (US) than the United Kingdom (UK) and more
pronounced on highly routinised processes (Taylor and Bain
2006b: 84–100). While the 'push' of working conditions contributes to turnover, of greater significance are 'pull' factors,
whereby employees (and managers) move between facilities in
order to leverage improvements in pay and rewards. Evidently
these labour market conditions have manifold consequences
for union organising. High attrition has contradictory effects:
labour is potentially in a strong bargaining position but, con-
trarily, turnover encourages employees to pursue individual
means to capitalise on relative scarcity.

A profile of the industry reveals characteristics that might impact further on the potential for collective organisation. There is its heterogeneous structure with companies falling into distinct categories. 'Captives', essentially in-house providers for global companies (for example, HSBC, Dell) own and directly control their operations. Conventionally included as 'captives', although distinctive in that they act as outsourcers, are multinational corporations (MNCs) such as Hewitt or Accenture. Both can be distinguished from Indian third-party providers—classic outsourcers—as a diverse category encompassing companies that emerged as dedicated outsourcers and the BPO arms of software companies. That sharp distinctions cannot always be drawn is evidenced by General Electric's (GE) metamorphosis from captive to global third-party player Genpact. Finally, there is the domestic BPO sub-sector which is growing rapidly (NASSCOM 2007b: 79). Differentiation extends to other aspects of BPO and carries additional implications for the potential to organise. There is the question of scale. While prominent 'captives' and third-party suppliers are very large employers,[3] and their facilities may accommodate several thousand employees, there remains a plethora of small and medium enterprises (SMEs), many in the domestic sub-sector, which conduct niche activities. Batt et al. (2005: 7) showed that international call centres were seven times larger than 'domestics'. There are obvious distinctions in types of work, the most significant being between call centre services and back-office processes. 'Voice' accounts for 60–65 per cent of employment and the diverse back-office activities 35–40 per cent (Taylor and Bain 2006b: 22). However, it should be acknowledged that a proportion of agents do undertake both voice and non-voice activities.

Relatedly, there is differentiation in work timings since much back-office work is conducted during daytime hours while voice processes are synchronised to customers' times across the different English-speaking geographies.[4] The result is a multiplicity of shift patterns which further fragments the construction of BPO work as a unified experience. Pay and rewards too are distributed unevenly across the 'sector'. Surveys (for example, NASSCOM-Hewitt's Total Rewards Study) show that remuneration tends to be higher for back-office employees than for voice-based agents (NASSCOM 2007a: 148) but, more significantly, captives/MNCs tend to pay more than Indian third parties and both considerably more than domestics. This brief profile indicates that union organising efforts will have to engage with an industry and a workforce that are internally differentiated in important respects.

WORKING CONDITIONS

Notwithstanding differences, certain common themes have been identified in working conditions and employees' experiences. The nature of work for captives, MNCs and international facing third-party centres, stems largely from the place that India occupies in global servicing chains. Accordingly, work organisation in Indian call centres may well constitute an exaggerated form of the mass production model (Taylor and Bain 2005: 269), a result of what might be termed 'Taylorism through export'. Recent evidence (Taylor and Bain 2006b: 46–71) strongly suggests that the BPO industry as a whole, whether captive or third party, call-centre or non-customer facing, still *tends* to deliver standardised and routinised services of lower complexity, despite limited moves up the value chain to knowledge process outsourcing. Tight monitoring, surveillance and a plethora of quantitative and qualitative controls are implemented (D'Cruz and Noronha 2006; Remesh 2005) which minimise employee discretion. Batt et al (2005) reported 71 per cent of managers saying their employees had little or no discretion over daily tasks and 76 per cent had little or no discretion over work procedures. Workers widely complain of infrequent breaks and the compulsion to remain engaged on calls for long periods.

Consequently, although Remesh's (2005) 'cyber coolie' metaphor may be overdrawn, many voice and non-voice agents report an experience of work as pressurised and frequently stressful and contributing to burnout and 'exit'. It is not being argued that highly-pressurised working conditions lead automatically to a propensity to collectivise. As D'Cruz and Noronha (2006) remind us, BPO professionals imbued with a strong customer servicing ethos, may well internalise these pressures. Nevertheless, these workplace experiences provide an inescapable quotidian reality. From the perspective of unionising possibilities, the contradiction between the expectation, encouraged by employers, of a stimulating job and rewarding career and the actuality of performing industrialised white-collar work may be a salient factor.

Distinctive characteristics of Indian BPO exacerbate pressures—nocturnal call-handling for overseas customers, long commuting times, extended shifts, unpaid overtime ('extra time'). Agents confirm the prevalence of symptoms of work-related ill-health and disruptions to work–life balance and family life, which may impact most upon women employees. There are the complex issues of identity construction, as Indians navigate the tensions between their culture and the requirements of service provision for Western customers, including practices such as locational masking, adopting pseudonyms and accent neutralisation, which may result in abuse from customers. Such issues have preoccupied many researchers (Cohen and El-Sawad 2007; McMilan 2006; Mirchandani 2004, 2008). While further study is required to explore the interrelationships between employees' psychological responses and the potential for collective organisation, it cannot be assumed that agents are simply more intensely exploited units of capital, but rather are active economic and cultural participants who, in constructing their own meanings of work, may develop forms of 'objection' or 'resistance' rather than 'assimilation' or 'accommodation' (Poster 2007).

Finally, researchers identified a 'democratic deficit'. There is evidence that customary Indian hierarchical work cultures have been transposed to BPO, and not merely to its third-party and domestic segments (Taylor and Bain 2006a). Employees report managerial and supervisory arbitrariness and authoritarian treatment, including disciplinary action and even dismissal on trivial grounds. An emerging concern is the practice of managers withholding 'leaving' or 'relieving' certificates, preventing employees from changing employer, which are part of concerted NASSCOM-facilitated attempts to control attrition (NASSCOM 2005). Top–down methods dominate staff communications systems (NASSCOM 2003) and employee involvement practices are task-based, geared to increasing productivity and improving quality, and not intended to give employees a voice let alone participate in decision-making (Batt et al. 2005: 17). Finally, it is worth recalling that many United Kingdom (UK) offshorers do recognise trade unions, but have not extended this to their Indian operations (Bain and Taylor 2008), a failure which underscores the democratic deficit in workplace governance.

UNITES AND TRADE UNIONISM

Despite strong traditions in telecoms, banking and insurance (Kuruvilla et al. 2003) established unions displayed a reluctance to organise these new workforces. Presaging subsequent academic studies (Noronha and D'Cruz 2006; Sandhu 2006), officers interviewed before the sector's dramatic expansion expressed the belief that these professional employees, coming from middle-class backgrounds and given attractive status titles such as 'executive', would not identify with collective workers' organisations (Taylor and Bain 2003: 127). Employee interviews have provided some support for this. The youth and inexperience of workers, their professional identity, career aspirations and relatively high earnings were seen as disincentives to joining unions (D'Cruz and Noronha 2006; Taylor and Bain 2006a). Several reported an antipathy based on their perceived association of unions with blue-collar work, strikes and demonstrations, at odds with their aspirant world view. High attrition, too, was regarded as a deterrent not just because continual churning makes it difficult to organise, but because the ability to change employer for higher pay fosters individualistic attitudes which undermine collectivism. Evidence exists of employers 'excluding' both union members and 'difficult' employees. Remesh (2005: 17) reported firms 'nipping out any sprouts of organisation' by forcing agents 'who are vocal against management decisions to quit…through carefully planned retrenchment mechanisms'. Cooke (2005: 6) described the peremptory sacking of a Wipro-Spectramind employee who protested against enforced unpaid work, lack of breaks and intimidatory management. Several unionised employees believed that if they were to 'come out' they would be disadvantaged in respect of promotion, appraisals, pay rises, and task and shift allocation (Taylor and Bain 2008). Others were convinced they would be 'terminated' (Indian parlance for sacked) if the management knew of their membership.

Employer resistance is widespread, notably among MNCs with industrial relations histories opposed to trade unionism (for example, IBM) and Indian third parties. The position of the CEOs of Wipro and WNS (Sandhu 2006: 4319), that unions should be resisted because their presence would dissuade clients from sourcing from India, is quite representative. NASSCOM repeatedly dismisses trade unions on 'inclusivist' grounds as summarised by its president, 'In the BPO industry the grievances of the workers are addressed promptly and the wages are good so there is no need for unions…' (http://www.rediff.com/money/2005/oct/17bpo.htm). Yet, limited breaches in the employers' Maginot line are detectable. BPO founding father, Raman Roy (http://www.upi.com/Hi-Tech/view.php?StoryID=20051107-094041-5729r), and Progeon's CEO (*Economic Times* 17 November 2005) have conceded that unions might help control attrition.

UNITES was formed in September 2005, following preparatory organising by the Centre for Business Process Offshoring Professionals (CBPOP). UNITES was the first explicit attempt to give BPO employees an independent voice and represented an organisational break from an earlier initiative, the Information

Technology Professionals Forum (ITPF) which oriented more on software/IT professionals (Hirschfeld 2005). The ITPF had rejected the union title, defining itself as 'a community of professionals' providing educational and training services for its career-minded members. UNI's justification for creating UNITES as a separate organising initiative was grounded in the understanding that BPO employees' working conditions were sufficiently distinct from those of IT professionals. Nevertheless, UNITES constituted only a partial departure from ITPF's ethos. The officers forming UNITES recognised the salience of employer hostility to overt unionism and, more importantly, of employees' powerful professional identity. An officer at UNITES founding conference emphasised, 'If we talk only about unionism, it's going to be a waste of time...we need to talk about a knowledge professionals forum' (interview conducted by Phil Taylor, 11 September 2005). UNITES record indicates genuine, if modest, progress (UNITES 2006). Overcoming bureaucratic obstacles, it secured legal status through the Labour Commission in Karnataka and gained 'provisional affiliation' to the Indian National Trade Union Congress (INTUC). It has organising centres and claims six viable 'chapters' (Bangalore, Hyderabad, NCR, Chennai, Mumbai and Kochi). One difficulty in stating exact membership stems from the distinction between fully paid-up members (Rs 600 or approximately US$ 11.99 per annum) and those paying an initial registration (Rs 100 or approximately US$ 1.99). Since, as officers report, it has proved difficult to translate those initially signing-up into full membership, it is helpful to think of UNITES as composed of a committed activist core and a looser peripheral membership, surrounded by non-members who comprise a broader, interested constituency.Accordingly, although 7,000 recruits were claimed by late-2006, the general secretary thought fully-paid membership numbered 700–1,000 (interview conducted on 19 November 2006).

Analysis of UNITES activities (Taylor and Bain 2008) demonstrates some success through much-publicised campaigns on behalf of employees. The first tranche of recruits followed protests organised in the wake of the rape and murder in

December 2005 in Bangalore of Hewlett-Packard worker, Prathibha Srikanth Murthy, by a man purporting to be her driver. UNITES' demands for improvements in the safety of the transportation provided by companies resonated with many (http://www.indianexpress.com/res/webpIe/full_story. php?content_id=84118). Other notable interventions included representing employees of Bangalore-based BelAir who had been summarily dismissed without pay, pursuing through the Karnataka Women's Commission the case of a woman who had been 'put on the bench' (suspended without pay) and instances of non-payment to trainees by HCL in Noida. UNITES has also succeeded in negotiating four collective bargaining agreements (Excel Outsourcing Services, e-Merge Business Processing, Infopoint, Transact Solutions), although these breakthroughs are confined to domestic SMEs. UNITES has striven to reflect the professional aspirations of its putative constituency, evidenced by its delivery of career-enhancing skills training. It recognises that to declare itself a trade union and to emphasise only what employers might perceive to be adversarial issues might isolate it from potential members, leaving it vulnerable to employer counter-mobilisation. Nevertheless, its conscious immersion in the experiences of BPO employees has compelled it to address questions of justice, fairness and rights and to represent individual workers over diverse issues. Taylor and Bain (2008) concluded tentatively that UNITES' future progress would depend on its ability to straddle the contradictions between becoming a BPO professionals' network and acting more explicitly like a trade union in the making.

METHOD

Questionnaire Distribution and Design

The distribution strategy aimed to capture as many UNITES' members as possible working in domestic, third-party and captive operations between April and July 2007. Using UNITES' membership databases, independent social science graduates were employed under the direction of the Indian researchers to approach members and complete the questionnaires as structured interviews. This strategy produced 1,206 completed questionnaires from Bangalore (30 per cent), Chennai (17 per cent), Hyderabad (16 per cent), Cochin (16 per cent), Mumbai (14 per cent) and Delhi (8 per cent). However, 13 per cent of respondents claimed not to be UNITES members. This was because some questionnaire completion occurred during UNITES' meetings when non-members were present. Non-members were excluded from analysis leaving a total of 879 completed questionnaires which, we are confident, reflects UNITES' active membership.

As there are no previous surveys of Indian BPO professionals' emerging union representation, we developed new questions as well as drawing on existing UK surveys of trade union members and/or call centre workers. The research team piloted the questionnaire in February 2007 in Chennai and refined it on the basis of qualitative feedback. The questionnaire structure followed the research aims as follows: to provide a demographic profile; to understand how employees became aware of UNITES and the actual process of recruitment; to identify the primary influences prompting members to join;[5] to distinguish between collective and instrumental/individualist reasons for joining (Waddington and Whitston 1997); to evaluate the importance of factors relating to working conditions which may dispose employees to join UNITES;[6] to evaluate perceived barriers to increasing membership within Indian BPO; to evaluate perceptions of management's effectiveness in relation to key aspects of the job; to evaluate general attitudes towards management and to evaluate the efficacy of HR in solving employees' problems.

Employee Interviews

Supplementary semi-structured interviews with UNITES members followed the questionnaire structure and enabled deeper exploration of members' experiences. The research team carried these out in four locations–Chennai, Delhi, Hyderabad and Bangalore. A cross-section of members was chosen across genders and company type producing a total of 45 interviews, each lasting approximately one hour. All interviews were voluntary and were taped and transcribed.

EXPERIENCES AND ATTITUDES OF UNITES MEMBERS

Membership Profile

The majority of UNITES members responding (70 per cent) were based in Indian domestic companies with 22 per cent in captives and 8 per cent in Indian third parties. This is an important finding, demonstrating the concentration of UNITES members in the domestic sub-sector, and a lesser penetration amongst captives and particularly third-party providers. The even gender balance reflects what we know about the industry (Batt et al. 2005). Positively, this suggests that to the limited extent that UNITES has made headway, it has succeeded in recruiting equally from both genders. Membership also reflects the strikingly youthful nature of the workforce; the mean age of UNITES members surveyed was 24. That most respondents were employed full-time is also consistent with what is known about the BPO workforce. Batt et al. (2005: 9) found 99 per cent of international call centre agents to be working full-time. More outstanding are the statistics on working hours. The mean of 216 hours per month (54 hours per week) demonstrates the prevalence in Indian BPO of a long hours culture, most pronounced in captives and domestic centres. Average tenure was one and a half years, although lower in domestic companies at just over one year. Given what is known about attrition, this may indicate that UNITES was more likely to attract employees who remained for longer periods with the same employer.

The evidence on career orientation provides fascinating insight into the intentions of this cohort of organised employees.

Overall, only one-in-four believed that their current job was one that they would stay in or was part of their career advancement. A majority in domestics (52 per cent) believed that their current job was part of a career that would take them to other BPO companies, compared to 30 per cent in captives and 22 per cent in third parties. Interview data reinforces the supposition that members in domestics, in common with their non-unionised colleagues, perceive a job in that sub-sector as a stepping-stone to employment in better paying and higher status international companies. Evidently, there is a multiplicity of career motives amongst UNITES members. While a willingness to move employer in order to better oneself was reported, a number of interviewees expressed their desire to build a career in their 'dream job'. A call centre worker in a Bangalore-based captive effectively expressed the duality of his colleagues' orientations:

> Every second company is willing to pay you very well irrespective of your experience. If the things don't work out well in one company they don't care, they can go elsewhere. Having said that, there are lots of people who really don't like doing this. Security of job is also important for them. It is a kind of mixture at times.

Aware of this contradiction, UNITES responds pragmatically. On the one hand, inter-company migration is providing an opportunity for UNITES to establish itself in areas where it has little presence. The general secretary (interview conducted on 4 August 2007) emphasised the importance of recruiting members from UNITES' domestic pockets of strength and then sustaining individuals' membership as they become dispersed throughout BPO. On the other hand, UNITES has developed agendas which emphasise the need for companies to develop career pathways for employees. The creation of more stable workforces is seen as important if UNITES is to put down firmer roots. Around 70 per cent of respondents in domestic and third parties were engaged purely in call centre work. In captives, however, 67 per cent combined call centre with other business process work. Over 70 per cent overall reported primarily receiving inbound sales, technical or general customer service calls rather than being engaged in outbound telesales. Night shifts were most common in Indian third parties at 35 per cent of that sub-sample (see Table 7.1).

Table 7.1: Sample Characteristics

	Captive (N = 192)		Indian Third Party (N = 69)		Domestic (N = 618)		Total (N = 879)	
	N	%	N	%	N	%	N	%
Gender								
Male	111	58	44	66	293	48	448	52
Female	80	42	23	34	314	52	417	48
Contractual status								
Full-time	187	100	57	85	544	90	788	92
Part-time			10	15	59	10	69	8
Career intentions								
A long-term job I will stay in	72	39	26	41	109	18	207	24
Career advancement in this company	46	25	19	30	157	26	222	25
Part of career that will take me to different BPO companies	54	30	14	22	318	52	386	44
Part of career that will probably take me outside BPO	19	10	5	8	16	3	40	5
Not part of a career/uncertain	13	7	11	18	30	5	54	6
Nature of work								
Combine call centre/ BPO work	125	67	19	28	204	33	348	40
Call centre work only	62	33	48	72	413	67	523	60
Inbound calls (sales, technical support, customer service)	98	77	33	83	398	69	529	71
Outbound calls (telemarketing, sales)	30	23	7	18	180	31	217	29
Night shifts	24	22	15	35	25	16	64	21
	N	Mean	N	Mean	N	Mean	N	Mean
Age	192	27.0	69	25.6	618	23.4	879	24.3
Tenure (months)	192	25.9	69	29.5	618	13.4	879	17.4
Monthly contracted hours [a]	95	206	48	191	520	219	663	216

Note: [a]Based on a restricted sample range (79 per cent) who provided calculable responses.

Recruitment to UNITES

The youth of the workforce and the fact that almost all were graduates means that very few respondents had been union members before joining UNITES. Recruitment from domestic companies appears to be the primary source of new membership, with the majority recruited in the last year (see Table 7.2). Those with longest periods of membership tended to be from Indian third-party operators, but the rate of recruitment has slowed. Encouragingly, the overwhelming majority found the process of joining easy. Only 11 per cent overall reported difficulties that were largely attributed to lack of awareness of UNITES' existence or of direct contact with the organisation.

Members' awareness of UNITES came primarily from friends or relatives, either in the same workplace or working in different BPOs. Here there was some difference between recent and older members, with recent recruits more likely to report workplace colleagues, and older members, friends/relatives in other call centres. This is perhaps to be expected given that UNITES 'started from scratch'. Interviews with longer-standing members confirms that they heard about UNITES through social or family connections with those initiating UNITES. For example, a Chennai member reported that her knowledge of UNITES came from her father who was a unionised employee of Bharat Sanchar Nigam Limited (BSNL), the national telecom provider. However, established workplace members are easily now the most important source of information and recruitment. Consequently, 80 per cent overall stated that they had been signed up by a UNITES member in their workplace. Making due allowance for the differing national contexts, the findings confirm knowledge of union growth in UK call centres, where the key role of workplace representatives as recruiters stands out (Bain and Taylor 2002). While in Indian BPO, of course, there is no structure of workplace representatives, one can suggest parallels with the role played by informal leaders. Two significant examples come from a captive in Bangalore and a third-party company in Noida, where emergent leaders have

Table 7.2: UNITES Recruitment

	Captive		Indian Third Party		Domestic		Total	
	N	%	N	%	N	%	N	%
Date of joining UNITES								
Within last year	87	49	18	28	452	80	557	69
More than 1 year ago	92	51	46	72	111	20	249	31
How did you find out about UNITES?								
Colleague/friend at work	151	79	43	63	451	73	645	74
UNITES website	10	5	13	19	211	34	234	27
Friend/relative working in different call centres/BPO	52	27	31	45	73	12	156	18
UNITES leaflet	2	1	5	7	51	8	58	8
How did you join UNITES?								
UNITES member at my workplace signed me up	127	67	32	47	541	88	700	80
Colleagues at my workplace encouraged me to join	51	27	35	51	106	17	192	22
I joined after receiving a leaflet	0	0	2	3	55	9	57	11
I asked a UNITES member at my workplace	13	7	4	6	58	9	75	9
My team leader/manager encouraged me to join	0	0	11	16	57	9	68	8
I made contact myself with UNITES	5	3	1	1	6	1	12	7
Friend/family member outside workplace encouraged me to join	9	5	10	15	79	13	98	5
I joined online	5	3	5	7	13	2	23	4
I sent form to UNITES office	13	7	9	13	21	3	43	3
I joined at UNITES meeting	13	7	8	12	13	2	34	1

recruited clusters of members through face-to-face discussion, persuasion and a willingness to pursue grievances.

Following 'workplace members/colleagues' and 'friends/ family elsewhere' as sources of information were the UNITES website and leaflets. This was especially so for more recent members. Other sources, such as newspaper advertisements or articles, emails, radio/television programmes or specific campaigns were cited by only a handful of respondents. It seems that forms of remote contact and individuals taking the initiative to join (joining online, posting a form) are much less important. Surprisingly and perhaps an issue of some concern is the fact that only small numbers reported joining at UNITES meetings. When asked what UNITES could do to improve recruitment, a higher profile and greater media coverage were mentioned. Several stressed how successful UNITES has been in its early days in gaining publicity through the much-publicised Prathiba and BelAir cases, but that recently declining media coverage had reduced public awareness. This was hampering attempts to build UNITES and needed to be rectified.

> UNITES has to unite really and march ahead. Take serious steps and move fast, now it moves slowly. The faster you move, the faster the processes are going to be. This means you start your media campaign, your one-to-one campaign, so they start getting educated, knowing. If you have any problems in your call centre, please log onto our website or on this number. (Voice agent, Hyderabad)

Reasons for joining UNITES

While employees join UNITES for multiple reasons, the most-frequently cited were primarily instrumental (see Table 7.3). In particular, 77 per cent identified UNITES as helping to improve pay and conditions. Of course, for members in those companies where collective agreements exist, joining the union might be directly related to UNITES' ability to improve pay and conditions. However, where collective bargaining does not exist, as for example in captives, the importance of this reason (81 per cent) may be interpreted differently. Interview evidence reveals several instances where UNITES had intervened on behalf of employees over pay-related grievances (for example, withholding pay/bonuses, unpaid overtime, underpaying). Others expressed the view that, while UNITES would not impact pay rates in the short term, its future ability to do so influenced their decision to join.

Table 7.3:   Reasons for Joining UNITES

	Captive		Indian Third Party		Domestic		Total	
	N	%	N	%	N	%	N	%
Improve my pay and conditions	155	81	27	40	472	77	654	77
Information/advice about my rights	133	69	25	37	407	66	565	66
Help my career	96	50	18	27	205	33	319	33
I believe in trade unions	119	62	16	24	195	32	330	32
Other people at work are members	102	53	35	52	149	24	286	24
UNITES provides training to enhance my skills and knowledge	100	52	19	28	135	22	254	22
UNITES will help me find out about pay/conditions in other workplaces	129	67	21	31	133	22	283	22
In UNITES I found people with the same attitudes	107	56	28	42	131	21	266	21
BPO professionals should have their own independent organisation to represent their interests	101	53	28	42	111	18	240	18
I wanted to help improve conditions in the industry	95	49	18	27	83	13	196	13
UNITES gave me support with a problem at work	109	57	39	58	68	11	216	11
UNITES campaigns to improve conditions in BPO firms	101	53	25	37	62	10	188	10
UNITES' community activities	134	70	16	24	52	8	202	8
UNITES provides housing/welfare information	100	52	19	28	42	7	161	7
UNITES provides good social activities	93	48	14	21	24	4	131	4

Two-thirds cited UNITES' ability to provide information or advice about rights as a reason for joining. Interviewees provided insight into the fundamental importance some attached to rights and representation issues.

I think it [UNITES] is very useful for people who are trying to enter the BPO industry…when they have nowhere to go and they feel they do not have that voice to speak up, and when they feel that there is a lot of prejudice and…so many problems. (BPO agent, captive, Bangalore)

In the early days there was nowhere for an employee to go in terms of whatever issues–claims, insurance–they might have. Here UNITES is calling people and saying if there is a problem [with your rights] we will represent and help you. (Voice agent, domestic, Bangalore)

One-in-three overall saw joining UNITES as assisting in career development, a proportion that rises to one-in-two for members in captives. Additionally, members reported the importance of UNITES providing training that would enhance 'skills and knowledge'. For members in captives particularly (67 per cent), joining UNITES enabled them to access information on pay and conditions across BPO. Clearly, these findings resonate with arguments stressing the importance of BPO employees' professionalism and aspirant careerism. Nevertheless, the data also provides evidence of a trade union orientation. As many as 62 per cent in captives stated that one reason for joining was that they believed in trade unions, although this was less pronounced amongst members in third parties and domestics. Further, a majority in captives and slightly less than a majority in third parties believed that BPO professionals should have their own organisation to represent their interests. Collective impulses emerge also when we consider that a majority of members in captives and third parties report that they joined because 'other people at work are members'.

There are some differences between members' attitudes across the sub-sectors. Those in third parties were more likely to have joined because others in their workplace were members, or that UNITES would support them over a specific work problem. Those in captives were more likely to cite UNITES community activities. Also notable is that those in domestic companies were less likely to relate to the attitudinal or value-based reasons for joining, such as the belief that BPO professionals should have an independent organisation to represent their interests.

The findings presented in Table 7.4 are important for they are the responses of UNITES members reflecting upon working conditions likely to prompt their non-member colleagues to join. The most significant was working hours—cited by 65 per cent overall as very important. This has several dimensions (shift length, night-time working, effects on well-being) and is closely associated with issues related to travel-to-work times, explicitly cited by 47 per cent as very important. Next in terms of overall importance were concerns over safety and security which remain prominent despite claimed improvements in companies' practices following Prathibha's murder. Given BPO's continued growth it is interesting that so many (62 per cent) consider colleagues' concerns over job security as very important in prompting employees to join. Interview evidence suggests that the cause might lie as much in management's treatment of individual workers and their sense of vulnerability, particularly in SMEs and domestics, than general concerns regarding downsizing or closures. A member from a Bangalore domestic BPO firm reported:

> ...certain employees could not do anything except succumbing to the managerial discretion. They have nobody to fall back to rather in the sense somebody they could look for some help and support...once in a while where there are people who seem to be targeted, who absolutely have no rights whatever of any kind. Because they are helpless, they are victimised or probably they have to succumb to the entire thing. Eventually they leave sacrificing the salary...

Pay, bonus and benefits issues were also identified, as were the task-related concerns of pressure of work and targets, which employees have long complained about in UK call centres (Taylor and Bain 2001). Interview evidence provides innumerable illustrations of these essential characteristics of Indian BPO/call centre work. We have the space only to cite one of the most graphic.

> ...daily targets are given because it is a typical call centre. Obviously the call centre is a target concept. At a stretch, a technician is supposed to take at least 50–60 calls, that is typically a Herculean task. Time is

Table 7.4: Work Conditions Prompting Employees to Join UNITES

	Overall 'Very Important' (%)	Captive	Indian Third Party	Domestic	Total
		Mean	Mean	Mean	Mean
Working times[a]	65	3.53	3.43	3.66	3.61
Employees' security, e.g., transport[a]	64	3.41	3.37	3.68	3.60
Job insecurity[a]	62	3.34	3.12	3.65	3.55
The need for employee voice[a]	59	3.51	3.17	3.55	3.51
Travel-to-work time	47	3.32	3.05	3.23	3.24
Pay[a]	46	3.29	3.06	3.38	3.34
Targets	45	3.35	3.39	3.40	3.39
Health and safety issues[a]	45	3.57	3.35	3.37	3.41
Pressure of work[a]	40	3.47	3.35	3.33	3.36
Bonuses and other benefits	37	3.11	3.17	3.23	3.20
Management goes back on promises	37	3.18	3.06	3.10	3.12
Demanding supervisor	29	3.05	3.03	3.16	3.13
'Apple polishing' (favouritism)[a]	22	2.82	2.95	2.68	2.73
Employers making it difficult to leave for another job[a]	17	2.83	2.95	2.57	2.65

Notes: Statements rated on four-point scale: 1–'not important', 2–'somewhat important', 3–'quite important', 4–'very important'.
[a]Differences were statistically significant at 95 per cent level of confidence.

money. But there should be something called time for relaxation. Huge call volumes. People are stopped from going for their breaks or their breaks are postponed to a large extent, their brain stops working and they start shouting at customers. Once they find that the person has shouted at the customer, he is thrown out of the job. But they don't address what is the problem or the reason for that action. (Voice agent, Chennai captive)

Supervisory pressure was also seen as a reason why colleagues might join.

No time to freshen up. I will be looking for the first break. We were not given paper cups. We were not allowed to get it inside also. So no water, three hours continuous talking, without taking a glass of water. We were supposed to be happy with the lunch-break, run, drink water, have lunch, come running back because 30 minutes is over. As the three teams will be having their break, there is hardly any place in the rest-room to rest. You will log-in late at least by 2–3 minutes and you will have red marks. The leader will yell, come to each and every person and scream. (Agent, Chennai domestic)

The team leader should be an example and that has not happened... There is a TL in IBM who used to scream for every small thing at the top of her voice. (Agent, Chennai captive).

Finally, perhaps the most significant finding is that almost six-in-10 believed the need for employee voice might be a very important factor in prompting employees to join.

Main Problems Facing UNITES over Recruitment

The main problems facing UNITES in recruiting additional members are shown in Table 7.5. In order, members perceived as 'very important' companies' opposition to UNITES (57 per cent), that BPO employees see themselves as professionals (54 per cent), a fear that companies might terminate someone for joining UNITES (54 per cent), the youth and inexperience of the workforce (53 per cent), high attrition leading to an unstable membership base (48 per cent), that many employees do not believe in trade unions (47 per cent), that employees think that joining UNITES would affect their careers (45 per cent). That many BPO employees see themselves as professionals received the highest mean rating (3.42). The survey thus provides evidence supporting claims regarding the effectiveness of employers' 'exclusivist' and 'inclusivist' strategies (Noronha and D'Cruz 2006). Interview data delivers insights into employers' overt anti-unionism, notably the testimony of the member who maintained UNITES' website. He reported the frequency with which employees contacting UNITES would say, 'Can I join in secret?' or 'I am a member but please do not let it be known', fearful of 'termination' if their membership became known to management.

Table 7.5:   Main Problems Facing UNITES over Recruitment

	Overall 'Very Important' (%)	Captive	Indian Third Party	Domestic	Total
		Mean	Mean	Mean	Mean
Companies are opposed to UNITES	57	3.33	3.03	3.15	3.18
BPO employees see themselves as professionals	54	3.26	3.23	3.50	3.42
Fear that companies might terminate someone for joining UNITES	54	3.33	2.83	3.33	3.29
Much of the workforce is young and inexperienced	53	3.29	2.97	3.23	3.22
High attrition makes it hard to recruit and build stable membership	48	3.06	3.03	3.48	3.35
Many BPO employees do not believe in trade unions	47	3.14	3.08	3.20	3.18
Employees think joining UNITES will affect their careers	45	2.81	3.14	3.43	3.28
Employees believe the employer is all they need	38	3.26	2.75	2.89	2.96
High salaries mean that employees do not need to join UNITES	38	3.49	2.79	3.38	3.36
Many BPO professionals do not see the need for UNITES	37	3.02	2.86	3.09	3.05
Many BPO professionals think they will be promoted	34	3.15	3.02	3.21	3.18
Employees believe any problem they have will be solved by managers	33	3.28	2.68	2.99	3.03
Unions in BPO are seen as damaging to Indian industry's growth	26	2.01	2.95	2.82	2.66
Employers have captured employees' hearts and minds	14	2.48	2.97	2.13	2.27

Note: Statements rated on four-point scale as for Table 7.4.

In cases where there is a person who is courageous and does not bother, [they] will not have to have a particular reason to terminate a person. Being a union member can be one of those reasons. Again, when they sign their contract letter initially, they sign and say they will not be a member of a union. This is another reason why they do not want to say they are a member.

Reprisals were reported not just against union members, but against any employee who raised his voice. A Bangalore call centre agent revealed:

Whenever we go to the smoking zone or elsewhere, when there is a problem, people discuss it. We used to discuss among ourselves how things go on, how to improve things, etc. We cannot raise our voices because once we do that there will be a black mark there. That will affect our appraisal and this fear was there in everybody. Normally, we are scapegoats, keep working and get out. If anyone raises his voice, there is trouble for him.

'Inclusivism' presents UNITES with obstacles as it seeks to increase its presence, particularly in respect of employees' powerful professional identity. Nevertheless, companies' cultural control strategies appear to have limited purchase. Only minorities viewed employers' capture of 'hearts and minds' and the potential for unions to damage Indian BPO as important deterrents.

Perceptions of Management

Space constraints prohibit full dissemination of perceptions of management, in respect of operational effectiveness and members' general attitudes. First, management was seen as particularly unsuccessful in the following respects: listening to employees' ideas (73 per cent very/quite unsuccessful), understanding job pressures (71 per cent), managing call volumes (71 per cent), preventing excessive work pressure (71 per cent), providing career progression (70 per cent), varying tasks (69 per cent), involving employees in target setting (68 per cent), being sensitive to family/personal responsibilities (67 per cent), involving employees in decisions that affect them (65 per cent), fair allocation of tasks (64 per cent), providing sufficient training (62 per cent) and fair treatment of the workforce (60 per cent). Domestic operators consistently received the lowest ratings and third-party operators the highest. These perceptions of managerial ineffectiveness suggests ways in which UNITES, by raising issues of equity and fairness, may potentially enhance its status as providing a voice for employees. Evidently, where members can act openly there may be opportunities to champion employee interests at the workplace level. This need not always involve adversarial representations but could form part of a broader initiative intended to persuade employers that involving employees may enhance performance. At a national scale, UNITES could judiciously highlight instances which reveal the democratic deficit in Indian ITES-BPO in order to advance the case for employee representation. Approaches that are employer-friendly in tone *and* those which expose malpractice and injustice could be utilised at both scales.

Second, attitudes to management in general reveal a scepticism that challenges the belief in the universal prevalence of unitarist values. For example, as many as 97 per cent overall agreed/agreed strongly that management are only interested in statistics and efficiency and only 28 per cent that management has the welfare of employees at heart. Arguably, in joining UNITES, members have already expressed to some degree certain values and attitudes at variance with those of their employers. Nevertheless, the fact that, for example, there is widespread disagreement (71 per cent) with the statement that management and employees have common interests does indicate that this cohort has attitudinal characteristics at least compatible with collectivisation (Bain et al. 2004). How far these attitudes extend throughout the workforce cannot be answered here and would constitute a valuable subject for further research.

The Role of HR

As might be expected from a survey of UNITES members, a small number (16 per cent) believed that the presence of HR removed the need for trade unions, yet this overall finding conceals significant variations. While only 10 per cent of domestic members consider that HR obviated the need for unions, this proportion rose to 28 per cent for captive members and 44 per cent for those in third-party firms (see Table 7.6). Furthermore, while only 15 per cent in domestics had turned to HR to get problems resolved, 32 per cent in third parties and 43 per cent in captives had done so. Such figures reflect differences in HR practice between the BPO segments. From interviews and other evidence it is clear that HR practice is far less developed in the domestic sub-sector than in captives and third parties. Of those respondents who had turned to HR to seek the resolution of problems, those in captives and third parties were considerably more positive about HR's success than those in domestics. Most strikingly, only 7 per cent of domestic members thought HR had successfully taken action to resolve their problems compared to 40 per cent of captive and 59 per cent of third-party members. From another perspective, though, these figures indicate that a majority of members in captives (60 per cent) and a sizable minority in third parties (41 per cent) who turned to HR did *not* have their problems resolved to their satisfaction. Furthermore, for those who had not turned to HR with a problem, the two most frequent responses was to do nothing (55 per cent captives, 27 per cent third parties) or to seek support from friends and personal networks (23 per cent captives, 25 per cent third parties). The latter suggests a potential role for UNITES either in providing advice or in advocacy to the extent that it can become embedded in social networks within companies.

Thus, it does not follow that sophisticated and effective HR practices prevail in the international-facing centres. Budhwar et al. (2006) emphasise limitations in career progression, development and retention policies, while focused sessions at NASSCOM conferences have been dominated by discussions of the need to develop coherent HRM approaches in place of existing ad hoc and 'firefighting' practices (Taylor and Bain 2006b: 76–100). Recalling the telling critique of HRM as it emerged in the UK, there is often a contradiction between

Table 7.6:   Role of HR

| | Indian | | | | | | | |
| | Captive | | Third Party | | Domestic | | Total | |
	N	%	N	%	N	%	N	%
The presence of HR to solve problems removes the need for trade unions (Yes)	49	28	28	44	60	10	137	16
I turned to HR to get problems resolved (Yes)	75	43	20	32	89	15	184	22
HR's success at making themselves available to listen to problems [a]	69	56	27	68	113	19	209	28
HR's success at listening to and understanding problems [a]	65	53	26	65	107	18	198	27
HR's success at taking actions that solve problems [a]	49	40	23	59	43	7	115	15
How did you deal with your problems?								
I did nothing	80	55	24	27	429	43	533	43
I sought support from my friends and personal network inside the company	34	23	22	25	68	7	124	10
I sought support from my friends and personal network outside the company	10	7	15	17	136	14	161	13
I tried to ignore the problems/ think differently about them	10	7	6	7	135	14	151	12
I decided to quit and look for another job.	5	3	11	13	138	14	154	12

Note: [a]Represents % answering very/quite successful of the 184 who turned to HR.

'rhetoric' and 'reality' (Legge 2004). Interview evidence provides scathing criticism of HR, particularly by this employee with seven years' experience of domestic, third-party and captive call centres:

> I disagree that HR would solve all the employees' problems. That is absolutely a misconception. They have made it a rule that the employees have to turn to the HR whatever happens. Though the HR department is approachable by employees, they are not too friendly or responsive to respond to employees' concerns...In the last seven

years, no HR department has ever helped me with my problems...HR
is misguiding the people that they can be approached. We [UNITES]
are the people whom they should be approaching.

In sum, sufficient evidence exists to question the notion that
HR departments and their supposedly increasingly sophis-
ticated policies have the effect of 'rendering unions redundant'
(Noronha and D'Cruz 2006: 2118).

CONCLUSIONS

It is not that the pessimistic scenario that emphasises the
difficulties facing UNITES is entirely incorrect. There is considerable evidence that members perceive, and may experience,
companies' combative anti-unionism, which causes a reluctance to declare their membership for fear of reprisals. Evidently
the messages issuing from NASSCOM and employers that trade
unionism is unwanted and unnecessary in Indian BPO do have
some purchase amongst employees, whose middle-class backgrounds, youth and lack of experience do not predispose them
to think in collectivist terms. In addition, many employees do
possess a profound professional identity (D'Cruz and Noronha
2006) and aspire to pursue careers in BPO. High attrition and
rapid growth undoubtedly contribute to many employees be-
lieving that individualistic solutions, notably moving to secure
better paid employment and/or promotion, are possible rather
than the less obvious collectivist route in conditions where
UNITES has barely established a presence.

Nevertheless, a singular focus on the obstacles neglects
the fact that a majority of UNITES members do not see their
interests and those of their employers as identical. Very few
believe that their colleagues have had their 'hearts and minds'
captured through cultural control strategies. Nor is there universal support for the view that HRM practices act as a substitute for, and render unnecessary, independent employee

representation. Both objectively and in terms of the unionised employees' attitudes expressed here, there is a democratic deficit in the Indian BPO industry. Of course, we must emphasise that what the survey has captured are the attitudes of employees who have already indicated through joining UNITES their belief in the need for independent representation. We cannot generalise these findings to the BPO workforce *in toto*. Yet, the manifold grievances uncovered, from the seemingly trivial indignities of favouritism to heavy-handed and arbitrary supervisory treatment, or to the material issues of pay or workload, or the plethora of complaints over work times, or even profound concerns over safety, suggest that employee concerns are widespread, even though they may be experienced with differing degrees of intensity and regularity depending on segment, company or process.

It is not being argued that highly-pressurised working conditions alone create the conditions for trade unionism to flourish. Nevertheless, the position occupied by the Indian BPO industry in the transnational supply chains of the corporations of the global North has created lean servicing regimes in which cost-cutting imperatives dominate. The fundamental dynamics of this broader political economy ultimately create an experience of work as intense, pressurised and often stressful. There is evidence that Indian BPO employees in both voice and business processes are being driven harder through the euphemistically-named process excellence agenda (NASSCOM-McKinsey 2005: 126) in order to compensate for rising costs. The significance of this intensification is to highlight further the potential gap between employees' expectations that the BPO industry will provide stimulating work and a prestigious career and the reality of repetitive and tightly-monitored work routines. While promotion and career prospects undoubtedly exist in such a rapidly-growing industry, many are unable to escape the phones or routine data processing. Notwithstanding the attractions of pay levels generally unavailable elsewhere for these graduates, the quotidian experiences for many of demanding work provides an inescapable context and a potential source of dissatisfaction. The evidence is unequivocal. UNITES has a constituency in the Indian BPO industry, notwithstanding contradictions in the orientation of employees. To repeat, the broader task facing UNITES is how to reconcile the tension between the requirement to resonate with the professional aspirations of its members and the need to act more overtly as a trade union. Members made diverse suggestions, reflecting this tension, on how UNITES can increase membership. Some urge UNITES to be bolder, to challenge the employers more stridently through media coverage and activities, while others urge continued caution emphasising the need to win employers' trust and to advance professional interests of its members. It is only through experience that UNITES will develop the understanding of what tactics are helpful in particular sets of circumstances.

The principal immediate challenge facing UNITES is, to paraphrase Marx, the primitive accumulation of members. Despite some recruiting success, for UNITES to be relevant it must broaden its membership base and develop clusters of self-reliant members in workplaces and across companies. One priority must be for UNITES to break out of its concentration in the domestic SME sector and to gain greater implantation in captives and third-party operations. While all membership sources are welcome and domestic employees can carry the unionisation message to international companies, agendas must be developed to attract members specifically from captives and third parties. Particularly in respect of captives, growth *within* India can be shaped partly by *external* developments, by the actions and interventions of unions in the global North and of international federations (Taylor and Bain 2008). Where trade union recognition exists in developed countries, attempts can be made to extend arrangements to India either directly or through global framework agreements. At the very least, UNITES can benefit hugely from external union support, information exchanges and reciprocal visits.

Ultimately, UNITES' progress will depend crucially on its own organising activities, in which the issues and methods relevant in the global North cannot be mechanically transplanted to India. Many matters of importance to Indians cannot be anticipated by reference to UK or US experience. While UNITES has made progress, there are indications that in order to achieve future growth it must overcome internal difficulties stemming from organisational immaturity, members' inexperience, limited financial resources and identifiable tensions between the different geographical centres. In conclusion, we agree with Ofresno et al. (2007: 552) that the BPO 'represents an entirely new frontier for organising trade unions' and UNITES' record suggests that a cautiously positive evaluation of its early achievements is appropriate.

Notes

1. D'Cruz, Noronha and Taylor participated in UNITES founding conference in Mumbai.
2. Despite the fact that an average Indian student receives 15 years of education in English, India does not possess inexhaustible supplies of graduates with the linguistic capability and depth of cultural understanding deemed acceptable by Indian providers and/or their clients (Taylor and Bain 2005). Only 10–15 per cent graduates have the skills for direct employment (NASSCOM-McKinsey 2005: 90) and the industry hires 3–5 of every 100 applicants.
3. For example, Genpact employs around 23,000 in India, HSBC 17,000, IBM-Daksh 25,000, Wipro 20,000+, Firstsource 10,000+ and EXL 9,000.
4. North America accounts for around 70 per cent of Indian BPO business and Europe (principally UK) around 20 per cent.
5. These broadly captured three types of recruitment identified as important (Waddington and Whitston 1997): direct union approaches, informal methods such as through friends or one's own initiative, and efforts initiated by the workplace.
6. Previous research has identified these factors typical of contact centres generally (Taylor et al. 2003) and in India (D'Cruz and Noronha, 2006; Taylor and Bain, 2006a).

REFERENCES

Bain, P. and P. Taylor. 2002. 'Ringing the Changes? Union Recognition and Organisation in Call Centres in the UK Finance Sector', *Industrial Relations Journal*, 33(3):246–61.

——. 2008. 'No Passage to India? The Initial Responses of UK Unions to the Migration of Call Centre Jobs', *Industrial Relations Journal*, 39(1): 5–23.

Bain, P., P. Taylor, K. Gilbert, and G. Gall. 2004. 'Failing to Organise–or Organising to Fail? Challenge, Opportunity and the Limitations of Union Policy in Four Call Centres', in G. Healy, E. Heery, P.Taylor, and W. Brown (eds), *The Future of Worker Representation*, pp. 62–81. Basingstoke: Palgrave.

Batt, R., Kwon H. Doellgast, M. Nopany, P. Nopany, and A. da Costa. 2005. *The Indian Call Centre Industry*. Ithaca: Cornell University.

Batt, R. and L. Moynihan. 2002. 'The Viability of Alternative Call Centre Production Models', *Human Resource Management Journal*, 12(4): 14–34.

Budhwar, P., A. Varma, V. Singh, and R. Dhar. 2006. 'HRM Systems of Indian Call Centres: An Exploratory Study', *International Journal of Human Resource Management*, 17(5): 881–97.

Castree, N., N. Coe, K. Ward, and M. Samers. 2004. *Spaces of Work*. London: Sage.

Cohen, L. and A. El-Sawad. 2007. 'Accounting for "Us" and "Them": Indian and UK Customer Service Workers' Reflections on Offshoring', *Economic and Political Weekly*, 26 May: 1951–57.

Cooke, M. 2005. *Stretched to the Limits–CBPOP, BPOX and Call Centre Unionisation in India*. London: Amicus.

D'Cruz, P. and Noronha, E. 2006. 'Being Professional: Organizational Control in Indian Call Centres', *Social Science Computer Review*, 24(2): 342–61.

Ellis, V. and P. Taylor. 2006. 'You Don't Know What You've Got Till It's Gone: Re-contextualising the Origins, Development and Impact of the Call Centre', *New Technology, Work and Employment*, 21(2): 107.

Frenkel, S., M. Korczynski, K. Shire, and M. Tam. 1999. *On the Front Line: Organisation of Work in the Information Economy*. Ithaca: Cornell University Press.

Glucksmann, M. 2004. 'Call Configurations: Varieties of Call Centre and Divisions of Labour', *Work, Employment and Society*, 18(4): 795–811.

Hirschfeld, K. 2005. *IT Professionals Forums in India: Organisation at a Crossroads*. Nyon: Union Network International.

Kelley, P.F. 2002. 'Space of Labour Control: Comparative Perspectives from Southeast Asia', *Transactions of the Institute of British Geographers*, 27: 395–411.

Kuruvilla, S., S. Frenkel, and D. Peetz. 2003. 'MNCs as Diffusers of Best Practice in HRM/IR in Developing Countries', in W. Cooke (ed.), *Multinational Companies and Global Human Resource Strategies*, Westport: Qurom.

Legge, K. 2004. *Human Resource Management: Rhetorics and Realities* (2nd edition). Basingstoke: Palgrave.

McMillin, D. 2006. 'Outsourcing Identities: Call Centres and Cultural Transformations in India', *Economic and Political Weekly*, 21 January 2006: 235–41.

Miozzo, M. and L. Soete. 2001. 'Internationalization of Services: A Technological Perspective', *Technological Forecasting and Social Change*, 67: 159–85.

Mirchandani, V. 2004. 'Webs of Resistance in Transnational Call Centres', in R. Thomas, A.J. Mills, and H.J. Mills (eds), *Identity Politics at Work: Resisting Gender, Gendering Resistance*, pp. 179–95. London: Routledge.

———. 2008. 'Transnationalism in Indian Call Centres', in Mohan Thite and Bob Russell (eds), *The Next Available Operator: Managing Human Resources in Indian Business Process Outsourcing Industry*, pp. 83–111. New Delhi: Sage.

NASSCOM. 2002. *Strategy Review 2002: The IT Industry in India*. New Delhi: NASSCOM.

———. 2003. *Strategy Review 2003: The IT Industry in India*. New Delhi: NASSCOM.

———. 2004. *Strategy Review 2004: The IT Industry in India*. New Delhi: NASSCOM.

———. 2005. *Nasscom's Handbook for Indian ITES-BPO Industry: Background and Reference Resource*. New Delhi: NASSCOM.

———. 2006. *Strategy Review 2006: The IT Industry in India*. New Delhi: NASSCOM.

———. 2007a. *India ITES-BPO Strategy Summit 2007–Background and Reference Source*. New Delhi: NASSCOM.

———. 2007b. *Strategy Review 2007: The IT Industry in India*. New Delhi: NASSCOM.

NASSCOM-McKinsey. 2005. Extending India's Leadership of the Global IT and BPO Industries. New Delhi: NASSCOM-McKinsey.

Noronha, E. and D'Cruz, P. 2006. 'Organising Call Centre Agents: Emerging Issues', *Economic and Political Weekly*, 27 May: 2115–21.

Ofresno, R.E., C. Ng, and L. Marasigan-Pasumbal. 2007. 'Voice for the Voice Workers: Addressing the IR Concerns in the Call Centre/BPO Industry of Asia', *The Indian Journal of Industrial Relations*, 42(4):534–57.

Peetz, D. 2002. 'Decollectivist Strategies in Oceania', *Relations Industrielles/Industrial Relations*, 57(2): 252–81.

Poster, W.P. 2007. 'Who's on the Line? Indian Call Centre Agents Pose as Americans for US Outsourced Firms', *Industrial Relations*, 46(2): 492–97.

Remesh, B.P. 2005. *Labour in Business Process Outsourcing: A Case Study of Call Centre.* Noida: V.V. Giri National Labour Institute.

Richardson, R. and J.N. Marshall. 1996. 'The Growth of Call Centres in Peripheral Areas of Britain', *AREA*, 28(3): 308–17.

Sandhu, A. 2006. 'Why Unions Fail in Organising India's BPO-ITES Industry', *Economic and Political Weekly*, 14 October: 4319–22.

Taylor, P. and P. Bain. 2001. 'Trade Unions, Worker Rights and the Frontier of Control in UK Call Centres', *Economic and Industrial Democracy*, 22: 39–66.

———. 2003. *Call Centres in Scotland and Outsourced Competition from India.* Stirling: Scotecon.

———. 2004. 'Call Centre Offshoring to India: The Revenge of History?', *Labour and Industry*, 14(3): 15–38.

———. 2005. '"India Calling to the Faraway Towns": The Call Centre Labour Process and Globalisation', *Work, Employment and Society*, 19(2): 261–82.

———. 2006a. 'Work Organisation and Employee Relations in Indian Call Centres', in J. Burgess and J. Connell (eds), *Developments in the Call Centre Industry*, pp. 36–57. London: Routledge.

———. 2006b. *An Investigation into the Offshoring of Financial Services Business Processes.* Glasgow: Scottish Development International.

———. 2007. 'Reflections on the Call Centre–A Reply to Glucksmann', *Work, Employment and Society*, 21(2): 349–62.

———. 2008. 'United by a Common Language?: Trade Union Responses in the UK and India to Call Centre Offshoring', *Antipode*, 40(1): 131–54.

Taylor, P., C. Baldry, P. Bain, and V. Ellis. 2003. 'A Unique Working Environment: Health Sickness and Absence Management in UK Call Centres', *Work, Employment and Society*, 17(1): 435–58.

UNITES. 2006. *Review of UNITES@One.* Bangalore: UNITES.

Waddington, J. and C. Whitston. 1997. 'Why Do People Join Unions in a Period of Membership Decline?', *British Journal of Industrial Relations*, 35(4): 515–46.

Walker, M. and J. Gott. 2007. 'A Global Market for Services: Highlights of A.T. Kearney's Global Services Location Index', in NASSCOM, *India ITES-BPO Strategy Summit 2007–Background and Reference Source*, pp. 28–31. New Delhi: NASSCOM.

8

Outsourcing Careers: Western Theories in an Indian Context

Laurie Cohen, Amal El-Sawad and John Arnold

This chapter explores the career experiences of Mumbai-based customer service employees working for a leading United Kingdom (UK) financial services organisation.[1] At the time of the research, the company was operating four contact centres: three in the UK and one in Mumbai. The Indian operation was the company's youngest and fastest growing unit, and can be regarded as an example of business process outsourcing (BPO). In this chapter, we examine Mumbai employees' ideas about career, success and their own career development in light of current debates in the careers literature—a literature which, it has been argued, has thus far paid only limited attention to careers enacted outside of Western national/cultural contexts and in emerging forms of organisation. Our aim in this chapter is twofold: to investigate the insights existing career theory can offer to our understanding of Indian workers' career meaning-making and action, and conversely to reflect on what our Indian data can tell us about the value and the limitations of this body of knowledge, thereby opening up possible avenues for future research and theory building.

The emergence and successful growth of the BPO sector is seen as a major highlight of India's new economy (Arora and Athreye 2002; Dossani and Kenney 2007). According to a recent estimate by NASSCOM (2007), revenues from this sector are likely to reach US$ 33 billion in the financial year 2007. While some of these companies are indigenous, often operating as third-party contractors, many multinational companies also run their own operations in some of India's major cities and towns (Arora et al. 2001; Arora and Gambardella 2005). They are popularly known as 'captive units' (Baruch and Budhwar 2006; Mehta et al. 2006). Our case study organisation was a captive, a wholly owned subsidiary of the UK parent company. As we will argue, this structural difference was significant to employees' career experiences.

While some commentators have described such arrangements as providing hitherto unknown opportunities for economic and social prosperity, security and freedom (Friedman 2005), others see India as a source of cheap labour, and this form of modernisation as ultimately leading to even greater inequality (Mishra 2006). Arguments that the technology-enabled sector is offering high wages and unprecedented career prospects to aspirational young people (Dossani and Kenney 2003; NASSCOM 2007) are set against a view of Indian customer service workers as 'insecure' and 'vulnerable' casualties of the new economic order (Ramesh 2004). Underpinning this highly polarised debate are questions about what it is like for individuals to develop a career in such a context. However, with some recent exceptions (Baruch and Budhwar 2006; Cohen and El-Sawad 2007; Mehta et al. 2006), these questions have largely failed to capture researchers' imaginations.

We envisage this chapter as an iterative dialogue between debates in the careers literature and the data generated in the course of the study. In contrast to a conventional structure in which a literature review is followed by empirical findings, we propose to organise these 'dialogues' more thematically, moving back and forth between the theory and the data. We will focus on four themes arising in the data which we see as particularly pertinent to the careers field at the present time: changing contexts and their implications for career thinking and enactment; boundaryless and protean careers; career success; and work/life balance. First, though, we briefly introduce our case study organisation and research design.

RESEARCH DESIGN

As mentioned, this chapter is based on ethnographic case study research (Bryman 2004; Hammersley and Atkinson 1995) into the customer service division of a multinational financial services company (referred to here as FinanceCo). At the time of the fieldwork (2004–2006), the organisation was operating three customer service centres in the UK (England, Scotland and Northern Ireland) and one in Mumbai. Our fieldwork was conducted at all four sites (Cohen and El-Sawad 2007) but in this chapter we are focusing on the Indian dataset. In terms of structure, the 'captive' Indian unit is a wholly-owned subsidiary of the parent company. Indian employees work in the same regulatory environment as their UK counterparts, within the same overall structural context, and are managed with reference to very similar human resources (HR) policies and practices, opportunities and constraints, with minor differences reflecting aspects of the local environment. Telephone calls between the continents are made as if they are local and information and communication technology (ICT) systems enable customer service representatives in two different continents to work off what is effectively the same computer screen. In contrast to the image depicted in some of the literature, Indian employees are not expected to hide their Indian-ness by taking on pseudonyms or false addresses. It is also significant that the Mumbai site operates on UK time rather than United States (US) time, so employees do not work through the night. Notably, whereas turnover rates within the BPO sector can be upwards of 65 per cent (sometimes reaching as high as 80 per cent), here in Spring 2006 it was calculated at 25 per cent.

This chapter is based on fieldwork conducted at the Mumbai site. The bulk of the data was generated through semi-structured interviews (Kvale 1996) with 30 employees, ranging from entry-level agents through consultants, team leaders and coaches (termed process leaders in Mumbai), middle managers and up to the managing director of the Mumbai subsidiary. The majority of the Indian cohort was between 20 and 30 years old, while the senior managers were in their late 30s and 40s. Although numerically the sample was split evenly in terms of gender, all of the middle and senior managers we interviewed were men. All of the respondents had completed first degrees and several had masters. In addition, many had acquired professional qualifications during their time at the organisation.[2]

The agents and consultants in our dataset were all involved in servicing customer accounts on a range of products including life insurance, pensions and annuities. New products were frequently being rolled out, and respondents spoke at some length about who got selected to work on these. Furthermore, whilst some respondents focused on one particular product or process, others were cross-trained to service several at once. This was generally seen as a good career move, and an opportunity people wanted. Agents and representatives dealt with a wide range of customer enquiries, from the provision of basic account information through to more complex processes like claims, complaints and customer retention. Mumbai operated back office and customer-facing processes, and we talked to employees involved in both. Notably, there were two sorts of customers: account holders and independent financial advisors (IFAs). Of these, the IFAs were seen as more difficult, and also as having more status. It was explained to us that because IFAs frequently complained, and on many occasions had refused to speak to Indians, the company had decided to handle them exclusively in the UK. However, because IFAs tended to present the most complex and interesting problems, and were at the same time seen as the most prestigious customers, some Indian employees were unhappy about being sidelined in this respect.

Interviews focused on employees' experiences and perceptions of work in this organisation, factors which enabled them and constrained them, the impact of factors such as gender, class, caste, faith, family, etc., on their progress in work and career, and their aspirations for the future. Interviews were recorded, transcribed verbatim and were subjected to template analyses (King 2004), managed through NVivo software. In addition to these interviews, we generated extensive data through non-participant and participant observation. We were given a room to work in, with open access to the open-plan offices of the agents and consultants. We had lunch in the employee canteens, joined employees for coffee and tea in the staff rooms. We held feedback sessions with senior and middle managers. We were also able to observe a training session. During our time in Mumbai, we stayed in a nearby hotel which visitors and people on secondment to the centre regularly use. We spent social time with company staff at the hotel, and travelled between the hotel and the offices with them in the company cars.

Our Mumbai case study was conducted in two stages. The first was when we conducted most of the interviews and the most extensive observation. A year later we went back for a seminar which we ran jointly with the organisation. Academics from Delhi, Kolkata, Mumbai and the UK attended and participated, and presentations were also made by two of the organisation's senior managers. The delivery of this seminar depended on close collaboration with contacts in the organisation. This process, together with the seminar itself, was an excellent opportunity for us to engage in participant observation, providing insights into organisational processes and practices that otherwise might not have been available. Field notes were written up throughout the observations and later transcribed. We used the feedback workshop and this seminar as opportunities for further data collection.

CHANGING CAREER CONTEXTS

There is a growing consensus that irreversible change has been, and still is, occurring in the organisation of working lives and the structures and cultures of working environments. Deregulation and the liberalisation of trade, particularly in financial, telecommunications and transport sectors, have had a significant impact on how work is experienced and organised around the world. The extent of change and the permanence of putative organisational forms have been debated (Baruch 2006; Jacoby 1999). In addition, questions have been raised about the sustainability (and indeed the desirability) of accepted career forms and structures and the emergence of new ways of thinking about career development and success (Arthur and Rousseau 1996; Arthur et al. 1999; Hall 2004).

The managing director at FinanceCo, Mumbai, explained these changes in the Indian context:

> India had kind of aligned itself with the Eastern Bloc countries and the Soviet Union and, you know, had a more socialistic pattern of economy... Overnight the government was forced to liberalise and push into allowing people, the private sector, to develop, remove the licenses, remove the barriers to trade... it was the start of liberalisation, the start of unshackling all the chains for a capitalist economy.

In the careers field, contextual changes have been examined from a predominantly Western vantage point. The central discourse has been one of flexibility and adaptability at organisational and individual levels in the face of increasing global competition, with some attention to how this may confer (or force) greater scope for proactivity and even liberation on some individuals (Hall 2002). This is not entirely inconsistent with the managing director's views discussed earlier, but the flavour is certainly different. For India the new environment is an opportunity for freedom and a break with communism, whilst for the West it is a threat, at least in part.

Challenging claims that globalisation will lead toward greater homogeneity, Storey (2000) argues that it could instead result in diverse arrangements depending on national cultural and economic contexts, local labour markets and sectoral considerations. However, with regard to processes like outsourcing and offshoring, scholars have been much more interested in examining implications for the source country than the destination, more interested in exploring the consequences of India's deregulation and low cost, highly skilled labour force for Western careers than in finding out how these changes are experienced by Indians themselves. We suggest that this ethnocentric focus has led to something of a blind spot in our understandings of the implications of globalisation for career sense making and enactment.

As noted, technological developments and intense competition have encouraged companies searching for cost savings and the promise of 'acceptable or better' quality (Dossani and Kenney 2003; Taylor and Bain 2005; Walsh and Deery 2006) to move between geographical areas, and in particular to offshore certain business processes to less economically developed countries. Here the Indian labour market, with its high levels of English language competence, expertise in mathematics, science and engineering, and its unique demographic profile (with over 50 per cent of the population being under 25 years of age) (NASSCOM 2007) is seen as offering particular advantages in terms of levels of skill, knowledge, aptitude and attitude (Walsh and Deery 2006). However, it is significant that when they were younger none of the young people we interviewed had anticipated a career in the BPO sector, quite simply because until a few years ago it did not exist. Discussing his childhood career aspirations one respondent explained:

> I didn't actually [think I'd be working here], no, because even when we were in college this kind of industry was… just mushrooming. It wasn't stabilised.

Another commented:

> We never dreamt that the BPO industry would come here. We never knew that this kind of industry ever existed when I was in school. I had no dreams as such during my school life.

In contrast, in the UK (at the Scottish site in particular), many respondents' mothers had also worked at FinanceCo and they had always expected to end up there themselves. In the UK data generally we found a striking level of apathy, monotony and a sense of resignation. A notable difference in the Indian data was respondents' emphasis on India's changing economy and their own sense of being part of that change.

It's changing every day and it's changing rapidly.

If I was to sum it up in one word, the one word would be 'energy'. I think people are more energetic here. They want it. The key is they want it.

Across the Mumbai dataset, respondents described the sector in hugely optimistic terms, as offering unprecedented opportunities for career 'learning and growth':

> India's still a developing place so everybody in the BPO sector will get opportunities, everybody can and will fit in somewhere or other and will have the chance to lead a good life.

> What's happened is that our industry has grown tremendously and if you just look at business transfer/offshoring every year we have a growth here of upwards of 50 to 52 per cent. So the industry is doubling its size every year; with it comes more opportunities.

The newness of the industry was a central theme in the Mumbai accounts. On an organisational level, in much of the literature on changing work organisations, inextricably linked to the more macro features we touched on earlier are ongoing processes of restructuring, typified in de-layering and down-sizing initiatives whose espoused aims are to increase flexibility and responsiveness, often by reducing the headcount (Cascio and Wynn 2004; Noon and Blyton 2002). Indeed, a few years before we conducted our fieldwork, FinanceCo's site in England had been drastically downsized, and shortly after we completed our study, the decision was taken to close the Northern Irish operation. Echoing Sennett (1998), such initiatives were justified to employees in terms of flexibility and increased market responsiveness. It was therefore not surprising that underpinning much of the UK data was a gloomy sense of insecurity—particularly with respect to Mumbai as the place where processes were being migrated to. In sharp contrast, the Mumbai employees saw themselves very differently—as part of an exciting, new, rapidly expanding entrepreneurial adventure. When we did our first round of interviews, the organisation was celebrating its second birthday, and many of our respondents had been there from the start. They typically began their interviews by telling us their employee number, and spoke of their feelings of optimism and excitement in those early days:

> When I joined FinanceCo it was the hottest, the best company in Mumbai.

> There was this new company. It was a start-up company and I was the sixth employee.

> I was employee number three. Rakesh was number one and Chandra [Rakesh's personal assistant] was number two.

> I met Rakesh [the founder], and actually I met three or four people before. They were living in an office which was a quarter of the size of the floor behind and he said, 'It's a dream which we have... Do you want to join the company?'

> Rakesh sold me a dream.

This 'dream' image came up time and again in the Indian accounts, which we see as consistent with the sense of aspiration and possibility which we found in so many of the stories we heard. Interestingly, though, when asked about just what these dreams entailed and what they aspired to, alongside lofty ideals (like becoming the 'next Rakesh'), respondents spoke more pragmatically of financial security. Indeed, we were struck by how alongside the sense of promise and opportunity in the data, there was an embedded discourse of insecurity. We found that the development of a career was seen by many respondents as underpinned by a deeper quest for security. As one agent explained:

> Here [in the BPO sector] you have to at least have an undergraduate degree to get a basic job. I need to have an MBA to get a job like this, whereas in the UK it would fetch me a management position. And the material abundance that you have over there in the UK, you have everything, availability of loans, social security systems etc. Whereas I have to manage that sense of security all on my own. My family is dependent on me...

This feeling was reiterated by another:

You tend to think in terms of security. I was looking at getting married about a year after [starting here], so I wanted some stability, some security.

On one hand, our data are reminiscent of Baruch and Budhwar's (2006) research into the Indian BPO sector which revealed a deep insecurity and short-termism created by the presence of foreign operators, free to take their contracts elsewhere if labour market conditions so dictated. However, we would argue that here it is important to look at the wider social setting. For the UK employees (particularly those who had been in the organisation for some time), increasing insecurity was described as a fairly recent phenomenon, something that they were gradually learning to come to terms with. In contrast, for Mumbai respondents it appeared not as a consequence of recent economic developments, but as a normal and wholly expected feature of life. Indeed, most respondents spoke about a sense of precariousness that pervaded the Indian context generally, as it always had. They argued that although in purely financial terms they were much better off than their parents' generation, they were still some distance away from the quality of life people enjoyed in Europe and North America. This contrast was particularly apparent to our respondents who, as employees in the financial services sector serving a UK market, were well aware of the value of life insurance and pensions (until recently unavailable in India) in creating feelings of security and safety—and by contrast their absence in the Indian context. In the words of one respondent:

Here we work longer hours. There it's more stable, it's more secure working in the UK. Here it's very volatile, the call centre industry. Even though it's not a call centre, it's a captive, but still. I mean [in the UK] you just feel a kind of security because of the laws there about working. You know, there people aren't forced to do anything. I mean, you're not supposed to be working after 5. If you're working after 5 you're supposed to be paid over-time. Here there's no concept at FinanceCo in India.

Notwithstanding its inherent volatility, our respondents saw outsourcing and offshoring as potentially offering a prospect of financial security previously unknown for all but the very wealthy. Significantly, FinanceCo employees also drew a sharp distinction between their own organisation and others in the sector. For one thing, their parent organisation was a long-standing, established firm with an excellent brand image and a reputation throughout Mumbai for stability, tradition and long-term employment prospects. As a customer service agent explained:

> It's a very big brand company. It's not going tomorrow. If the project is going, the process is not working, the company won't shut down.

The managing director, who had been involved with the Mumbai operation from the start, talked about his career progression within the company:

> It's fundamental and very important to be in the right environment, so that's something that I would seek, and if FinanceCo provides that, I would definitely stay with FinanceCo.

Furthermore, as a 'captive' unit, the Mumbai operation does not depend on particular contracts for its survival and is not subject to quite the same competitive pressures as third-party operations. As two customer service agents explained:

> A BPO is something which is dependent on the client and anytime a client wants they can withdraw the process.

> Insecure feelings would be there if you were in a BPO and if you were in a captive you would feel very secure.

This sense of confidence in the organisation, as both a captive and as part of a 'safe' and established UK firm, permeated the Mumbai account. As we have argued elsewhere (Cohen and El-Sawad 2007), the distinction respondents drew between the different types of offshoring could be an argument for taking a more in-depth look at the sector itself. The sector is often described in rather monolithic terms that fail to recognise its inherent diversity.

The Pursuit of Learning and Growth and the Discourses of Boundaryless and Protean Careers

Linked to the contextual changes we have discussed thus far, within the last decade there has been some convergence around the notion that careers are changing in form, that the 'traditional', bureaucratic career with its implicit sense of advancement from humble beginnings to more senior positions is in decline, and being replaced by new, more holistic and integrated versions (Arthur et al. 1999; Hall 2002; Sullivan and Arthur 2006). Although the extent to which most careers ever did conform to this model is debatable, such patterns are increasingly being discredited as stultifying of the individual spirit and promoting an unhealthy dependence on organisations (Briscoe and Hall 2006; Herriot and Pemberton 1995). In contrast to notions of career which arguably serve to fragment and separate aspects of human experience, emerging conceptualisations, based on the accumulation of skills and knowledge and the integration of professional and personal spheres of life, are being promoted. Metaphors of boundaryless and protean careers have been developed to capture this changing landscape (Arthur and Rousseau 1996; Briscoe and Hall 2006; Mirvis and Hall 1996; Sullivan and Arthur 2006). As DeFillippi and Arthur stated, 'Put simply, boundaryless careers are the opposite of "organizational careers"—careers conceived to unfold in a single employment setting' (1996: 5). Whereas boundarylessness typically describes both physical and psychological dimensions of career, the protean metaphor highlights the latter, and specifically on the achievement of 'subjective career success through self-directed vocational behaviour' (Briscoe and Hall 2006: 31). At the heart of both metaphors, however, is a turn away from hierarchical advancement as the main marker for career progress.

Our data raise significant questions about the salience of these emerging discourses in offshoring and outsourcing contexts. While at first glance the idea of migrating business processes around the globe could be seen to exemplify boundary crossing, this is at a corporate rather than an individual level. The accounts of our Indian respondents tell a very different story. A pervasive feature of this dataset is employees' strong attachment to the organisational hierarchy and their commitment to bureaucratic advancement (Weber 2003). As noted, the emerging careers literature sees weakening ties with organisations as an increasingly important feature of today's careers. In particular, writers on protean careers have highlighted the shift away from the organisation, and towards the individual as the driver for career development. However, in our accounts, respondents drew no such distinction. On the contrary, an organisational orientation was seen as entirely compatible with individual development, and respondents explained how it was possible to achieve both organisational and personal goals in the course of developing one's career. As a process leader explained:

> Well, personally I would rate myself on the performances that I've shown in the last quarter or half year or the year gone by... every time you get a new profile you get a visibility on what's expected of you and you get a brand new set of KPIs [key performance indicators]. Right? If you work on that, if you drive on that you get a visibility of what you will be doing for the next quarter or for the next half year or for the year ahead and what's going to be your personal contribution into where the business wants to move itself or where the company wants to head.

This close alignment of personal and organisational interests was a notable feature of our data, and we might tentatively argue that this is related to the idea of the Mumbai operation as an entrepreneurial venture, and of the important role employees play in their organisation's success. It is certainly a far cry from the apparent assumption, evident in some writing about the boundaryless career, that individual and organisational interests are likely to be in conflict (Briscoe and Hall 2006).

Within the protean career literature in particular, a distinction is drawn between organisational and self career management. Our accounts are interesting in this sense, as they somewhat paradoxically depict an exceptionally high level of personal responsibility (echoing aspects of the protean metaphor), but within clearly defined organisational structures (reminiscent of a much more 'traditional' careers discourse). Here we cite two respondents, both process leaders aiming for a team leader position:

> I think I'm ready for my boss' job now. I think I have probably another six months of some stuff to do, which if I finish and deliver on those I think I'll be able to justify the need for me to move into that role.
>
> I've spent 2 years on this particular designation and learnt quite a lot. I've sharpened and bettered my skills to handle a team now. I've looked at how the other team managers operate and how they've handled situations... I think I'm now ready for a team manager's designation.

As mentioned earlier, the dominant discourse in these accounts was 'learning and growth'—a discourse which is likewise very popular within the new careers literature. However, within this literature the meanings of these terms appear to be quite different from those expressed in our accounts. Writers on boundaryless and protean careers clearly differentiate the quest for learning from the quest for promotion—indeed this distinction is a central feature of their argument. However, for our Mumbai respondents, they are one and the same—learning involves the acquisition of the relevant knowledge and skills necessary for bureaucratic advancement. Indeed, employees in FinanceCo's HR department were keen to show us the firm's growing library (which included books and magazines on a whole range of issues—not just the finance industry), and were especially delighted by the extent to which employees made use of it. For their part, customer service representatives spoke of the importance of such learning for their career progress. In the case of 'growth', the protean metaphor sees growth as psychological development. As Hall, the founder of the protean concept, suggests: 'the individual, not the organization, is in charge, the core values are freedom and growth, and the main success criteria are subjective (psychological) vs. objective (position, salary)'

(2004: 4). In contrast, at FinanceCo 'growth' means upward movement, and everyone wants it. As one agent put it:

> Everybody's thinking about growth here. Every minute you're thinking about growth...

And another:

> Obviously getting vertical growth, that was one of my main motives [in joining this firm].

Proponents of the boundaryless career concept suggest that movement across organisational boundaries as one of its defining features (Arthur and Rousseau 1996). In the previous section we talked about the volatility of the BPO labour market. In this rapidly expanding sector, people swiftly change organisations as contracts between purchasers and providers of services come and go.

> If I don't get growth here, then I'll start looking out for the job that's going to [give me that].

> In case I don't get growth I can't afford to stay here. I'll have to look for opportunities where I get to be a process leader with some other company.

However, we would argue that notwithstanding the extent and pace of this movement across organisational boundaries, as demonstrated in these quotes, employees are still deeply oriented to hierarchy, still searching for progression upwards. In our data, far from challenging the notion of bureaucracy, respondents respected hierarchical order and worked within its terms. Indeed, a senior HR manager explained how early on in the Mumbai operation, FinanceCo introduced many more hierarchical levels than they had in the UK in order to satisfy employees' expectations of growth:

> In this organisation we have five levels, but it's only in Mumbai that within the five levels all the levels are calibrated with three levels in between because the desire for somebody to grow from Level 1 to a Level 2 is so high that we've got to calibrate Level 1 into three broad

divisions. So you have 1A, 1B and 1C and then 2A, B and C, and 3A and B and then there is 4 and 5...

Within this tightly defined structure, positions and career paths were fixed, and consistent with bureaucratic modes of organising, the criteria for upward movement were clearly outlined:

> We have a career path for us, so they say if you're at this role and if you want to go to this role these are what the requirements are, and only if you meet the eligibility you will be promoted. If you meet the eligibility you can apply for it.

A key strand within the 'learning and growth' discourse was serving time. Implicitly, there was also an acceptance of organisational performance management systems. As mapped out by a team leader, at FinanceCo movement up the hierarchy was rigidly time-bound:

> It's defined on paper. So everyone knows right from day one how to develop and how to grow and what is the ultimate goal. We also know how to groom people to get them to that level. Should I be a process leader? I have another 15 months to go. In the next 15 months I can prepare myself to become a team manager... I'm a team manager today, I have another two years exactly to develop myself to jump to the next level of senior manager. I get a good rating, two more years in service. Should I be a manager, then how do I become a senior manager. So everything has a time. So at the end of it I'm not left clueless that I'm three years in the organisation and nothing has happened to me. Why not? If nothing has happened to me I just look over my rating, or maybe my behaviour was not so good at that point of time and maybe I missed by SLAs [service level agreements–part of the regulatory framework they must adhere to] in so and so month and that's why I was not selected.

Most people spoke of the need to be in a post for between 15 months and two years before considering promotion. Asked if anything could be done to speed up the process, the answer was 'nothing at all'. Given that FinanceCo was celebrating its second birthday, at the time of our first round of interviews many employees were coming up to that mark. There was therefore a high degree of nervous tension around as people competed for those internal promotions. In light of emerging career discourses, we found it interesting that although a number of respondents were critical of how these rules were enacted in practice and at times experienced them as unfairly applied, in our data the legitimacy of the rules themselves was never once questioned, and nobody offered alternatives to 'learning and growth'.

CAREER SUCCESS

In the course of their accounts our respondents spoke at length about what career success meant to them. Likewise, research interest in career success has been high for many years. Two broad strands of research into career success have emerged in the careers literature. One focuses on different interpretations of career success and their relationship to one another (for example, Heslin 2005; Sturges 1999). The other concerns predictors of career success. FinanceCo employees spoke at length about the former and in a more limited way about the latter.

A conceptual distinction between seemingly objective and subjective measures of success is often made. Here objective success criteria include salary and rate of salary growth, hierarchical advancement, proximity to the chief executive officer (CEO) and number/rate of promotions. Measures of subjective career success typically include career satisfaction, life satisfaction, job satisfaction and beliefs about one's employability (see Arthur et al. 2005 for a listing of the labels given to objective and subjective criteria).

As we have already indicated, amongst the Mumbai respondents, growth, in the sense of upward hierarchical movement, was the key indicator of career success, and many respondents aspired to positions at the very top of the organisation:

> There's somebody called Sailesh… He's a director. I like his way of managing things. I hope to get his designation one day.

A bigger, higher designation every year.

I want to be CEO

Underpinning this objective view of success, though, was a deeper quest for security. For a number of employees, providing for oneself and one's family was described as an important indicator of career success:

> I mean it's like a dream come true working at FinanceCo and growing in the industry, it's like, the feel of it is so amazing and most important is that I'm able to support my family and take care of it.

> You think in terms of security.

Notably, security was not only an issue for those employees with children. As we mentioned earlier, the majority of our Indian respondents was between 20 and 30 years old. Although many did not yet have their own young families, they nevertheless had financial responsibilities within their joint family arrangements. Here a few points are worthy of note. First, conceptualising career success in terms of security is not something that we found in the UK FinanceCo accounts, nor does it feature much in the literature which, as we have argued, is largely based on research conducted in the West. Perhaps this is surprising given the insecurity felt by staff at the UK call centres and the growing academic literature about job insecurity and the rise of the 'contingent' workforce (Feldman 2006; Guest 2004), and underemployment and unemployment (Feldman et al. 2002; Ranzijn et al. 2006). While security could be part of satisfaction or employability criteria, it certainly has not been highlighted as a central concern. Its prevalence in the Indian dataset thus elucidates the relevance of the wider social and economic contexts for how careers are understood. At the same time, it makes us wonder whether a more explicit focus on security as an indicator of career success in Western contexts might yield interesting findings. More generally, in terms of the objective/subjective distinction noted here, we might question how security should be classified, given that it arguably contains both objective and subjective elements.

Recent work has also included discussions of how ostensibly subjective and objective success factors relate to each other (Hall 2002). As in many other studies, our respondents included both in outlining what career success meant to them. This is illustrated in the two following examples. The first links emotional satisfaction with monetary reward, while in the second success is described in terms of both personal/intellectual development and hierarchical progression:

> A successful career would be a career where I see myself happy with what I am doing. I see passion in my work and I like what I'm doing and, well, obviously if I am rewarded handsomely

> [To me career success] means personal development, not exactly a jump in designation, but more additional responsibilities, personal growth, knowing more and more about products, processes. Basically personal development is more important than a designation. I will probably look for a bigger, higher designation every 2 years. I look to be a director sometime in the next 5 years.

In her research into conceptions of career success amongst telecommunications managers, Sturges (1999) highlights the importance of social reputation as a salient success criterion, in particular being seen as an expert by others and having informal influence, findings which are further developed in Lau, Shaffer and Au's more recent study of Chinese entrepreneurs' notions of success (2007). Regarding the objective/subjective dichotomy, both of these studies serve to further obfuscate this distinction; indeed, as we have argued elsewhere (Arnold and Cohen 2007), it might be better framed as one's own subjectivity versus somebody else's. That matter aside, the importance of social reputation certainly resonates with some of our Indian data, where being seen to be doing well was important to many respondents. An interesting issue which emerged in the Indian data is the importance of corporate reputation to employees' feelings of success, and more particularly the importance of that reputation in their wider community of friends and family. Many of our interviews started with respondents telling us how delighted they were to be working for this established, well-reputed brand, a brand which was recognised by their family and friends. As their accounts progressed, this was developed as an important dimension of their conceptualisations of career success.

> I really feel proud to work at FinanceCo.

> In India FinanceCo has a really good brand name. You know, working for FinanceCo is something like, 'Okay, fine, you're working for FinanceCo. Lovely...', it gives you an edge.

> I talk to myself and I motivate myself, 'I'm working with FinanceCo'. It's really something very nice. And my parents have heard so much about FinanceCo.

Researchers have paid some attention to the role of corporate image and reputation in employee attitudes and behaviour, particularly commitment (Carmeli 2005) and intention to stay or leave (Mignonac et al. 2006). However, corporate reputation has scarcely been used as an indicator of career success (except, oddly, for academics–Judge et al. 2004). We suggest that the emphasis on corporate reputation could be related to the unpredictability of the BPO space in India, where firms come and go almost on a daily basis. We learned that in this context, an established UK-based firm carries considerable cultural capital, which, it is argued, works as a valuable commodity for FinanceCo employees as they compete in this volatile market.

A considerable literature has developed which has examined the relative disadvantage women experience with regard to variables such as salary, promotion and career satisfaction (Ng et al. 2005). Whilst the majority of writers in this area have attributed this difference to the effects of discrimination (Chenevert and Tremblay 2002), Hakim's 'preference theory' (2006) proposes an alternative explanation, that the main reason for women's disadvantaged position is consistent sex differences in personal styles, values and life goals, which mean that many women place less importance on conventional career success than most men do. Consequently, they tend to choose different life paths.

Here our Indian data raise some interesting issues. All of the respondents maintained that at FinanceCo, as in India's technology-enabled sectors more generally, there is no gender discrimination when it comes to promotion through the hierarchy. However, this is set against a social backdrop in which many women still expect, and are expected to, leave work once they are married. As respondents explained:

> As far as girls are concerned, but then when they become like 20, 24, in India ... you get married and then you start leaving and then there's no career.

> Because all of them [families] are similar in regards with these situations: they prefer the girls back home by 8, let's say, and they don't like girls working. Many a time religion [impacts] in the sense that they don't like girls working after marriage. You need to sit at home.

> [Women] would leave in the case of their spouse doesn't want them to work or perhaps, probably they're leaving the country or elsewhere to another state. That would be the reason [for women leaving].

Of course not everyone subscribed to this, and as the following quote illustrates, some respondents spoke of how things were beginning to change with regard to married women working:

> Now it's not like what used to happen—like when you were 16 or 17 you got married. In India it used to happen a lot, but now people are very career oriented. The girls also now, 'we don't want to get married. We want to achieve something. We want to stand on our feet'. They will achieve something and then when they are 29, 30 years or something like that, then.

However, notwithstanding these changing views, at FinanceCo newly married women accounted for by far the largest proportion of people leaving. At the seminar we held it struck us that although attrition is a real challenge for FinanceCo and although they continue to search for new and better ways to retain staff, young women appeared as a kind of 'no go' area—it was inevitable and entirely normal for young women to leave, even in this very modern organisation. It appeared to us that this is such a deeply embedded aspect of social and organisational life, that it did not even warrant discussion. While we had no evidence of explicit discrimination, neither did women describe their decisions to leave in terms of 'preferences'. Rather, they spoke of social pressure, expectations, rules and norms. Here again, the issue of social context becomes central to our understanding of career sense-making and enactment.

Our second point on predictors of career success relates to ethnicity. Whilst there is limited research into the significance of ethnicity for career success, what there is suggests that in the US at any rate, Black people are disadvantaged relative to their White counterparts with respect to pay (although critics argue that much more nuanced research is needed to understand the complexity of the findings) (Bevelenader and Veenman 2004; Kenny and Briner 2007). At FinanceCo Mumbai, several respondents explained how in the old 'brick and mortar' Indian companies there were very strict divisions with respect to caste, religion and related issues like regional background and language. However, there was a consensus that in Mumbai's new sectors, such divisions were no longer relevant. Indeed, many said they did not even know of their colleagues' caste or religious backgrounds. Rather, in this global marketplace, what mattered was performance. As two respondents explained:

> As you know, we have thousands and thousands of classes of castes and religions, but it is all outside the organisation. When we are inside this building, personally I don't see any [differences]... I think it's a culture which is growing across all organisations in India today. We are far away from those orthodox cultures that we had from our traditions basically. We're not detaching ourselves from our culture, but we're just trying to modernise it or modify it to the betterment of everyone because today it's not the religion or the culture of a person which will determine the success of the organisation. It's the talent that the person carries out, it's the hard work that the person does. Irrespective of if he's a Muslim, a Hindu, or a Catholic or a Protestant or whatever for that matter, he is a good employee and for us that's what really matters... especially in this industry we have moved away from those things.

> [In] today's organisation we don't even have any kind of discrimination because we are, we have to keep pace with the world. Now that we're joining hands with more and more companies from abroad we can't afford being [left behind].

Here our findings echo Baruch and Budhwar (2006) who found that India's new economy, with its focus on rationalised human resource management (HRM) and career management practices, is posing a challenge to traditional organisations in which promotion was sometimes based on 'ascribed status and political connections' (Baruch and Budhwar 2006: 88). Perhaps what is surprising in our study is the apparent consensus, and lack of controversy, about this change. However, the still widespread assumption that women will stop work upon marriage shows that not everything has changed.

WORK–LIFE BALANCE

Recent conceptualisations of career have emphasised not only paid work, but have also included other dimensions of life as integral to the construction and enactment of career as it unfolds across time and space (Collin and Young 2000; Sullivan and Arthur 2006). The way in which individuals understand and then manage work and personal spheres of life has emerged as a key issue in debates on new forms of career (El-Sawad et al. 2006; Collin 2006). Proponents of the boundaryless career idea have taken issue with what they see as a tendency to fragment and separate these spheres within earlier interpretations, and certainly in conventional career practice. In contrast to these patterns, an important aspect of the boundaryless career is the notion of life-work balance, with a particular focus on the integration of work and home (Arthur and Rousseau 1996; Sullivan and Arthur 2006), where distinctions between these realms become blurred (Nippert-Eng 1995).

Our concern with much of this literature, particularly as regards its relevance to our Indian data, is that it appears to be almost exclusively based on Western notions of the 'home' sphere of life, and particularly on versions of the nuclear family. However, as many Indians live in joint families, with married women often moving into their husbands' households, the applicability of these debates is questionable.

In their recent 'mapping' of the work/balance landscape, Lewis, Gambles and Rapaport (2007) see the work/life balance literature as comprising two distinct, though related discourses: a 'personal control of time' discourse, and a discourse of 'workplace flexibility'. The first focuses on how relatively affluent men and women workers in Western countries manage the time they allocate to work and non-work spheres of life. The second, on the other hand, has an organisational orientation, and is concerned with workplace policies which promote and support flexible work arrangements to enable their employees to cope more effectively with the varied demands on their time. Central to both of these discourses are questions about how people living in nuclear families manage their various arrangements, and the demands placed on them, at home and work. Our respondents explained how in joint family settings such demands can look very different:

> The social milieu that we live in in India is a little different and I think life is easier in India if you are able to make enough money. Domestic help, access to family and support. My wife, you know, lives alone [this respondent's family home is outside of Mumbai] but I'm not worried because I have my father and mother, mother-in-law, father-in-law, her brother, her sister. My daughter goes to school and I don't have to worry because there will be somebody who'll dress her, feed her up, take her to school, bring her back and I have no worries. It will just happen.

Clearly in this type of context home-work balance must mean something other than it does in the West, if indeed it means anything at all. Furthermore, the spirit behind notions of work-life balance and integration appear to be gender-neutral (although in our view this could be contested): that they assume that both men and women will potentially participate in work and home life, and will both need to find ways of managing the boundaries between them. However, we have already noted that in India there is an enduring propensity for married women to leave paid employment, and likewise in our data we found little evidence of men's extensive engagement in domestic arrangements or childcare. Thus, the applicability of frameworks for understanding based on less differentiated roles is questionable in the Indian context. Interestingly, we suggest that our Indian data might also encourage us to identify aspects of sex role differentiation which persist in the West, and which one might argue are quite neatly wiped away, or ignored, in the apparent gender neutrality of the rhetoric of work-life integration.

That said, at FinanceCo we found instances of work/life integration that have never been apparent to us in Western contexts, and certainly did not feature in the UK. First, the organisation provides transport for their employees, collecting them from and returning them to their homes—which are often quite far from the offices—at any time of day or night. In fact, this has become a common feature of life in the BPO sector where the norm is working unsocial hours and where, given the young age of many of the staff and parental concern about their children, especially their girls, being out late, the organisation is acting *in loco parentis*. In addition, a number of respondents also spoke of how upon joining FinanceCo, their families were invited in to meet the other staff and have a look round the site. As a customer service agent explained:

> We've got an activity wherein your parents can come in and they can check ... probably they'll spend a day here and we've got people who would look after them, taking them through each and every department and tell them, 'this is where your son, this is where your daughter works and this is the environment that they are in'... It's to create an intimacy, a close relationship with employees, saying that it's very important while you are contributing to us as a company, but we would also be interested to know about where you belong and what is your background, who your parents are.

The various ways in which the organisation appeared to value and welcome respondents' families was echoed throughout the dataset. We heard one especially poignant story from a young man who had recently lost his father. He was on secondment in Scotland when the death occurred, at which point FinanceCo immediately flew him home. Shortly after his return, Rakesh, the managing director, paid a visit of condolence to the family. The employee told us how touched he was by this gesture.

As noted earlier, FinanceCo Mumbai is a multicultural organisation, with employees from a range of religious backgrounds. While there was a consensus that in terms of working practices this was not a relevant issue, culturally it certainly was, and the organisation expended considerable effort on celebrating the festivals of the diverse groups represented. These events were described in glowing terms by respondents:

> We appreciate each and every religion and we've got festivals over the year. A particular month would be something crucial for a Hindu, like we celebrate Diwali... so we've got a lot of celebrating happening here. For Muslims as well we've got Eid so there a lot of celebrations, good food... We've got a specific team which just concentrates on [festivals].

It might be argued that in the West, organisational policies around work-life balance are designed to prevent work demands from interfering with home life, so that autonomous individuals can balance the two separate worlds as they see fit. Here, on the other hand, the two worlds are brought together much more actively. Celebrations are held for all religious festivals, rather than giving individuals time off to attend the celebration (somewhere else) of their choice. There is a sense of accountability of the employer to the wider family of each employee, and again this is expressed by bringing the two worlds together, rather than giving individuals space to cross the boundaries as they see fit.

CONCLUSIONS

In some ways, recent Western analyses of careers can be seen to have some applicability to the BPO context in India, at least in a general sense. The economic conditions, and consequently career opportunities, are seen as increasingly global and subject to change. Conceptions of career success are somewhat varied and if not competing then at least existing in parallel. People often describe their careers in the language of growth and development. There is some corporate attention to issues of work-life balance.

Yet, in some important ways, those Western approaches either do not apply, or apply in ways which seem not to be considered by their originators. Particularly notable is the tendency for elements of so-called protean or boundaryless career thinking and traditional bureaucratic career thinking to co-exist. So, although staff in the FinanceCo call centre talked repeatedly about their growth, the way they thought about that growth was closely linked to climbing the rungs of the corporate ladder—and furthermore, some of those rungs had been inserted especially for them. Corporate policies linked promotion to the demonstrable and consistent mastery of work tasks, so in that sense expansion of personal capacity really was connected to hierarchical advancement. But perhaps more powerfully, there were also strong requirements to do a job for a certain length of time before being considered for promotion. This is one of the hallmarks of a 'bureaucratic career' (Kanter 1989). This co-existence and inter-twining of the old and the new seems not to be considered by most career theorists, and even the literature pointing out that perhaps changes in careers are not as great or as pervasive as some would claim (for example, Pringle and Mallon 2003), tends to portray the issue as 'either-or' rather than 'both'.

Extending this point, it is notable that much of the writing on boundaryless and protean careers tends to treat individuals and organisations as likely to be in conflict. This conflict is not usually portrayed as inevitable, but organisations are seen as prime suspects in the suppression of individual freedom and growth (Briscoe and Hall 2006). In contrast, in the context examined here, the organisation was the vehicle for growth and learning. It even provided a clear and welcome structure for it to happen. This leads us to suggest that recent Western analyses of career are not so much rooted in an increasingly globalised economic context per se, but in wealthy post-industrial economies that are experiencing globalisation at least in part as a threat that requires an agile response.

This also alerts us to the importance of the context, particularly recent history. This customer service centre was part of an expanding new industry in India, and was perhaps not quite established enough to have accumulated a large number of disillusioned people who felt they were in dead-end jobs. India as a country can be seen as moving to some extent from a state-controlled bureaucratic to a free market economy, which will present some people, especially the better educated, with expanding opportunities. Although Arthur and Rousseau (1996) amongst others tend to portray the boundaryless career as being liberating for individuals in the West, they acknowledge that it is partly a consequence of organisations having to become more flexible and faster-moving, with job security harder to find than in the past. Some writers (for example, Hirsch and Shanley 1996; Lips-Wiersma and McMorland 2006) have emphasised that downside, pointing out that it takes a certain kind of person with certain levels of marketable skills to flourish in the new career environment. It seems that the UK and India staff of FinanceCo are experiencing all this from opposite starting positions: in the UK, security is hard to find and in less plentiful supply than it used to be. For those in India, security is far from guaranteed, but it is a possibility and one that is worth working for, especially from a starting point of having little or none. Perhaps our data signal that in the West it is now time to use job security as one indicator of career success, rather than going along with the rhetoric that you just will not find it these days. Certainly there is evidence that people value it highly and that the consequences of insecurity for health tend to be negative (Hellgren and Sverke 2003).

Another significant element of context is of course the nature of family life in India. As noted earlier, the work-family debate and the extent to which the two facilitate or conflict with each other (for example, Grandey et al. 2005; Greenhaus and Powell 2006) assumes, almost without realising it, that families are nuclear and that support from the wider family is not the norm. The ways in which work and family intersect, and corporate policies in that area, clearly need to be re-thought in this more communal context.

Finally, we believe that work on the boundaryless and protean career has been helpful in illuminating elements of our data that might otherwise have gone unnoticed. For example, the overwhelmingly bureaucratic orientation of much that the Indian employees said about careers might have led us to miss the acceptance of personal responsibility to meet required levels of performance and keep oneself visible. Given the historically bureaucratic nature of much of the infrastructure in India, perhaps our interviewees were accustomed to and comfortable with promoting their own interests within a rigid structure. Indeed, this alerts us to the possibility that even in the (semi-mythical?) era of lifetime organisational employment in the West, it was advisable to push yourself forward and not accept organisational career management.

In sum, we would argue that while the concept of career does translate across national/cultural contexts, as ever we researchers must be wary of the assumptions implicit in our interpretations but which we often take for granted. In particular, we argue that our work shows that: (*a*) the economic changes brought about by globalisation vary in different parts of the world and have correspondingly diverse implications for careers; (*b*) phenomena that are often considered incompatible in Western careers research, such as organisationally managed careers and personal growth, can in some senses co-exist; and (*c*) cultural contexts such as extended families can fundamentally change the meaning and nature of organisational policies to support work–life balance. These insights should inform future careers research in non-Western contexts. More subtly, they also alert us to the possibility that some aspects of what we found in FinanceCo in India may be more applicable to the West than it might first appear.

NOTES

1. This research was supported by the British Academy and the UK's Economic and Social Research Council.
2. Where individuals are identified we have used pseudonyms.

REFERENCES

Arnold, J. and L. Cohen. 2008. 'The Psychology of Careers in Industrial-Organizational Settings: A Critical But Appreciative Analysis', in G.P. Hodgkinson and J.K. Ford (ed.), *International Review of Industrial/Organizational Psychology*, Vol. 23, pp. 1–44. Chichester: Wiley.

Arora, A., A. Arunachalam, J. Asundi, and R. Fernandes. 2001. 'The Indian Software Services Industry', *Research Policy*, 30(8): 1267–87.

Arora, A. and S. Athreye. 2002. 'The Software Industry and India's Economic Development', *Information Economics and Policy*, 14(2): 252–73.

Arora, A. and A. Gambardella. 2005. 'The Globalization of the Software Industry: Perspectives and Opportunities for Developed and Developing Countries', National Bureau of Economic Research (NBER), *Innovation Policy and the Economy*, 5(1):1–32.

Arthur, M.B., S.N. Khapova, and C.P.M. Wilderom. 2005. 'Career Success in a Boundaryless Career World', *Journal of Organizational Behavior*, 26: 177–202.

Arthur, M.B. and D. Rousseau (ed.). 1996. *The Boundaryless Career: A New Employment Principle for a New Organizational Era*. Oxford: Oxford University Press.

Arthur, M.B., K. Inkson, and J. Pringle. 1999. *The New Careers*. London: Sage.

Baruch, Y. and P.S. Budhwar. 2006. 'A Comparative Study of Career Practices for Management Staff in Britain and India', *International Business Review*, 15: 84–101.

Baruch, Y. 2006. 'Career Development in Organizations and Beyond: Balancing Traditional and Contemporary Views', *Human Resource Management Review*, 16: 25–138.

Bevelenader, P. and J. Veenman. 2004. 'Variation in Perspective: The Employment Success of Minority Ethnic Males in the Netherlands, 1988–2002', *International Migration*, 42(4): 35–64.

Briscoe, J.P. and D.T. Hall. 2006. 'The Interplay of Boundarylessness and Protean Careers: Combinations and Implications', *Journal of Vocational Behavior*, 69: 4–18.

Bryman, A. 2004. *Social Research Methods*. Oxford: Oxford University Press.

Carmeli, A. 2005. 'Perceived External Prestige, Affective Commitment, and Citizenship Behaviors', *Organization Studies*, 26: 443–64.

Cascio, W.F. and P. Wynn. 2004. 'Managing a Downsizing Process', *Human Resource Management*, 43: 425–36.

Chenevert, D. and M. Tremblay. 2002. 'Managerial Success in Canadian Organizations: Is Gender a Determinant?', *International Journal of Human Resource Management*, 13: 920–41.

Cohen, L. and A. El-Sawad. 2007. 'Lived Experiences of Offshoring: An Examination of UK and Indian Financial Service Employees' Accounts of Themselves and One Another', *Human Relations*, 60(8): 1235–60.

Collin, A. 2006. 'Conceptualizing the Family Friendly Career: The Contribution of Career Theories and a Systems Approach', *British Journal of Guidance and Counselling*, 34: 295–308.

Collin, A. and R. Young (ed.). 2000. *The Future of Career*. Cambridge: Cambridge University Press.

DeFillippi, R. and M.B. Arthur. 1996. 'Boundaryless Contexts and Careers: A Competency-based Perspective', in M.B. Arthur and D.M. Rousseau (eds), *The Boundaryless Career: A New Employment Principle for a New Organizational Era*, pp. 116–31. Oxford: Oxford University Press.

Dossani, R. and M. Kenney. 2003. 'Went for Cost, Stayed for Quality? Moving the Back Office to India', *Asia Pacific Research Centre Working Paper*, Stanford, CA, USA. Available online at: http://APARC.stanford.edu.

Dossani, R. and M. Kenney. 2007. 'The Next Wave of Globalization: Relocation Service Provision to India', *World Development*, 35(5): 772–91.

El-Sawad, A., L. Cohen, and P. Ackers. 2006. 'Critical Perspectives on Careers and Family-friendly Policies: Introduction to the Symposium', *British Journal of Guidance and Counselling*, 34: 273–78.

Feldman, D.C. 2006. 'Toward a New Taxonomy for Understanding the Nature and Consequences of Contingent Employment', *Career Development International*, 11: 28–47.

Feldman, D.C., C.R. Leana, and M.C. Bolino. 2002. 'Underemployment and Relative Deprivation Among Re-employed Executives', *Journal of Occupational and Organizational Psychology*, 75: 251–471.

Friedman, T. 2005. *The World is Flat. The Globalized World in the 21st Century*. New York: Penguin Books.

Grandey, A. A., B. Cordiero, and A.C. Crouter. 2005. 'A Longitudinal and Multisource Test of the Work Family Conflict and Job Satisfaction Relationship', *Journal of Occupational and Organizational Psychology*, 78: 305–23.

Greenhaus, J. H. and G.N. Powell. 2006. 'When Work and Family are Allies: A Theory of Work-Family Enrichment', *Academy of Management Review*, 31: 72–92.

Guest, D. 2004. 'The Psychology of the Employment Relationship: An Analysis Based on the Psychological Contract', *Applied Psychology: An International Review*, 53: 541–55.

Hakim, C. 2006. 'Women, Careers and Work-Life Preferences', *British Journal of Guidance and Counselling*, 34: 279–94.

Hall, D.T. 2002. *Careers In and Out of Organizations.* Glenview: Scott, Foresman.
——. 2004. 'The Protean Career: A Quarter Century Journey', *Journal of Vocational Behavior,* 65: 1–13.
Hammersley, M. and P. Atkinson. 1995. *Ethnography: Principles in Practice,* second edition. London: Routledge.
Hellgren, J. and M. Sverke. 2003. 'Does Job Insecurity Lead to Impaired Wellbeing or Vice Versa? Estimation of Cross-Lagged Effects Using Latent Variable Modeling', *Journal of Organizational Behavior,* 24: 215–36.
Herriot, P. and C. Pemberton. 1995. *New Deals: The Revolution in Managerial Careers.* London: Wiley.
Heslin, P.A. 2005. 'Conceptualizing and Evaluating Career Success', *Journal of Organizational Behavior,* 22: 223–47.
Hirsch, P.M. and M. Shanley. 1996. 'The Rhetoric of *Boundaryless*–or, How the Newly Empowered Managerial Class Bought into its Own Marginalization', in M.B. Arthur and D.M. Rousseau (ed.), *The Boundaryless Career: A New Employment Principle for a New Organizational Era,* pp. 218–34. Oxford: Oxford University Press.
Jacoby, S.M. 1999. 'Are Career Related Jobs Headed for Distinction?', *California Management Review,* 42: 123–45.
Judge, T.A., J. Kammeyer-Mueller, and R.D. Bretz. 2004. 'A Longitudinal Model of Sponsorship and Career Success: A Study of Industrial-Organizational Psychologists', *Personnel Psychology,* 57: 271–303.
Kanter, R.M. 1989. 'Careers and the Wealth of Nations: A Macro Perspective on the Structure and Implications of Career Forms', in M.B. Arthur, D.T. Hall and B.S. Lawrence (eds), *Handbook of Career Theory,* pp. 506–28. Cambridge: Cambridge University Press.
Kenny, E.J. and R.B. Briner. 2007. 'Ethnicity and Behaviour in Organizations: A Review of British Research', *Journal of Occupational and Organizational Psychology,* 80: 437–57.
King, N. 2004. 'Using Interviews in Qualitative Research', in C. Cassell and G. Symon (eds), *Essential Guide to Qualitative Methods in Organizational Research,* pp. 11–22. London: Sage.
Kvale, S. 1996. *Interviews.* London: Sage.
Lau, V.P., M.A. Shaffer, and K. Au. 2007. 'Entrepreneurial Career Success from a Chinese Perspective: Conceptualization, Operationalization and Validation', *Journal of International Business Studies,* 38: 26–146.
Lewis, S., R. Gambles, and R. Rapaport. 2007. 'The Constraints of a "Work-Life Balance" Approach: An International Perspective', *International Journal of Human Resource Management,* 13: 360–73.
Lips-Wiersma, J. and J. McMorland. 2006. 'Finding Meaning and Purpose in Boundaryless Careers: A Framework for Study and Practice', *Journal of Humanistic Psychology,* 46: 147–67.
Mehta, A., A. Armenakis, N. Mehta, and F. Irani. 2006. 'Challenges and Opportunities of Business Process Outsourcing in India', *Journal of Labor Research,* 27(3): 323–38.

Mignonac, K., O. Herrbach, and S. Guerrero. 2006. 'The Interactive Effects of Perceived External Prestige and Need for Organizational Identification on Turnover Intentions', *Journal of Vocational Behavior,* 69: 477–93.

Mirvis, P.H. and D.T. Hall. 1996. 'The New Protean Career: Psychological Success and the Path with a Heart', in D.T. Hall and associates, *The Career is Dead, Long Live the Career: A Relational Approach to Careers,* 237–55. San Francisco: Jossey-Bass.

Mishra, P. 2006. *Temptations of the West. How to be Modern in India, Pakistan and Beyond.* London: Picador.

National Association of Software and Service Companies (NASSCOM). 2007. Available online at http://www.nasscom.in/Default.aspx

Nippert-Eng, C.E. 1995. *Home and Work.* Chicago: University of Chicago Press.

Noon, M. and P. Blyton. 2002. *The Realities of Work,* second edition. London: Palgrave.

Ng, T., L.T. Eby, K.L. Sorenson, and D.C. Feldman. 2005. 'Predictors of Objective and Subjective Career Success: A Meta Analysis', *Personnel Psychology,* 58: 367–408.

Pringle, J. and M. Mallon. 2003. 'Challenges for the Boundaryless Career Odyssey', *International Journal of Human Resource Management,* 14: 839–53.

Ramesh, B. 2004. '"Cyber Coolies" in BPO. Insecurities and Vulnerabilities of Non-Standard Work', *Economic and Political Weekly,* 31 January. Available online at: http://www.epw.org.in

Ranzijn, R., E. Carson, A.H. Winefield, and D. Price. 2006. 'On the Scrap Heap at 45: The Human Impact of Mature-aged Unemployment', *Journal of Occupational and Organizational Psychology,* 79: 467–79.

Sennett, R. 1998. *The Corrosion of Character. The Personal Consequences of Work in New Capitalism.* London: Norton.

Storey, J. 2000. ' "Fracture Lines" in the Career Environment', in A. Collin and R.A. Young (eds), *The Future of Career.* Cambridge: Cambridge University Press.

Sturges, J. 1999. 'What it Means to Succeed: Personal Conceptions of Career Success Held by Male and Female Managers at Different Ages', *British Journal of Management,* 10: 239–52.

Sullivan, S. and M.B. Arthur. 2006. 'The Evolution of the Boundaryless Career Concept: Examining Physical and Psychological Mobility', *Journal of Vocational Behavior,* 69: 9–29.

Taylor, P. and P. Bain. 2005. '"India Calling to Far Away Towns": The Call Centre Labour Process and Globalization', *Work, Employment and Society,* 2005, 19(2): 261–82.

Walsh, J. and S. Deery. 2006. 'Refashioning Organizational Boundaries: Outsourcing Customer Service Work', *Journal of Management Studies,* 43(4): 557–82.

Weber, M. 2003. *The Protestant Ethic and the Spirit of Capitalism.* New York: Dover Publications.

SECTION THREE

COMPARATIVE PERSPECTIVES

9

Employment Systems in Call Centres in the United States and India

Rosemary Batt, Virginia Doellgast and Hyunji Kwon

The explosive growth of call centres in India has gained wide-spread attention because of its potential impact on employment in the United States (US) and other advanced economies. Media accounts report that Indian operations are more likely to use college-educated workers while paying one-tenth of US wages. Some argue that these advantages may allow Indian centres to outcompete US centres on both cost and quality (see Dossani and Kenney 2004). Nonetheless, complaints about poor quality and security, as well as consumer backlash, have led some firms to pull out of India, while leaders in the offshoring business such as General Electric have sold their Indian operations altogether. High turnover rates have become a particularly serious problem in recent years as an expanding number of employers compete for a small pool of educated employees, a trend that both increases costs and undermines service quality.

With heated debate more prevalent than systematic empirical investigation, our understanding of this emerging sector is based largely on anecdotal evidence. National figures on employment, industry trends and the percentage of centres operated in-house (as opposed to outsourced or offshore) are unreliable.[1] Our own national survey of US call centres suggests that after two decades of rapid growth, the outsourced sector represents less than 15 per cent of the market, and Indian offshore centres cover a tiny fraction of the US market.

In addition, there has been little or no research on management and employment practices in this sector, either in the US or in India. In this chapter, therefore, we consider two questions. First, how similar or different are call centre management strategies and employment systems in each country? Here our goal is to map the management practices adopted by three types of operations: in-house centres in the US, outsourced centres in the US, and offshore centres that are owned and operated by subcontractors in India and serve the US market. Are there systematic differences in these practices, or is there a call centre 'production model' that has diffused across very different institutional and organisational contexts? Second, what are the implications of different management practices for outcomes such as turnover? In other words, which practices explain the high levels of turnover in the industry?

To answer these questions, we draw on an original establishment-level survey of 330 call centres in the US and India. We focus on customer contact rather than back-office operations such as cheque processing or online order fulfilment. For each centre, the survey provides information on the customer base, market and ownership conditions, organisational characteristics, work functions, workforce skills and training, call centre technology, work organisation, compensation and outcomes such as absenteeism and turnover. In the next section, we discuss prior research that informs our study. The third section presents the study methods and analytic strategy and the fourth section, our findings. Finally, we outline the study's limitations and implications for policy.

PRIOR RESEARCH

The first question we address in this study concerns the extent to which call centre management practices vary across markets and institutional settings. Call centres represent a new industrial model driven by advances in information technologies that are now ubiquitous. These technologies facilitate the automation of services through interactive voice recognition units, standardise customer transactions through skill-based routing systems, create machine-paced operations through automated call distribution systems and routinise work through widespread use of scripting and electronic monitoring.

However, research shows that service management strategies and employment systems vary substantially across centres that serve different industry and customer segments, and that perform different work functions—from professional approaches to service to highly transactional or cost-driven ones (Batt 2000; Frenkel et al. 1998; Shire et al. 2002). In this line of research, work and employment systems typically are defined to include three dimensions: (*a*) the level of education and training required; (*b*) the level of discretion and collaborative problem-solving embedded in the design of work; and (*c*) the level and type of compensation system designed to motivate effort (Appelbaum et al. 2000; Batt 2002).

The professional service model includes a set of employment practices based on high skills and training, employee discretion and collaborative problem-solving and high relative pay (Batt 2002; Heskett et al. 1997). This approach to service management is typically found in business-to-business centres and information technology (IT) help desks or technical service centres. By contrast, centres that focus on simple transactions, such as telemarketing, reservations, or credit card handling, require relatively low skills, and jobs are likely to be highly routinised with low pay. Quality control is ensured through extensive use of electronic monitoring systems (Heskett et al. 1997).

A more complex question is how to explain the variation in customer contact centres that fall between these two extremes: centres that target the mass market or a mixture of markets and that provide service and sales for products that entail some degree of complexity along with opportunities to bundle services and customise offerings. These represent the overwhelming majority of contact centres serving customers in such sectors as financial services, insurance, telecommunications and a variety of manufacturing industries. Here, management strategies vary considerably in how much weight they give to competing on quality and mass customisation versus focusing primarily on cost (Pine 1993).

IN-HOUSE VERSUS OUTSOURCED STRATEGIES

How does the variation in call centre management strategies and employment systems align with their ownership status—that is, with whether call centres are in-house, outsourced, or offshore operations? There are many reasons to believe that outsourced and offshore centres will adopt management strategies that focus more on controlling costs than on investing in employees. First, outsourcing allows firms to avoid paying the high wages associated with internal equity norms and internal labour markets or union contracts (on internal labour markets see Abraham 1990; on union contracts see Pfeffer and Baron 1988). Several studies have found that subcontractors hire workers at lower pay and benefits to do the same work (see, for example, Davis-Blake and Uzzi 1993). Erickcek, Houseman and Kalleberg (2003) found that this is particularly true for low-skilled work, where subcontracting led to the loss of union representation as well as lower pay and benefits.

Second, the literature on transaction cost economics suggests that outsourced centres will focus on cost reduction because, as work is turned over to a third party, the client firm must absorb the costs of monitoring and contract enforcement (Williamson 1985). Thus client firms are likely to exert pressure on subcontractors to keep costs low in order to justify the additional transaction costs of managing the vendor relationship. In addition, client firms worry about the operational risks associated with third-party subcontracting and as a result are likely to outsource those processes that are easily standardised or codified and monitored through objective performance metrics. As research by Aron and Liu (2005) shows, the more work processes are codified and the higher the number of performance metrics agreed upon by the buyer and seller, the lower the operational risk. Other research also demonstrates that subcontractors drive efficiency through greater work intensity and capital utilisation than in-house operations (Marsden 1999). Grugulis, Vincent and Hebson (2003) examined outsourcing in three functions requiring radically different levels of skill and complexity and found that in each case the process of subcontracting led to higher levels of employee monitoring, adherence to specific performance metrics and lower levels of employee discretion. For consumers, high levels of process standardisation also reduce service quality by limiting options for customisation and relying on menus and self-servicing.

In the call centre industry, these issues are likely to be particularly salient because arm's-length contracting and attention to the bottom line are widespread, and contract enforcement typically is ensured through ongoing monitoring and adherence to performance metrics (Kinnie and Parsons 2004). Performance management technologies such as electronic monitoring systems provide real-time measures of talk times, adherence to schedules and scripted texts and sales productivity, allowing client companies to regularly monitor the employees of subcontractors. Thus subcontractors are under intense pressure to contain costs and meet these efficiency goals.

The work of Levy and Murnane (2004) on computers, skills, and the organisation of work provides additional insights into the process of subcontracting. They have argued persuasively that computers are best able to automate jobs that require rules-based logic, such as data management and order processing—precisely the kinds of jobs frequently found in call centres. Automation does not eliminate all jobs, but creates standardised work processes that reduce operational risk and allow electronic monitoring of a wide range of performance metrics. Once these processes are computerised and standardised, they are more easily outsourced to third-party vendors. However, more complex processes with higher levels of uncertainty are more likely to be retained in-house, where companies have direct control over operations that require more tacit knowledge and entail more nuanced interactions with customers.

The strategic management literature on core competencies provides another perspective on how and why outsourced work systems are likely to be more cost-focused and standardised than those managed in-house (See Prahalad and Hamel 1990; Quinn 1992). Core competencies are defined as those that contribute value to customer benefits and end products, that provide access to a wide variety of markets and that are difficult for competitors to imitate (Prahalad and Hamel 1990). In theory, firms should retain functions that they consider to be their core competency while outsourcing those functions that are non-core. When applied to the choice of employment systems, the theory suggests that firms should retain human capital that creates value for the firm, is rare or unique and is difficult to imitate (Barney 1991; Williamson 1981). For example, firms are likely to choose internal employment systems for operations that involve firm-specific knowledge and skills, team-based systems, or work processes that involve 'social complexity', 'causal ambiguity', or 'idiosyncratic learning' (Lepak and Snell 1999: 35). They are likely to externalise or subcontract work that is more generic, involves lower-order skills, or is transactional in nature. Much call centre work appears to fall into this latter category and thus would be viewed as a prime candidate for outsourcing.

According to this argument, whether call centre work is outsourced depends on whether customer relationship management is considered central to a firm's competitiveness. If the products and services offered by a company are relatively complex, involving firm-specific knowledge of products, processes, or customers, then firms are likely to retain their customer service and sales functions in-house. Similarly, if companies seek to compete on quality service or customer loyalty, they are also likely to keep call centre work in-house because they do not want to lose control of their customer base or have their customers treated generically, in the same fashion as the customers of their competitors, who may be using the same call centre subcontractor.

For high-value-added customers, such as business customers, firms are particularly likely to use a strategy of service quality, customisation and loyalty and therefore retain business-to-business channels in-house (Batt 2002). For mass-market service channels, the costs and benefits of keeping operations in-house are more ambiguous from a strategy perspective, and there appears to be considerable variation in what companies actually do. Although the number of call centre subcontractors grew dramatically in the 1990s in the US, at least 85 per cent of contact centres in this country continue to be in-house operations (See Batt and Moynihan 2006; Datamonitor 2001, 2003). This would suggest that a large majority of firms view their customer service and sales operations as central to their competitiveness–or at least have not yet become convinced that they should outsource them.

The implications of these arguments for the design of work and employment systems are straightforward. Companies are more likely to retain in-house services that are complex, that involve customer transactions that are nuanced or uncertain, and that provide services to highly valued customers. In order to meet the demands of these types of products and customers, they are more likely to use a strategy of service quality and customisation, and therefore to adopt a more professional approach to service. Centres that are operated by subcontractors, either in the US or offshore, by contrast, are more likely to compete on costs through lower wages and benefits, more standardised work processes and higher levels of performance monitoring.

OUTSOURCED VERSUS OFFSHORE STRATEGIES

The academic literature provides much less guidance for predicting the differences between US outsourced and offshore centres operated by Indian subcontractors. On the one hand, arguments regarding the likelihood of a more cost-based strategy in outsourced operations may be equally or more relevant to offshore subcontractors. US companies have sent work overseas to take advantage of lower wages, but at the same time they are concerned about the level of service quality provided. They also worry about consumer backlash and the security and privacy of financial databases. A recent survey of US executives reported that the top driver for moving operations offshore was cost savings while the top reasons for staying onshore were security and service quality (see Ventoro 2005).

For these reasons, US companies may impose tighter constraints on managerial discretion in Indian centres and higher levels of performance monitoring and adherence to call centre metrics. If so, then we would expect the work and employment systems in Indian call centres to be more tightly constrained and standardised than those found among US subcontractors. But unique conditions in the Indian labour market suggest that both the reasons for moving work to this segment and the incentives for investing in employees may differ from those in the US outsourced sector. First, the offshore workforce tends to be drawn from a relatively small pool of college-educated, middle-class Indians. We might expect these employees to be more self-motivated, allowing managers to rely on more professional, or at least quasi-professional, employment practices to motivate their workforce. Moreover, given the large cost advantages that Indian centres enjoy, there is opportunity to relax adherence to performance metrics such as talk time so that employees can use their skills to respond more effectively to customer requests.

In addition, the growing competition for these employees has put pressure on employers to invest in benefits intended to promote commitment and reduce turnover. Many call centres serving the international market occupy sprawling complexes outfitted with gyms and canteens. They often provide employees with free lunches and door-to-door taxi services and seek to create a 'fun' environment with games and prizes. The additional investment in 'accent neutralisation' training required by many companies, which averages one to two weeks, makes it particularly costly to lose employees. Moreover, the use of fixed employment contracts in India also means that there is a long wait for new employees, which increases the expense of recruitment. One manager of a multinational third-party centre explained:

> You have to think about hiring way, way ahead…. Let's say I was trying to hire someone from another company in India; she has to give 30 days' notice, so I have a delay for the 30 days. And once I get her, she has to do the normal products training, but she also goes through two-and-a-half to three weeks of accent neutralisation training. So there is a long, long wait for employees offshore. It's a month longer than in the US, easy. (Interview, March 2005)

In sum, the unique labour market conditions and cost advantages of Indian offshore centres suggest that they will adopt a less cost-driven approach to work and employment systems than subcontractors located in the US.

MANAGEMENT PRACTICES AND TURNOVER

The second question we ask in this chapter is how the different management strategies adopted across segments of the market translate into organisational outcomes. Empirical research on the performance effects of alternative approaches to service management has expanded in recent years. There is growing evidence that a more professional, or at least quasi-professional, approach is associated with higher employee satisfaction and customer satisfaction, higher sales productivity, lower turnover and higher sales growth and higher service quality and higher net revenues.[2]

Low-cost systems, by contrast, typically are associated with high levels of employee dissatisfaction, absenteeism and turnover, and these in turn often produce added costs, reduce options for customisation and lead to lower service quality. For example, several studies of call centre workers have found that routinised work design and high levels of electronic monitoring lead to stress, anxiety, depression, emotional exhaustion and burnout (Carayon 1993; Deery et al. 2002; Holman 2004; Holman et al.

2002; Singh 2000). Deery, Iverson and Walsh (2002) found that customer interactions, scripts, routinisation, workloads and managerial emphasis on quantity predicted emotional exhaustion, which in turn predicted absenteeism. Singh (2000) demonstrated that as worker burnout with customers increased, call centre workers were able to maintain their productivity levels, but their self-reported quality was lower.

In this chapter, we focus on turnover because it is extremely high in the industry and viewed as a major problem by employers. Industry analysts estimate that it averages between 30 and 70 per cent in the US, but in our interviews some managers reported rates of 100–150 per cent annually. In India, news reports suggest that turnover rates are often 50 per cent or higher. Voluntary turnover, or the employee quit rate, is of particular interest to organisational researchers because it represents a large cost to employers. When employees leave, their experience and the firm's investments in training are lost. Moreover, as noted earlier, the factors that influence turnover also influence other important outcomes, including employee motivation, service quality and labour costs.

Empirical studies of voluntary turnover have found that it is significantly related to human resource (HR) practices (Arthur 1994; Huselid 1995), particularly with respect to work design and compensation. Shaw, Delery, Jenkins and Gupta (1998) found that quit rates were lower when monitoring and work intensity were lower and pay and benefit levels were higher. Similarly, Batt, Colvin and Keefe (2002) found that greater discretion and collaboration at work coupled with high relative pay predicted lower quit rates while high levels of electronic monitoring and use of commission-based pay led to higher quit rates.

Expected Findings

We have argued here that ownership status is likely to be associated with particular approaches to work and employment practices. Based on the theoretical and empirical literature, we expect that in-house, outsourced and offshore establishments will differ systematically in their service management and employment systems. In comparison with outsourced or offshore centres, in-house establishments are more likely to adopt employment practices that involve a higher educated and better trained workforce, that provide employees with more discretion and problem-solving capability, and that offer higher relative pay. We also expect differences between outsourced and offshore centres, with the latter more likely to adopt a professional approach to employment management than the former. These differences in choice of employment system, in turn, should explain variation in turnover rates, with the more professional approach associated with significantly lower turnover. In other words, work and employment practices should partially explain the relationship between ownership status and turnover. To examine these arguments, we developed a model of turnover that includes controls for market and organisational characteristics, while examining the independent variables of ownership status and employment system characteristics, as follows:

Turnover = f (market and organisational characteristics, ownership status, education and training, work organisation, compensation strategy).

METHODS

Sample

The sample for this study is based on two identical establishment-level surveys conducted in the US and India between mid-2003 and mid-2004. The US survey was administered to a stratified random sample of 472 call centres drawn from the subscriber lists of *Call Center Magazine* (60 per cent of the sample) and the Dun and Bradstreet listing of establishments in the telecommunications industry (40 per cent of the sample). Using the two

lists was necessary to identify call centres in different industries. A survey team conducted the survey by telephone with a
40-minute average interview, yielding a 65.4 per cent response
rate. The sample was reduced to 464 after eliminating outliers
and observations that were missing substantial data.

The Indian survey was administered to a non-random sample
of 60 Indian call centres compiled from internet sites and the
membership list of the National Association of Software and Service Companies (NASSCOM) in India. The research team focused on six cities with large call centre concentrations (Chennai,
Kolkata, Bangalore, Mumbai, Hyderabad and Delhi). In each
city, the research team had one week to contact the call centres on
the list, make appointments and conduct the survey, which aver-
aged 95 minutes in length. The team did not target any particular type of centre, but rather conducted surveys on a first come,
first-served basis as appointments were made.

All survey respondents were asked to answer questions pertaining to the 'core' workforce in their establishment: the largest
group of customer contact employees who carry out the primary work activity at that location. Owing to variations in the
sample, we use a portion of the full dataset in this analysis. First,
we restrict our sample to three market segments: large business,
mass market and all markets. We dropped 106 small business
centres and 10 operator services centres from the US sample,
since these segments were not present in the Indian sample.
Second, we excluded 16 call centres that serve only the Indian
domestic market (located primarily in Kolkata) because only
the international centres serve the US market. These exclusions
reduced the sample size to 392. Because of randomly missing
observations in the dataset, our regression analyses are based on
a sample of 310 call centres (237 US in-house, 42 US outsourced
and 31 Indian offshore).

In both the US and India, we conducted extensive site visits
in different industry segments to aid with the design of the survey and the interpretation of results. In the US we visited 12 in-
house call centres and six outsourced call centres, where we
interviewed managers, supervisors and employees on various
aspects of their HR policies and work design strategies. In India,

each survey was administered onsite, allowing the researcher to cross-check responses and providing an additional test of the reliability of survey responses.

Measures

The independent variables of interest include the ownership status of the centre (in-house, outsourced, or offshore), and the work and employment system, as defined along three dimensions: human capital (employee education and training), work design (opportunities for discretion and problem solving) and rewards (compensation practices). To determine whether an establishment was in-house or outsourced in the US sample, respondents were asked how they would best describe the call centre: as an in-house centre providing services to their company or as a subcontractor providing services to other companies. The offshore segment includes Indian call centres that serve an international market. Almost all of the Indian centres were owned and operated by Indian subcontractors, with only a handful owned by US subsidiaries or US subcontractors.

To measure human capital, we control for the sex composition of the workforce and use two measures of education and training: the years of formal education of the typical worker in the call centre and employer investment in initial training (an additive index of the number of weeks of initial training an employee receives and the number of weeks to become qualified). For work design, three measures capture the extent to which employees have opportunities for discretion and problem solving. First, discretion over customer interactions is measured by the variable *script use*, based on a 1 to 5 Likert response to the question, 'To what extent are core employees required to use scripts when talking to a customer?' where 1 is 'not at all' and 5 is 'a great deal'. Second, we used three measures to construct a *work discretion index*, again based on Likert-type questions. Respondents were asked to rate the extent to which core employees had discretion over their daily work tasks; tools, methods, or procedures; and pace of work. The three measures were highly correlated ($p < 0.001$)

and were combined into a mean index. The third measure of discretion, *per cent in offline teams*, is the percentage of employees who participate with supervisors in problem-solving groups or teams.

The final group of variables measure compensation practices, including total compensation and per cent commission pay. We were unable to use average annual salary in the analysis owing to the large differences in pay between the US and India. While there are national statistics in the US on average compensation for customer service and sales employees, it is difficult to find accurate information on the typical pay of a call centre employee in India. We therefore constructed a *pay ratio* measure based on the ratio of a call centre's average gross annual pay to the median pay in each full country sample (US$ 29,000 in the US and US$ 2,444 in India). Informal documentation from industry publications gave similar estimates for average pay levels in the Indian mar-ket. The US median pay in our sample was also similar to esti-mates from the Bureau of Labor Statistics for the median pay of customer service representatives (US$ 28,720). *Per cent commission pay* is measured as the percentage of total annual pay that is based on individual commission.

Dependent Variable

The dependent variable of interest is the average annual quit rate, as reported by managers for the previous calendar year. A square root transformation was used to correct for the non-normal distribution of the variable.

Control Variables

We included additional controls for common turnover determinants. The primary customer segment served by employees has been found in several previous studies of front-line service workplaces to influence both management practices and turnover rates (Batt 2000). Call centres serving higher-value-added segments, such as large business customers, can be expected to invest more both in the skills of the workforce and in employee retention, as well as to be more selective in hiring, which reduces quit rates. Call centres serving multiple market segments typically have a broader skill base and more diverse job requirements. We thus control for whether the establishment serves primarily large business, mass market, or multiple market segments. We also control for union presence, which has been found in past studies to be negatively correlated with quit rates (Batt et al. 2002; Shaw et al. 1998). Employees in unionised establishments are able to exercise 'voice' versus 'exit', which leads to improved pay and working conditions and reduces turnover (Freeman and Medoff 1984).

In earlier analyses we tested the effects of several other control variables that have been used in past studies of turnover, including systematic selection procedures for hiring new employees, the ratio of applicants hired, whether the call centre was part of a larger organisation and the age of the call centre. We also analysed variation in outcomes when controls for industry and type of call centre work were added, including a control for whether the call centre predominantly handled sales or customer service. None of these had a substantial effect on the coefficients of the independent variables of interest and either reduced or had a negligible effect on the overall Chi square. Several of these additional controls were also highly correlated with other variables included in the model. For example, both the outsourced and offshore centres have a significantly lower average age than in-house call centres. Thus in the final model we included a more parsimonious list of control variables that captured key measures of markets and organisational characteristics.

RESULTS

Comparison of Mean Characteristics

Table 9.1 presents a comparison of organisational characteristics, workforce characteristics, employment system variables

and organisational outcomes for the in-house, outsourced and
offshore centres. We use a broader range of variables here than
were included in our analysis of turnover antecedents to provide a more comprehensive picture of how organisational characteristics and management practices differ across the segments.
In addition, in order to make comparisons more precise, we restricted the mean comparison in Table 9.1 to non-union call centres serving mass-market or multiple customer segments.

Table 9.1:   Mean Comparison: In-house, Outsourced and Offshore
Call Centres

	In-house	Outsourced	Offshore	p < 0.05
Organisational characteristics				
Establishment age in years	15.7	9.4	3.4	a, b, c
Part of a larger organisation (%)	79.6	75.9	78.9	
Sales-oriented call centres (%)	5.0	13.8	29.4	b
Workforce characteristics				
Female (%)	68.9	71.5	43.1	b, c
Tenure of less than one year (%)	28.1	36.8	61.8	a, b, c
Part-time (%)	17.6	35.6	1.0	a, b, c
Training and qualification				
Average years of education	13.3	12.6	14.0	a, b, c
Typical education (high school) (%)	38.3	69.0	36.4	a, c
Days of initial training	19.7	11.5	23.6	a, c
Days to become qualified	66.8	44.2	53.3	
Days of ongoing training per year	9.6	10.4	11.2	
Employee discretion				
Reliance on scripted texts[d] (%)	9.9	48.3	32.4	a, b
Discretion over work[d] (%)	9.9	3.4	5.9	
Discretion over handling customer requests[d] (%)	39.2	17.2	2.9	a, b, c
Participating in offline teams (%)	36.2	22.2	6.9	b, c
Performance monitoring				
Work time electronically monitored (%)	49.5	67.7	91.7	a, b, c
Frequency of supervisor monitoring[e] (%)	49.7	67.9	82.4	b
Frequency of feedback and coaching[e] (%)	46.0	55.2	94.1	b, c

(*Table 9.1 continued*)

(*Table 9.1 continued*)

	In-house	Outsourced	Offshore	p < 0.05
Compensation				
Average annual pay ($)[f]	27,713	23,881	2,635	a, b, c
Pay based on commission (%)	8.4	4.1	18.5	b, c
Turnover and absenteeism				
Quit (%)	15.8	25.6	24.5	a, b
Total turnover (quits + dismissals) (%)	24.6	41.2	29.6	a, c
Absenteeism (%)	5.5	8.9	5.3	a, c
Sample size	181	29	34	

Notes: [a] In-house and outsourced are significantly different.
   [b] In-house and offshore are significantly different.
   [c] Outsourced and offshore are significantly different.
   [d] Percentage answering 'a lot' or 'a great deal' (4 or 5 on a 5-point scale).
   [e] Percentage with weekly to daily performance monitoring
   [f] Gross annual earnings

We tested the significance of mean differences using one-way analysis of variance. In general, there are significant differences in most dimensions of organisational characteristics and work and employment systems across the three types of centres. The patterns are consistent with our expectations, but there are important exceptions and contradictory patterns as well. Overall, in-house centres tend to adopt a more quasi-professional approach to employment than either outsourced or offshore centres. They offer jobs with substantially more opportunities for discretion and problem solving, make significantly less use of electronic monitoring and performance management systems and offer higher pay. Associated with these patterns are significantly higher rates of organisational tenure and lower turnover rates than those found in either outsourced or offshore centres. For example, while 28 per cent of the workforce in US in-house centres has less than one year of tenure, the comparable rate in outsourced centres is 37 per cent and in offshore centres 62 per cent. The annual employee quit rate alone is reported at 16 per cent in in-house centres, 26 per cent in outsourced centres and 25 per cent in offshore sites–that is, it is over 55 per cent higher than in the in-house centres.

The exception to this pattern is that offshore centres rely on workers with somewhat more formal education than those in in-house locations. The typical worker in an Indian centre has 14 years of education (on average two years of college) compared to 13.3 years among US in-house establishments. Yet, these differences are not as great as often portrayed in the media. Close to 40 per cent of managers in both types of centres (38 per cent in-house and 36 per cent offshore) reported that the typical worker in their establishment has a high school education. Similar patterns hold for initial training, with offshore call centres providing 4.7 weeks on average and in-house centres 3.9 weeks. However, given that much of the initial training in Indian centres is focused on accent neutralisation, it appears that Indian centres do not provide more initial training for other aspects of the job.

The comparison between US outsourced and Indian offshore centres yields results that do not fit our expectations. On the one hand, the formal education levels of Indian centres are substantially higher than those found among US subcontractors, where the typical worker has an average education of 12.6 years and almost 70 per cent of managers report that the typical worker has a high school diploma only. Initial training in US outsourced centres is less than half that found in Indian centres. However, the amount of on-the-job training to become qualified and the annual rates of ongoing training are not substantially different.

On the other hand, despite relying on a more educated and full-time workforce, the Indian centres have work systems that are more tightly constrained and standardised than those found among US subcontractors, contrary to our expectations. With the exception of reliance on scripts, which is higher in the US outsourced centres, Indian managers report substantially lower levels of discretion in handling customer requests and use of problem-solving groups. For example, only 3 per cent of offshore call centres report giving employees 'a lot' or 'a great deal' of discretion in handling customer requests, compared to 17 per cent of outsourced centres and 39 percent of in-house centres. While in-house centres have an average of 36 per cent of employees working in teams, 22 per cent of employees in outsourced centres and only 7 per cent of those in offshore centres do so.

Measures of performance monitoring illustrate a similar pattern. Most call centres adopt a mix of practices to track employee performance on adherence to talk time, whether they follow the scripts provided and their effectiveness in both providing friendly service and resolving customer requests. In a sales environment, monitoring is also used both to control potential employee fraud and to provide coaching on selling techniques. Both electronic monitoring and supervisor monitoring and feedback are employed for this purpose, and the intensity of these practices varies substantially among the different sites. While about 50 per cent of work time in in-house centres is electronically monitored, this average jumps to 68 per cent in outsourced centres and 92 per cent in offshore centres. Similarly, supervisors provide feedback and coaching on a weekly or daily basis in 94 per cent of the offshore centres, but in only 46 and 55 per cent of the US in-house and outsourced centres.

With respect to compensation, the average median annual pay reported by managers is US$ 27,713 among in-house centres, US$ 23,881 in outsourced centres and US$ 2,635 in offshore centres. Thus in-house centres pay about 14 per cent more than outsourced centres and 90 per cent more than the offshore segment. The use of commission pay is surprisingly low across the in-house and outsourced segments, at 8 and 4 per cent, but significantly higher in offshore centres (19 per cent). This probably reflects the higher percentage of sales-oriented call centres in the offshore sample (29 per cent) than in the in-house (5 per cent) and outsourced (14 per cent) sites.

Finally, we compare turnover and absenteeism, both important organisational outcomes. High investments in training at many workplaces mean that turnover is costly and the often tight scheduling practices based on predicted fluctuations in call volume mean that excessive absenteeism has an immediate negative effect on customer satisfaction and sales. As noted earlier, quit rates as well as total turnover are the lowest among in-house centres and higher in outsourced and offshore centres. Absenteeism, by contrast, is highest in the US outsourced segment (9 per cent) and lower in both in-house and offshore centres

(6 per cent and 5 per cent respectively). These measures capture the motivation of the workforce to show up and meet performance expectations, and are largely in line with our other results that indicate outsourced centres tend to adopt a low-commitment employment system that combines low pay with intensive monitoring and low discretion.

Owing to variation in the industries represented in each sample, we checked to see whether these patterns held when the sample was further broken down. For example, we compared centres serving high-end customers as well as those in telecommunications and financial services and found similar patterns. That is, no particular sectors accounted for the variation found across in-house, outsourced and offshore sites.

Multivariate Analyses

Table 9.2 provides the means, standard deviations and pair-wise correlations of the variables included in the final model. For our analyses of turnover, we estimate left-censored Tobit models because the dependent variable is truncated at zero (Maddala 1992).

Predictors of Turnover

Table 9.3 reports estimates of models for quit rates at the establishments. The first equation, model 1, includes the market segment and organisational characteristics. The second equation adds controls for employee human capital, while the third and fourth add measures of work organisation and compensation practices.

In the first model, after controlling for market segment, outsourced and offshore centres have significantly higher quit rates (compared to the omitted variable, in-house centres), while unionised centres are associated with significantly lower quit rates.

In Model 2, both the length of initial training investment and years of education are significantly associated with lower quit

Table 9.2: Means, Standard Deviations and Pair-wise Correlations[a]

Variable	Mean	SD	1	2	3	4	5	6	7	8	9	10	11	12	13	14	15
1 Square root of annual quit rate	3.23	2.22															
2 Large business segment	0.34	0.47	-0.16														
3 Multiple market segments	0.19	0.40	0.02	-0.35													
4 Mass-market segment	0.47	0.50	0.13	-0.67	-0.46												
5 Union presence	0.08	0.27	-0.22	0.00	-0.05	0.04											
6 US in-house	0.76	0.42	-0.27	-0.04	-0.04	0.06	0.13										
7 US outsourced	0.14	0.34	0.13	0.12	-0.12	-0.01	-0.08	-0.71									
8 Indian offshore	0.10	0.30	0.24	-0.08	0.19	-0.08	-0.10	-0.60	-0.13								
9 Per cent female	0.64	0.25	0.08	-0.25	-0.04	0.27	0.24	0.11	0.12	-0.30							
10 Years education	13.53	1.64	-0.19	0.21	0.01	-0.21	-0.06	0.07	-0.19	0.12	-0.46						
11 Initial training investment	19.01	17.73	-0.23	0.06	0.00	-0.05	0.22	0.17	-0.15	-0.07	-0.04	0.06					
12 Script use	2.19	1.20	0.27	-0.03	0.03	0.01	-0.01	-0.43	0.26	0.31	0.07	-0.18	-0.17				
13 Work discretion index	2.60	0.92	-0.37	0.15	0.07	-0.19	-0.01	0.23	-0.09	-0.22	-0.16	0.24	0.04	-0.29			
14 Per cent in offline teams	0.36	0.38	-0.36	0.17	-0.05	-0.12	-0.01	0.27	-0.12	-0.25	-0.18	0.19	0.15	-0.16	0.25		
15 Pay ratio	1.19	0.60	-0.31	0.44	-0.11	-0.33	0.09	0.17	-0.16	-0.05	-0.46	0.50	0.30	-0.20	0.33	0.26	
16 Per cent of pay based on commission	0.11	0.20	0.04	0.11	-0.02	-0.09	-0.13	-0.05	-0.05	0.13	-0.29	0.08	0.08	-0.05	0.14	-0.04	0.39

Notes: [a] For all correlations greater than .11, $p < 0.05$.
SD: standard deviation.

Table 9.3: Tobit Estimates for Quit Rates[a]

Variable	Model 1 Coefficient	Model 1 Standard error	Model 2 Coefficient	Model 2 Standard error	Model 3 Coefficient	Model 3 Standard error	Model 4 Coefficient	Model 4 Standard error
Organisational and market characteristics								
Large business segments	-1.02^c	0.31	-0.61^b	0.32	-0.32	0.30	-0.17	0.31
Multiple market segments	-0.62^b	0.38	-0.50	0.37	-0.21	0.35	-0.20	0.34
Union presence	-1.99^c	0.54	-2.02^c	0.55	-2.15^c	0.51	-1.91^c	0.52
Outsourced	1.22^c	0.41	0.78^b	0.41	0.19	0.39	0.15	0.39
Offshore	2.03^c	0.47	2.30^c	0.48	0.57	0.50	0.40	0.50
Human capital								
Workforce: per cent female			1.10^b	0.68	0.22	0.64	0.19	0.67
Years of education			-0.20^c	0.09	-0.06	0.09	0.01	0.09
Initial training investment			-0.02^c	0.01	-0.01^b	0.01	-0.01^b	0.01
Work design								
Script use					0.22^b	0.12	0.23^c	0.12
Work discretion index					-0.73^c	0.15	-0.73^c	0.15
Per cent in offline teams					-1.84^c	0.37	-1.74^c	0.37

Compensation strategy

				Coef.	
Pay ratio				-0.52^b	0.32
Per cent of pay based on commission				1.47^c	0.71
Constant	2.27	5.47	6.28	5.70	
Sample size	310	310	310	310	
Chi square likelihood ratio	50.02	67.73	124.89	130.05	
Probability > Chi square	0.00	0.00	0.00	0.00	
Pseudo R^2	0.04	0.05	0.09	0.10	

Notes: [a]Unstandardised Tobit estimates are reported

[b]$p < 0.10$
[c]$p < 0.05$
[d]$p < 0.01$
[e]$p < 0.001$

rates. The percentage of the workforce that is female is positively associated with higher quit rates, but this relationship becomes insignificant in the full model. Offshore ownership status continues to be positive and significant at the $p < 0.001$ level, while the significance of outsourced status decreases but is still marginally significant. With the introduction of work design variables in Model 3, neither outsourced nor offshore status remains significant and human capital variables decline in significance. Work discretion and the use of problem-solving groups are significantly negatively associated with quit rates ($p < 0.001$), while script use is positively associated ($p < 0.10$). In the full model (Model 4), union presence, training investments, work discretion, use of problem-solving groups and the pay ratio are all significantly associated with lower quit rates, while script use and per cent commission pay are associated with higher quit rates.

We estimated the effect sizes of the Tobit coefficients by decomposing them into estimates of changes in outcomes above the left censored limit and changes in the probability of observing an outcome above the left limit (McDonald and Moffitt 1980). This provides an interpretation equivalent to ordinary least squares (OLS) regression estimates.[3] The Tobit coefficients in the model are 0.62 of the OLS coefficients. Thus when the work discretion index changes by one standard deviation, the effect on quit rates decreases by 0.5 percentage points (0.62 x –0.73); a one-standard-deviation increase in the percentage of employees who participate in offline teams decreases the effect on quits by 1.1 percentage points ($p < 0.001$).

DISCUSSION, LIMITATIONS AND POLICY IMPLICATIONS

In this study we examined the extent of variation in service management and employment strategies among in-house, outsourced and Indian offshore call centres that provide similar services to US customers. We found significant differences in the patterns of employment practices and related outcomes across these three settings, but not in ways that were entirely anticipated. In this sample of establishments, in-house centres tended to adopt a more coherent quasi-professional approach to service interactions than outsourced and offshore sites, with in-house jobs characterised by relatively higher levels of initial investments in training and pay, discretion and problem-solving opportunities. Offshore centres, by contrast, had somewhat higher levels of formal education and initial training than in-house centres, but significantly lower levels of employee discretion and problem solving opportunities and higher levels of electronic monitoring and performance management. From a managerial perspective, US outsourced centres seem to present the worst of both worlds: a workforce with lower levels of formal education and training than in-house or offshore centres, low levels of discretion and problem-solving opportunities that closely resemble those of offshore centres and levels of pay much closer to those found among in-house operations than among Indian centres.

In further multivariate analyses, we found that outsourced and offshore centres had significantly higher quit rates after controlling for the market segment served, union presence and measures of employee human capital. Systematic differences in work design explained most of the variation in quit rates, so the significance of ownership status disappeared when these practices were included in our equations. That is, ownership status is an important driver in the choice of management and employment practices, with outsourced and offshore centres more constrained to use standardised operating procedures and performance monitoring. It is these practices, in turn, that explain the higher quit rates in these centres.

There are several limitations to this study. One concerns the representativeness of our samples, which we discussed earlier. Because larger organisations are over-represented, if anything the study overstates the level of workforce education, pay and levels of employee participation in call centres. We have no reason to believe that the bias is greater in one sample or the other, but there is really no way to test this deficiency in the data. A second limitation is that these large-scale surveys provide only single-sourced data and external labour market data from India are not available to compare the relative value of call centre pay in that country with pay levels in the US.

A third limitation is that we cannot determine whether differences in management and employment systems are due to differences in the complexity of work functions or differences in business strategies based on quality and cost. Complexity and quality service strategies are highly correlated, such that companies tend to adopt quality strategies for higher-value-added functions, which typically are more complex in nature. In our analysis of average differences across ownership types, we used various methods to compare centres by industry and customer segment as well as work function. In each of these analyses, we found systematic differences based on ownership type. However, sample size restrictions prevent us from determining whether these differences are due to business strategies or service complexity, or some combination of both.

In addition, the outcome measured in this study is limited. On the one hand, turnover is a useful metric to analyse because the industry has unusually high levels of workforce churn, which is widely recognised to be problematic and costly. There is also considerable empirical evidence to show that turnover is associated with lower service quality and productivity. On the other hand, future research needs to examine a much wider array of performance measures that directly capture operational quality and productivity if we are to understand the relative costs and benefits of alternative service management strategies.

Despite these limitations, the findings are consistent with other research on subcontracting relations. For example, subcontractors are more likely to have standardised processes and to use more performance monitoring and metrics, a pattern that supports Aron and Liu's argument (Aron and Liu 2005) that these practices are central to reducing operational risk. Aron and Liu's finding that workforce training does not have a large effect on reducing operational risk is also consistent with our analysis. Despite the fact that offshore centres in India hire college-educated workers and offer considerable initial training, the high levels of process standardisation do not let employees use their human capital in ways that can improve operational performance. This point is reiterated in the work of Agrawal (2005), who demonstrates that the return to investment in technology in Indian call centres is far below that found in the US. He notes that this 'cookbook' approach to management reduces the incentives to innovate and constrains the ability to move up the value chain.

Our findings have several policy implications at the level of managerial strategy and broader public policy. For management, the evidence is clear that the extensive use of routinised work processes in call centres leads to high turnover, which limits options for customisation and is associated with lower service quality and productivity. Moreover, to the extent that call centres hire college-educated workers, the highly constrained and monitored work system creates an inefficient use of human capital: a particularly bad fit between selection and recruitment policies on the one hand, and between selection and work design policies on the other. The under-utilisation of human capital represents a substantial loss for Indian subcontractors, who are paying for skills that they are not using.

Thus, to the extent that companies have complex service offerings or want to compete on the basis of service differentiation, quality, or customer loyalty, they are likely to retain customer contact interactions in-house, consistent with the transaction costs perspective and core competency argument. To date this appears to be what most US corporations are doing: after two decades of rapid growth of US call centres, most industry estimates are consistent with our own survey that less than 15 per cent of US call centres are run by third-party subcontractors, and only a tiny fraction have moved offshore.

However, for those transactions that are simple and codifiable, it is likely that companies will continue expanding their operations offshore. Our data suggest that the strategy of outsourcing operations to US subcontractors is likely to be a transitory one because the modest reductions in labour costs (compared with those of subcontractors offshore) may be offset by the high costs of turnover and low levels of employee skill. According to this scenario, the US subcontracting sector, which grew dramatically in the 1990s, will be the hardest hit by Indian competition. If these findings hold across a larger and more representative sample of establishments, then the shift in customer contact employment from the US to India is likely to be considerable but will remain confined to stand-alone work functions that are relatively simple or transactional. Under this scenario, the problem for both US and Indian subcontractors is that stand-alone call centres appear to be failing (see Dossani 2005).

An alternative scenario is that Indian call centres will gain the ability to compete more fully on the basis of quality and customer service as well as price. In theory, this is possible. With an educated workforce and high relative pay for the Indian labour market, Indian centres could be poised to handle more complex and nuanced customer transactions and provide service that builds customer loyalty. However, the current work systems are not in any way geared toward that alternative, but rather contain fundamental contradictions that are reminiscent of the problems of high turnover among overqualified workers in the monotonous jobs found in US manufacturing industries in the 1960s and 1970s. Current analyses of the potential for high-quality service in offshore centres give too much weight to the level of formal education among workers and too little weight to the organisation of work and technology, which shape the effective use of that human capital (Jaikumar 1986).

However, case study evidence by Dossani (2005) shows that some call centres have been able to move up the value chain and expand their operations to include increasingly complex processes. Whether these examples of best practice can expand to the majority of call centres in India remains to be seen. This question turns on whether the current approach to managing vendor relations–through tight control by client firms–is considered so fundamental to limiting costs and operational risk that it will not be abandoned, or whether it is a temporary phenomenon that will give way over time to closer supplier relations built on trust. In the former case, the Indian call centre sector would continue to handle relatively simple, codifiable, low-value-added transactions. In the latter case, the offshore market could expand to cover a much larger portion of the US customer contact business. Even here, however, companies will need to learn much more about what kinds of tacit knowledge and contextual understandings are needed for which types of customer interactions. In service settings where 'bridging to sales' is a major source of revenues, for example, tacit knowledge of cultural norms may still be an important source of competitive advantage, thereby favouring US in-house or outsourced locations.

A third alternative could involve a combination of organisational forms, with companies using a number of in-house, outsourced and offshore venues to manage similar types of customer interactions. In our field research, we found several instances of this emerging strategy, and Aron and Liu (2005) demonstrate that this 'extended' model of organisation may hold the most promise for quality and productivity in the long run. This approach allows companies to create competition for cost and quality innovations among their own subsidiaries and vendors. It also allows for organisational flexibility, so that client firms can adjust volumes and vendor contracts to seasonal demand. Similarly, some US multinational subcontractors are offering a variety of venues to client firms, including a combination of onshore and offshore call centres, with volumes able to fluctuate according to seasonal demand. These strategies may help US subcontractors survive as client firms exert ongoing pressure to reduce costs.

These scenarios also depend on the role that public policy plays in human resource development. In India there is evidence that demand is outstripping the supply of skilled labour, at least in the short run, in call centres in cities such as Bangalore and Chennai. Thus, there is a need for the Indian government to invest in the skills and human resource infrastructure required to respond to external demand.

In the US the question is whether subcontractors will be able to improve the skill base of the workforce. They may be able to do so in locations where they have access to certification programmes and community college programmes in customer service management. Because centres are often co-located in 'call centre cities'–such as Jacksonville, Tucson, San Antonio, Omaha, or Phoenix–there may be opportunities to build a skilled labour pool with access to ongoing education and opportunities for multi-employer job ladders that help stabilise employment. Our survey results suggest that public support for the industry is available, with 49 per cent of outsourced call centres reporting that they use public training resources and programmes. Nearly all of the managers we interviewed in the outsourced industry relied heavily on local universities, community colleges and partnerships with welfare-to-work and public sector organisations to recruit employees. These resources offer the potential to improve the quality of the workforce. However, we found that they are often used to substitute for internal investments in employee skills and discretion rather than to support a more professional or high-commitment strategy. Thus while these types of innovations could allow US subcontractors to improve the quality of their workforce and employment practices, the limited evidence in our study suggests that public sector resources are being used to supplant, rather than complement, private investment in human resource systems. If this represents the future among US subcontractors, then they are unlikely to remain competitive with their Indian counterparts.

APPENDIX

Estimates of US Call Centre Workforce, 2004

To estimate the number of call centre jobs in the US, we used the May 2004 Occupational Employment and Wage Survey of the Bureau of Labor Statistics (BLS). We chose 'office and administrative support occupations' (NAICS 43-0000). Within that category, we chose the sub-occupations that were most likely to be located in call centres, based on the BLS description of work tasks and our own knowledge of call centre operations. We also included telemarketers from sales occupations. Table 9A.1 details the employment numbers, per cent of sample and mean wages for those sub-occupations. By this methodology, there were an estimated 3.97 million call centre workers in the US in 2004, representing 2.85 per cent of the working population. This estimate, however, undercounts some workers while overcounting others. Overcounting may occur because some of the workers in the categories provide face-to-face service. Undercounting occurs because this tabulation

Table 9A.1: Employment and Compensation in Typical Call Center Occupations, US

Call Centre Work Tasks	Number Employed	US Workforce (Per cent)	Mean Hourly Wage (Dollars)	Mean Annual Wage (Dollars)
Switchboard, answering services	206,370	0.15	10.81	22,490
Telephone operators	38,500	0.03	14.53	30,220
Bill and account collectors	445,180	0.32	13.95	29,010
Credit authorisers and checkers	66,010	0.05	15.15	31,520
New accounts clerks	96,560	0.07	13.55	28,180
Order clerks	289,830	0.21	12.85	26,730
Reservation agents, travel clerks (excludes travel agents, hotel clerks)	159,910	0.11	14.48	30,120
Insurance claims and policy processing clerks	239,250	0.17	14.70	30,580
Customer service representatives	2,021,350	1.45	14.01	29,130
Telemarketers	410,360	0.29	11.29	23,490
Total call centre workers	3,973,320	2.85	13.53[a]	28,147[a]

Source: Bureau of Labor Statistics, Occupational Employment Statistics, May 2004 (www.bls.gov/oes).

Note: [a] Weighted average, weighted by number employed by occupational group.

does not include other sales agents besides telemarketers, and many call centres define their work as primarily sales. If one sub-group of sales agents is also included ('sales representatives, services, other' [NAICS 41-3099]), then the estimated number of call centre workers rises to 4.33 million, or 3.11 per cent of the workforce. By these calculations, a reasonable estimate of the US call centre workforce in 2004 is between 2.5 and 3 per cent of the US workforce. This estimate is considerably higher than that found in reports by industry consultants. It may overstate the current numbers of jobs in call centres, but it includes jobs that, if not now organised into call centres, are prime targets for call centres in the future.

ACKNOWLEDGEMENTS

We thank the Alfred P. Sloan Foundation, the Russell Sage Foundation and the Cornell University Centre for Advanced Human Resource Studies for generous funding that made this study possible. Thanks also to the Survey Research Institute, ILR School, Cornell University, for administration of the US survey and to Priti and Mudit Nopany for conducting the Indian survey. This research is part of a broader international survey of call centre establishments in 20 countries in North America, Europe, and industrialising economies, coordinated by Rosemary Batt, David Holman and Ursula Holtgrewe.

This chapter is a reprint of R. Batt, V. Doellgast and H. Kwo. 2006. 'Service Management and Employment Systems in US and Indian Call Centres', in S. Collins and L. Brainard (eds), *Brookings Trade Forum 2005: Offshoring White-Collar Work—The Issues and Implications.* Washington DC: The Brookings Institution.

NOTES

1. Data on numbers of call centres and employment come largely from interested parties, such as India's National Association of Software and Service Companies (NASSCOM) and industry consultants such as Datamonitor in the US. NASSCOM put the number of call centre positions in India at

158,000 in 2004. For the US in 2001, Datamonitor estimated a total call centre workforce of 2.5 million, with 88.7 per cent located in in-house centres and 11.3 per cent in outsourced centres. It projected that by 2005, call centre employment would grow by 14 per cent, reaching a total of 2.86 million, with 13.4 per cent located in outsourced centres (Datamonitor 2001). That estimate is close to the 14.6 per cent of US centres outsourced that we found in our 2004 national survey.

Datamonitor bases its estimates on market research and the sale of call centre work stations and other technology. The numbers of work stations may underestimate employment because they may be used for two or three shifts of workers. More recently, Datamonitor (2004) estimated that the US call centre employment would fall to 2.7 million positions in 47,500 call centres by 2008. Our calculations, based on Bureau of Labor Statistics data, suggest a US call centre workforce in 2004 of 3.97 million, or an upper limit of 3 per cent of the workforce. These calculations are limited by the available data. See appendix for a technical note on these calculations.

2. On those issues, see, respectively, Loveman (1998); Batt (1999); Batt (2002); and Batt and Moynihan (2006).

3. The adjustment based on the second term in the McDonald and Moffit (1980) decomposition is calculated by multiplying the Tobit coefficients by $[1-z^*f(z)/F(z)-f(z)2/F(z)2]$, where $F(z)$ is the cumulative normal distribution function associated with the probability of cases being above the left limit, $f(z)$, the first derivative of $F(z)$, is the unit normal density associated with this probability and z is the corresponding z score for this probability. See Roncek (1992).

REFERENCES

Abraham, Katherine. 1990. 'Restructuring the Employment Relationship: The Growth of Market-Mediated Work Arrangements', in Katherine Abraham and Robert McKersie (eds), *New Developments in the Labor Market*, pp. 85–118. Cambridge, MA: MIT Press.

Appelbaum, Eileen, Thomas Bailey, Peter Berg, and Arne L. Kalleberg. 2000. *Manufacturing Advantage: Why High-Performance Work Systems Pay Off.* Ithaca, NY: Cornell University Press.

Agrawal, Vivek. 2005. 'Comment on Batt, Doellgast and Kwon, "Service Management and Employment Systems in U.S. and Indian Call Centers"', in S. Collins and L. Brainard (eds), *Brookings Trade Forum 2005: Offshoring White-collar Work–The Issues and Implications*, pp. 361–66. Washington, DC: The Brookings Institution.

Aron, Ravi and Ying Liu. 2005. 'Determinants of Operational Risk in Global Sourcing of Financial Services: Evidence from Field Research', in S. Collins and L. Brainard (eds), *Brookings Trade Forum 2005: Offshoring White-collar Work–The Issues and Implications*, pp. 373–98. Washington, DC: The Brookings Institution.

Arthur, Jeffrey. 1994. 'Effects of Human Resource Systems on Manufacturing Performance and Turnover', *Academy of Management Journal*, 37(3): 670–87.

Barney, Jay B. 1991. 'Firm Resources and Sustained Competitive Advantage', *Journal of Management*, 17(1): 99–120.

Batt, Rosemary. 1999. 'Work Organization, Technology, and Performance in Customer Service and Sales', *Industrial and Labor Relations Review*, 52(4): 539–64.

———. 2000. 'Strategic Segmentation in Front-Line Services: Matching Customers, Employees and Human Resource Systems', *International Journal of Human Resource Management*, 11(3): 540–61.

———. 2002. 'Managing Customer Services: Human Resource Practices, Quit Rates, and Sales Growth', *Academy of Management Journal*, 45(3): 587–97.

Batt, Rosemary and Lisa Moynihan. 2006. 'Human Resource Practices, Service Quality, and Economic Performance in Call Centers'. CAHRS working paper No. 06.01. Available online at: http://www.ilr.cornell.edu/cahrs/research/workingPapers/index.html

Batt, Rosemary, Alex Colvin, and Jeffrey Keefe. 2002. 'Employee Voice, Human Resource Practices, and Quit Rates: Evidence from the Telecommunications Industry', *Industrial and Labor Relations Review*, 55(4): 573–93.

Carayon, Pascale. 1993. 'Effect of Electronic Performance Monitoring on Job Design and Worker Stress–Review of the Literature and Conceptual Model', *Human Factors*, 35(3): 385–95.

Datamonitor. 2001. *U.S. Customer Relationship Outsourcing to 2005*. London: Datamonitor.

———. 2003. *Opportunities in North American Call Center Markets to 2007*. New York: Datamonitor.

———. 2004. *The Vertical Guide to Contact Centers in North America: Tracking Sector Needs in a Mature Market*. New York: Datamonitor.

Davis-Blake, Alison and Brian Uzzi. 1993. 'Determinants of Employment Externalization: A Study of Temporary Workers and Independent Contractors', *Administrative Science Quarterly*, 38(2): 195–223.

Deery, Stephen J., Roderick D. Iverson, and Janet P. Walsh. 2002. 'Work Relationships in Telephone Call Centers: Understanding Emotional Exhaustion and Employee Withdrawal', *Journal of Management Studies*, 39(4): 471–97.

Dossani, Rafiq. 2005. 'Globalization and the Offshoring of Services: The Case of India', in S. Collins and L. Brainard (eds), *Brookings Trade Forum 2005: Offshoring White-collar Work–The Issues and Implications*, pp. 241–78. Washington, DC: The Brookings Institution.

Dossani, Rafiq and Martin Kenney. 2004. 'Went for Cost, Stayed for Quality? Moving the Back Office to India'. Asia-Pacific Research Center, Stanford University.

Erickcek, George A., Susan N. Houseman, and Arne L. Kalleberg. 2003. 'The Effects of Temporary Services and Contracting Out on Low-Skilled Workers: Evidence from Auto Suppliers, Hospitals, and Public Schools', in Eileen Appelbaum, Annette Bernhardt, and Richard J. Murnane (eds), *Low-Wage America: How Employers Are Reshaping Opportunity in the Workplace*, pp. 368–403. New York: Russell Sage Foundation.

Freeman, Richard B. and James L. Medoff. 1984. *What Do Unions Do?* New York: Basic Books.

Frenkel, Steve, May Tam, Marek Korczynski, and Karen Shire. 1998. 'Beyond Bureaucracy? Work Organization in Call Centres', *International Journal of Human Resource Management*, 9(6): 957–79.

Grugulis, Irena, Steven Vincent, and Gail Hebson. 2003. 'The Rise of the Network Organization and the Decline of Discretion', *Human Resource Management Journal*, 13(2): 45–59.

Heskett, James L., Earl W. Sasser, and Leonard A. Schlesinger. 1997. *The Service Profit Chain*. New York: Free Press.

Holman, David. 2004. 'Employee Well-Being in Call Centres', in Stephen Deery and Nick Kinnie (eds), *Call Centres and Human Resource Management*, pp. 223–44. Basingstoke: Palgrave.

Holman, David, Claire Chissick, and Peter Totterdell. 2002. 'The Effects of Performance Monitoring on Emotional Labour and Well-Being in Call Centres', *Motivation and Emotion*, 26(1): 57–81.

Huselid, Mark A. 1995. 'The Impact of Human Resource Management Practices on Turnover, Productivity, and Corporate Financial Performance', *Academy of Management Journal*, 38(3): 635–72.

Jaikumar, Ramchandran. 1986. 'Postindustrial Manufacturing', *Harvard Business Review*, 64(6): 69–77.

Kinnie, Nick and Jon Parsons. 2004. 'Managing Client, Employee and Customer Relations: Constrained Strategic Choice in the Management of Human Resources in a Commercial Call Centre', in Stephen Deery and Nick Kinnie (eds), *Call Centres and Human Resource Management*, pp. 102–26. Basingstoke: Palgrave.

Lepak, David P. and Scott A. Snell. 1999. 'The Human Resource Architecture: Toward a Theory of Human Capital Allocation and Development', *Academy of Management Review*, 24(1): 31–48.

Levy, Frank and Richard J. Murnane. 2004. *The New Division of Labor: How Computers Are Creating the Next Job Market*. Princeton: Princeton University Press.

Loveman, Gary W. 1998. 'Employee Satisfaction, Customer Loyalty, and Financial Performance: An Empirical Examination of the Service Profit Chain in Retail Banking', *Journal of Service Research*, 1(1): 18–31.

Maddala, Kamaswari. 1992. *Introduction to Econometrics,* second edition. New York: Macmillan.

Marsden, David. 1999. *A Theory of Employment Systems: Micro-Foundations of Societal Diversity.* Oxford: Oxford University Press.

McDonald, John F. and Robert Moffitt. 1980. 'The Uses of Tobit Analysis', *Review of Economics and Statistics,* 62(2): 318–21.

Pfeffer, Jeffrey and James Baron. 1988. 'Taking the Workers Back Out: Recent Trends in the Structuring of Employment', *Research in Organizational Behavior,* 10: 257–303.

Pine, B. Joseph. 1993. *Mass Customization: The New Frontier in Business Competition.* Harvard: Harvard Business School Press.

Prahalad, C.K. and Gary Hamel. 1990. 'The Core Competence of the Corporation', *Harvard Business Review,* 68(3): 79–91.

Quinn, James Brian. 1992. *Intelligent Enterprise.* New York: Free Press.

Roncek, Dennis W. 1992. 'Learning More from Tobit Coefficients: Extending a Comparative Analysis of Political Protest', *American Sociological Review,* 57(4): 503–07.

Shaw, Jason D., John E. Delery, G. Douglas Jenkins Jr., and Nina Gupta. 1998. 'An Organization-Level Analysis of Voluntary and Involuntary Turnover', *Academy of Management Journal,* 41(5): 511–25.

Shire, Karen, Ursula Holtgrewe, and Christian Kerst. 2002. 'Re-Organising Customer Service Work: An Introduction', in Ursula Holtgrewe, Christian Kerst, and Karen Shire (eds), *Re-Organising Service Work: Call Centres in Germany and Britain,* , pp. 1–16. Aldershot: Ashgate.

Singh, Jagdip. 2000. 'Performance Productivity and Quality of Frontline Employees in Service Organizations', *Journal of Marketing,* 64(2): 15–34.

Ventoro. 2005. *Offshore 2005 Research: Preliminary Findings and Conclusions.* Hillsboro, Ore.: Ventoro.

Williamson, Oliver E. 1981. 'The Modern Corporation: Origins, Evolution, Attributes', *Journal of Economic Literature,* 19(4): 1537–68.

——. 1985. *The Economic Institutions of Capitalism.* New York: Free Press.

10

Managing Work and Employment in Australian and Indian Call Centres

Bob Russell and Mohan Thite

INTRODUCTION

As various contributions to this collection suggest, there are considerable differences regarding the effects and likely outcomes associated with the practice of business process outsourcing (BPO). From the receiving end of countries such as India, different positions have been mapped out that deal with the nature of the work that is being exported, the likely effects of this employment on the workforces that take it up and on the grander societal effects on host economies. From the employment-exporting zones, debate has flared up as to the costs and benefits of BPO and how they are distributed. Naturally, these are two sides of the one globalisation coin. In this chapter we advance a methodological case for a cross-national comparative treatment of these issues as a way of moving the analysis forward. This entails a comparison of work design and conditions at a number of Australian call centres and Indian BPO providers.

In depicting work design and conditions we deliberately take a broad view. We not only include the ways in which work is structured in specific jobs, but also consider the ways in which workers are socialised to such conditions as well as the implications of this for how they perceive their situations. Under the notion of job design we examine the constitutive elements that enter into the work of Indian and Australian call centre workers, including the skill sets that are associated with it and the manner in which skills are exercised. This covers concerns that normally fall under considerations of the labour process, including the pace and intensity with which work is carried out, the means by which this is determined and expectations around what constitutes reasonable work effort/outlay. Such expectations on the part of employers and workers entail a cultural element that we also consider. Organisations, especially in customer service provision, extend efforts to engage their employees in what it is they are doing. Often considerable endeavours will be made to influence staff subjectivities at work through the projection of a well-defined organisational identity. These both have a bearing upon work expectations and design and in turn reflect the structural elements of the work environment. In other words, our comparative treatment of work is of such a nature as to take into consideration what is normally considered under both labour process and human resource management (HRM) aspects of employment.

In the sections that follow, we take up these components of work dealing with the organisation of workflows, the implications of this for employee skills and work/job skill fit, as well as organisational/ social identities. While the Australian call centres considered here are mostly in-house operations and the Indian call centres/BPO are third-party offshore service providers, we use a common research instrument at both locations to examine the similarities and differences in what is essentially a continuum in a globalised information service environment. We find that comparisons of work intensity/effort, skill sets and employee identities are a good deal more nuanced than simple juxtapositions allow for.

Issues Surrounding BPO

As a first approximation, the existing literature on BPO can be divided between optimistic accounts which emphasise the overall benefits of this new phenomenon and more cautious accounts which are also cognisant of potential dark sides. The former body of work can be further sub-divided between more general journalistic accounts (Das 2002; Friedman 2005; Kamdar 2007; Sheshabalaya 2005) that announce the arrival of India on the global economic stage with titles like *India Unbound, Planet India* and *Rising Elephant* and more academic work that is beginning to appear in scholarly journals (D'Cruz and Noronha 2007; Raman et al. 2007; Shah and Bandi 2003; Srivastava and Theodore 2006). The more general accounts draw our attention to the stellar growth in information technology (IT)/ information technology enabled services (ITeS)/BPO employment, with approximately 700,000 employed in IT proper (2005) and an additional 350,000 in the sector of immediate concern in this chapter, ITeS/BPO (Thite and Russell 2007). Moreover, growth in front and back office ITeS is expected to continue apace and eventually outdistance employment in IT, with recent estimates forecasting a demand for 1.4 million workers as early as 2010 (Bhatnagar 2007; also Government of India 2003: 7; KPMG 2004: 17–18). Although these numbers must be set against a labour force totalling over 400 million (organised + unorganised sectors) (www.censusindia.net) nonetheless it does represent employment generation on a significant scale and especially for the college graduates the industry employs. As a result, IT/ITeS/BPO employment is very much identified with the creation of a new middle class and the prosperity that accompanies it. Symbolising this there is a common mantra that runs along the following lines: 'although we missed out on the first industrial revolution and the benefits that accompanied it, India will not miss out on the gains associated with the current information revolution'.

As for the work itself, some accounts draw attention to the real and further potential for articulation with skilled IT work in general as in the provision of help desk services for overseas clients (Shah and Bandi 2003). The professional ambiance of BPO customer service centres and its effects on employee mentalities have also been discussed in recent research which attempts to distinguish between electronic sweatshop operations and better quality employment (D'Cruz and Noronha 2006, 2007). While such contributions raise interesting points of variation with many Western customer contact centres, it must be kept in mind that they are based on one-off case studies or very small samples drawn from a number of case studies and this limits any generalisations that can be made about the general nature of BPO.

Another track of investigation along this path hypothesises the emergence of a knowledge process outsourcing (KPO) industry as a logical successor to BPO. KPO is taken to include such functions as the provision of legal services (contract drafting, document analysis and research), health and pharmaceutical applications (for example, non-invasive imaging, pre-clinical studies and clinical data management) and corporate investment and equity research (Raman et al. 2007). As overseas companies gain confidence in the capabilities of the Indian workforce, movement up the value-adding chain from BPO to more highly skilled KPO is considered to be a realistic outcome (Srivastava and Theodore 2006).

Offsetting this picture is a quite different one that commences by highlighting the mass production nature of much BPO work. A crude indicator of this is the simple size of Indian ITeS operations, which generally dwarfs most in-house contact centre work in countries such as Australia. With seating capacity for hundreds of workers at any one time and employment at the larger BPOs running into the thousands, it is argued that the industry has been established precisely to process simple, repetitive transactional work. This translates into a 'low value, low skill' model of employment, or what Taylor and Bain (2005) designate as 'an extreme form of the mass production model' (Taylor and Bain 2005: 269; also see Budhwar et al. 2006; Ofreneo et al. 2007). This can be contrasted with alternative work designs that encourage greater skill development and utilisation such as the high performance work systems, professional service delivery and mass customisation paradigms that have been identified in a host of other publications (Batt 1999, 2000, 2002; Batt and Moynihan 2002; Frenkel et al. 1999; Korczynski 2001; Korczynski et al. 2000).

To this picture of large customer and data-processing plants, BPO introduces other elements that distinguish it further from work in Western information processing organisations. BPO workers are often required to be people that they are not, that is, to adopt fictional identities including names, locations, cultures and forms of speech/accents that are not their own. Such processes of 'masking' have been pointedly referred to as a form of 'globalisation from above' (Mirchandani, this volume, and Chapter 5, this volume). Minimally such requirements could be hypoth-esised as enhancing the levels of emotional labour (Hockschild 1983) that are expected in this type of interactive service work while others have raised the possibility of more serious forms of psychological damage occurring as a result of such practices (Budhwar et al., Chapter 4, this volume).

An expanded theoretical rationale has also been advanced in support of arguments that BPO work entails higher levels of supervision and specification and that this is best accomplished through a Tayloristic mass production managerial paradigm. Invoking tenets of principal/agency theory (Eisenhardt 1989), Batt, Doellgast and Kwon (Chapter 9, this volume) maintain that the challenge of management control is substantially altered in outsourcing scenarios. Under such conditions, the principal is unable to directly monitor and control the work that is being conducted on its behalf. It is precisely this managerial labour that is being outsourced. Owing to this, the principal will make every effort to render what is being done as transparent as possible. This results in work being kept as simple (deskilled) as possible, with high levels of supervision, documentation and precise service level agreements specifying expectations and measuring compliance with them. Empirical results based upon large numbers of managerial interviews comparing workflows in American in-house and national outsourcing operations against Indian BPO operations lend support to these hypotheses (Batt et al., Chapter 9, this volume). Outsourcing and BPO in particular is associated with a cost-driven, work intensive, low skill approach.

The remainder of this chapter explores these themes in greater detail and from a different methodological angle which is explained in the next section.

THE CALL CENTRE/BPO STUDY

The results that are reported upon in this chapter are based upon employee surveys that were conducted at Australian case study call centres and case study BPO operations in India. Supplementing the surveys are managerial interviews that were conducted at the participating organisations and in the Australian context, additional field observations taken at the point of production. In this chapter it is mainly survey results that are reported, although qualitative evidence is introduced when it can usefully be employed in the interpretation of the quantitative results.

Customer service representatives at 20 Australian contact centres completed self-administered surveys as part of the study over the course of 2004–2005. The case study organisations were divided up between different industry sectors as follows: four in financial services (banks and/or insurers); two telecommunications companies; two firms in the transportation field; two in health care/health insurance; one online gaming centre (leisure services); and nine in the public/not-for-profit sector, representing various levels of government and state/social functions. All of the centres except for one were in-house, inbound operations, while the one exception provided inbound tendered services for the government. The survey was restricted to non-supervisory call centre agents who had a minimum of three months tenure in their current positions. This sampling frame generated 1,232 useable returns.

In India, permission was received to conduct the same employee survey at four BPO sites. Details of the organisation and employee profile of the Indian study are provided in our chapter in this volume on HRM in Indian call centres. These venues represented four large Indian companies that specialised in providing ITeS to overseas customers. In each case, this included both inbound and outbound work as well as non-voice services such as pay roll and benefit administration for foreign clients. Total employment at these companies ranged from 1,700 workers to over 12,500 workers spread across multiple city sites. For three of the companies, survey administration was conducted at a single work site, while at the fourth, employees from two of the company's operations participated in the study. As already indicated, employment totals include both customer service representative (CSRs) and non-voice active services. Thus, in order to compare like with like, instructions were provided that only telephone-based customer service workers should complete the survey. In total 638 useable returns were garnered from the Indian section of the study.

At all 24 interview sites, the survey was self-administered. Typical of the different workforce demographics that populate info-service work in India and Australia, the Indian sample fell almost completely within the 20–29 year old age bracket (90 per cent), was exclusively tertiary educated with two-thirds possessing an undergraduate degree and a further one-quarter a graduate qualification and was divided on a 60:40 ratio between male and female agents. By comparison, the Australian sample was well represented across the 20–49 age deciles, was fairly evenly divided in terms of educational qualifications, with the largest proportion (21 per cent) having some high school education and was mainly (that is, three-quarters) female. The questionnaire instrument was devised by the authors specifically to explore work experience in info-service, call centre based environments. Nominal, ordinal and interval inquiries of a factual nature as well as five-point Likert scale attitudinal questions were included in a five part structure that surveyed recruitment, selection and labour market factors, workflows and demands, employment relations (HR, organisational cultures, employee involvement), occupational health and safety issues and personal biographical data. In this chapter we are mainly interested in comparing the experience of work along the aforementioned dimensions on a country by country basis. For present purposes, inter-organisational differences are largely ignored, although we have added this dimension to our analysis in other publications (Russell and Thite 2008). We begin our comparison with an examination of the work flows including the effort and skills they embody as reported by our respondents in Australian call centres and Indian BPOs.

WORKFLOWS

In this section we consider the responses of Indian and Australian CSRs to various questions that were posed around how they experience work processes in voice-to-voice informational service work. The questions in Table 10.1 measure two components of work design. The upper portion of the table examines the expectations that are built into the work effort bargain and workers' perceptions regarding the fairness of such requirements, while the lower section of the table reports on the operationalisation of those expectations in the real-time execution of work.[1] With respect to the former, if anything, the Indian sample is more likely to agree with the reasonableness of workload expectations, while expressing confidence in their abilities to meet such demands. For example, a smaller proportion of the Indian sample registers concern about their capacity to meet the key performance indicators (KPIs) they have been set, while a higher proportion assents to the fairness of such targets, although overall the correlations (V) between country and these variables is not strong.

When it comes to examining the ways in which workflows are operationalised, however, different indications begin to emerge. While expressing no greater dissatisfaction with *work expectations,* Indian workers are more likely to acknowledge that their work is more intensive than their Australian counterparts. For example, the Indian cohort is more likely to agree/strongly agree that they are required to work very fast in order to keep up with

Table 10.1: Indian/Australian Responses to Labour Process Questions (%)

Statement	Country	Strongly/ Disagree	Neutral	Strongly/ Agree
Work expectations				
Difficult to consistently	India	51.0	24.6	24.4
meet my KPIs*	Australia	47.7	21.9	30.4
V = 0.063				
Work targets are	India	14.5	14.9	70.5
reasonable***	Australia	22.6	19.7	57.7
V = 0.124				
Management's	India	22.2	26.7	51.1
expectations of work	Australia	26.4	21.5	52.0
loads are reasonable*				
V = 0.063				
Operationalisation of work				
Management is	India	11.8	23.4	64.8
too focused on	Australia	24.1	26.5	49.5
statistics*** V = 0.154				
Work under a great deal	India	36.7	31.1	32.1
of pressure*	Australia	37.0	25.3	37.7
V=0.066				
Pace of work adequate	India	16.8	18.0	65.2
to meet expectations	Australia	13.3	10.7	76.1
of callers***				
V = 0.115				
Can take as much time	India	24.6	22.4	53.0
as required to complete	Australia	14.1	7.6	78.2
a call*** V = 0.257				
Have to work very fast	India	16.3	28.6	55.0
to deal with level of	Australia	32.4	26.4	41.2
call volumes***				
V = 0.163				
Need more employees	India	9.6	30.9	59.5
given levels of call	Australia	23.6	34.5	41.9
demand***				
V = 0.181				

Notes: *p ≤ 0.05
**p ≤ 0.01
***p ≤ 0.001

the volume of calls. Given such demands they are also likely to agree that under-staffing is an issue at their places of work. They also register greater pressure to quickly terminate customer queries so that they can move on to the next call. Such pressure is also reflected in higher levels of agreement that management at the BPO providers is overly focused on quantitative measurements of agent performance. Overall, we can say that while the BPO workers appear largely accepting of the work effort bargain, they also provide indications that it is a more intensive regime than the workflows at the Australian sites. In a comparative sense, this finding lends support to those who have suggested that the BPO model approximates a high intensity, mass production paradigm of informational work.

The other aspect of work effort that is relevant to this analysis involves considering the emotional labour that is required for performing the tasks at hand. Emotional labour has been defined as control of the self in order to induce a desired state of mind in others (Hockschild 1983). This may entail the suppression of one's own emotions in favour of 'feeling rules' which are adopted on behalf of the organisation that supplies employment. Emotional labour is rightly thought to be of particular importance in front-line service work, such as we are analysing here (Korczynski 2002, 2003). For a variety of reasons, the exercise of emotional labour in the BPO/outsourcing situation could be hypothesised as being at least as great if not greater than what is required in domestic info-service work. First of all, workers are struggling to understand, interpret and interact with members of alien cultures. This may place additional burdens on CSRs that no amount of cultural training is likely to overcome. Second, the possibilities for cultural misunderstandings, as well as resort to racist stereotypes, or other forms of abuse on the part of Western customers (see Carroll and Wagar as well as Budhwar et al., in this volume) are more than likely enhanced in such interactions.

Three questions on our survey were designed to canvass these points. Respondents were asked to agree/disagree with the following statements: (a) 'I have to become emotionally detached from callers when I am responding to them'; (*b*) 'I have to mask my true feelings when I am dealing with callers'; and (*c*) 'I can be my true self when I am on the phone with callers'. Unexpectedly, differences between respondents in the two countries are marginal. The Indian sample is only two percentage points more likely to agree with the notion of emotional detachment than the Australian cohort (45 versus 43 per cent). In a stronger version that takes up the question of masking emotions the differences are even more slender with 54 per cent of the BPO workers and 53 per cent of the Australian workers agreeing that this is an element of their work. Finally, Indian respondents are more likely than their Australian counterparts to agree that they can be their true selves in interactions with customers (51 versus 45 per cent).

If nothing else, these results suggest that employees in BPO organisations do not experience their work as any more emotionally taxing than domestic in-house Australian call centre workers. It may be that shorter, more transactionally-based calls lead to less emotional investment in work. Alternatively, the designation of ITeS/BPO as 'professional' work with information may lead to less emotional investment. Obviously, these suggestions require additional rigorous examination.

The other aspect of work design that concerns us in this chapter relates to the comparative skill requirements of BPO work. Recall that it is possible to entertain different positions on the skill aspects of the work, with some suggesting that it can/is morphing into more highly skilled knowledge based work (D'Cruz and Noronha 2007; Raman et al. 2007; Shah and Bandi 2003; Srivastava and Theodore 2006) and others maintaining that BPO is largely representative of a low skill outsourcing road (Batt et al., this volume; Taylor and Bain 2004, 2005, 2006).

Table 10.2 presents questions in the survey that pertained to different aspects of the skill question. Again, there are two dimensions that are taken into account in our approximation of work skill. First, respondents are asked about aspects of their work that are thought to reflect upon its skill demands. These refer to worker's perceptions of the objective features of the work, such

Table 10.2:   Indian/Australian Responses to Work Skill Questions (%)

Statement	Country	Strongly/ Disagree	Neutral	Strongly/ Agree
Work skill				
Have a great deal of	India	6.6	14.5	78.9
responsibility to	Australia	24.3	21.6	54.0
carry*** V = 0.254				
Work has a lot of	India	27.7	23.8	48.5
variety in it*** V =	Australia	55.3	15.3	29.5
0.258				
Opportunities to	India	16.3	21.7	62.0
advance with this	Australia	42.4	17.0	40.6
organisation***				
V = 0.260				
Lots of discretion	India	36.4	35.8	27.8
in responding	Australia	25.0	22.5	52.5
to customer's				
questions***				
V = 0.227				
Need greater	India	14.3	31.3	54.4
flexibility to meet	Australia	33.4	33.8	32.8
expectations of				
callers***				
V = 0.224				
Conversations are too	India	26.2	34.6	39.2
closely scripted***	Australia	44.1	23.5	32.4
V = 0.168				
Job could be designed	India	7.6	27.4	65.0
to be more	Australia	22.7	30.6	46.6
interesting***				
V = 0.206				
Job makes full use of	India	37.7	25.9	36.4
my education and	Australia	54.2	20.7	25.1
experience***				
V = 0.156				
Satisfied with	India	30.3	26.1	43.6
opportunities to use	Australia	39.9	23.1	37.1
skills***				
V = 0.094				

Notes: *p ≤ 0.05
   **p ≤ 0.01
   *** p ≤ 0.001

as the amounts of variety and discretion that is encompassed by the work as well as whether or not it embodies opportunities for further learning and advancement. A second line of questioning examines features of the work as measured against the skills and capacities that workers bring to it. Here the concern lies with the (mis)matching of job holders and the work they perform. Many analysts emphasise the human capital capabilities of the Indian economy such as the number of tertiary educational institutions that exist and the number of graduates pumped out each year (Raman et al. 2007), while others point to the potentials that exist for underemployment, with skilled university graduates performing semi-skilled, clerical tasks (Batt et al., this volume).

First we will consider how employees view their jobs, as reported in the upper section of Table 10.2. Along the first three components of skill, variety, responsibility and opportunity, the workers at the Indian BPOs clearly consider their work to be of a higher order. On responsibility, almost 30 percentage points separates Indian workers who (strongly) agree that their jobs carry heavy responsibilities from the Australian sample. While practically half of the Indian cohort considers their work to offer considerable amounts of variety, less than a third of Australian respondents fall into the same camp. A similar picture emerges with respect to how respondents evaluate opportunities for further learning and advancement with 20 per cent more Indian CSRs likely to *strongly /agree* that such opportunities are present in their current employment situation. All results are statistically significant at the 0.001 level and exhibit moderately strong levels of statistical association.

The direction of responses is similar in regards to the final two questions in Table 10.2, which examine respondent skills vis-à-vis the demands of the work. Once again, Indian BPO workers are more likely to agree that the work makes use of their education and experience (36.4 versus 25.1 per cent) and that the work provides opportunities for individuals to use the skill sets they bring to the job (43.6 per cent of Indian and 37.1 per cent of Australian respondents). Note, however, that the differences on these questions are not as great as on the initial questions that analyse how the work is objectively perceived and that the statistical correlations are considerably more modest. This overview is further complicated by the four middle questions in Table 10.2. Here the pattern moves in exactly the opposite direction, with BPO employees less likely to agree that they have the discretion required to meet the needs of customers and considerably more likely to agree that they require greater flexibility in dealing with the public. The BPO cohort is also more likely to *strongly/agree* that their work is too closely scripted (39 per cent versus 32 per cent) and is considerably more likely to concur with the notion that the work could be redesigned so as to be more interesting (64.9 per cent versus 46.7 per cent). Overall, the results suggest a more nuanced image than a stylisation of BPO work that is simply more skilled or less skilled than informational work in the West. Along certain dimensions of skill, (for example, responsibility, variety and opportunity) the work that the BPO employees carry out in these case study organisations appears to compare favourably with that conducted in Australian call centres, while in other respects (for example, flexibility), previous critical analyses of BPO seem to be upheld. In order to understand these patterns, it is useful to consider in a little more detail how BPO differs as a business model from the intra-organisational provision of information services that is common in economies such as Australia.

In the case study organisations included here, BPO is best represented as a loose amalgamation of a large number of project teams working for different overseas clients. At the time of interviewing, one of the organisations had 20 foreign client firms, 50 per cent of whom were Fortune 500 companies, while another firm operated six vertical organisations within it, covering insurance, health care, banking and capital, communications, business enterprise services and knowledge services (mainly financial research). Each client or process has numerous teams dedicated to it. What we are suggesting is that this business structure may account for the type of responses garnered on some of the questions. For example, the number of different teams/processes as well as the perpetual growth of new clients/service agreements could easily account for perceptions of opportunity and levels of work variety that are greater than within dedicated in-house operations. Agents may move from one process and team to another working on behalf of a different principal. At some organisations, teams are responsible for a host of different client functions and this may also provide variety and opportunity for workers to do different things. Meanwhile, greater levels of responsibility may be associated with the prominence of the financial, banking and insurance sectors in outsourcing and the flows of money associated with such work. Also, the phenomenon of having two bosses–the employer and the client–may lead to a greater sense of responsibility on the part of Indian CSRs, although at this stage of our research such relationships can only be put forward as hypotheses that require further examination.

According to our measures, the Indian respondents do not exhibit higher reported levels of underemployment, in spite of having higher levels of educational attainment than their Australian contemporaries, although here, it needs to be noted that higher proportions of workers in both countries exhibit dissatisfaction rather than satisfaction with the opportunities they are presented with in their work to make use of their education. Thus, while the BPO workers do not necessarily define themselves as underemployed according to the questions they were posed, neither are they complacent in their current positions. Clearly many of our respondents would be willing to assume greater scope in the work they carry out.

Workflows in India register tighter controls (for example, heavier scripting, more frequent monitoring) than is the case in Australia, but at the same time, the work appears to be more broadly based and subject to more frequent change. Thus, instead of more skilled or less skilled than call centre work in Australia, it appears to be a case of skilled in different ways. This follows from the different business structures that have organised call centre labour processes in the two countries. In the next section, we examine whether such differences are also apparent in the organisation/work cultures that are exhibited in the case studies and what this might mean for employee identities.

WORKPLACE IDENTITY AND SOCIALISATION

As other researchers have remarked, call centres not only feature high levels of technological control (Callaghan and Thompson 2001), as witnessed in the plethora of KPIs that individual employees and work teams are held accountable to, as well as in the capacities to covertly monitor both phone calls and computer/web use, but considerable effort also goes into making the workplace a fun and spirited environment in which to operate (Kinnie et al. 2000; Russell 2002). This element is also present in the Indian case studies examined in this chapter, however, as in the West it is still an open question as to *what* workers make of this complex and contradictory amalgam of control strategies and *how* they respond to it.

Responses arrayed in Table 10.3 represent an attempt to respond to these issues, by examining both the 'what' and the 'how' questions that we have posed. The top section of the table leaves little room for ambiguity. Workers in BPO engage to a greater extent with the organisational cultures that are presented to them than their Australian counterparts. This is clear right from the start, where BPO employees indicate a greater likelihood of participating in organisationally-sponsored cultural events and a greater appreciation of such practices. The Indian sample is also more than twice as likely to indicate that such rituals constitute an important aspect of their employment and by a similar margin would like to see more cultural events organised in their workplaces. Differentiation on these questions is stark and the correlations between location of the work and response are quite impressive. While Indian respondents emphasise the importance of social activities in their work, Australian workers attach little significance to such practices, with greater proportions disagreeing rather than agreeing that such activities are an important aspect of their employment or that they would like to see more in the way of cultural initiatives.

Table 10.3: Indian/Australian Responses to Organisational Culture (%)

Statement	Country	Strongly/ Disagree	Neutral	Strongly/ Agree
What workers make of the practice				
Usually participate in organised social activities*** V = 0.184	India	16.5	22.2	60.9
	Australia	34.4	18.0	47.7
Enjoy taking part in organised social activities (e.g., theme days)*** V = 0.148	India	13.3	19.6	67.2
	Australia	26.2	18.1	55.7
The games, social events, etc., are an important aspect of my job*** V = 0.371	India	16.2	25.0	58.8
	Australia	46.4	30.6	22.9
Wish we had more social events*** V = 0.357	India	11.5	22.7	65.8
	Australia	39.4	30.8	29.8
Performance competitions make working here more enjoyable*** V = 0.307	India	12.0	23.5	64.4
	Australia	33.7	32.3	34.1
Wish we had more performance competitions at this call centre*** V = 0.401	India	12.5	30.6	56.9
	Australia	45.1	34.4	20.5
Organisational identity				
Employing organisation recognises and rewards employee loyalty*** V = 0.208	India	21.0	29.2	49.8
	Australia	42.2	22.8	35.0
Employees can trust the organisation to do what is right by them*** V = 0.202	India	17.4	31.9	50.7
	Australia	37.0	27.7	35.2
Tends to be an 'us/them' relationship between employees and management at this organisation*** V = 0.153	India	27.6	35.1	37.3
	Australia	28.1	21.4	50.5

(*Table 10.3 continued*)

(*Table 10.3 continued*)

Statement	Country	Strongly/ Disagree	Neutral	Strongly/ Agree
Strongly identify with the mission and values of the organisation*** V = 0.164	India	5.2	18.6	76.3
	Australia	11.7	28.6	59.7
Working for this organisation provides me with an important sense of who I am*** V = 0.311	India	12.6	22.8	64.6
	Australia	33.8	33.8	32.5
Willing to work extra hours at regular rates of pay to help the organisation*** V = 0.143	India	28.0	21.2	50.8
	Australia	35.9	10.9	53.2
Try not to pick up calls before break and before finishing time*** V = 0.139	India	45.6	24.3	30.2
	Australia	42.0	14.9	43.1
Don't mind staying late after my shift to complete work*** V = 0.136	India	20.5	16.6	62.9
	Australia	34.2	14.7	51.1

Notes: ***p ≤ 0.001

Thus far we have counterpoised the hard edge of info-service work with its insistence upon adherence to quantity and quality benchmarks with the carnival-like atmosphere that is a feature of employment in many call centres. The use of performance competitions brings these two features of organisational life together. Such practices may be low key (for example, recognition of high performers), or they may be very explicit as when personal performance data of both above average and below average results are placed on public display. Also, such competitions may be organised at both individual and team levels. While majorities of both samples identify such practices with motivational campaigns, that is, efforts to obtain greater work effort, responses between workers in the two countries are decidedly different. Australian workers are equally divided on whether such competitions are a source of enjoyment or a source of irritation. Indian CSRs, on the other hand, are much more supportive of such practices, again with almost twice as many supporting such events as in the Australian sample. Meanwhile, a similar margin separates the two cohorts over whether they would be supportive of a greater emphasis on performance competition in the workplace, with over half of the Indian sample favouring such an initiative, but only a fifth of the Australian sample concurring.

Various factors may be hypothesised as being responsible for these observed differences. First of all, there is the diverse labour market demographic that is relevant to info-service employment in India and Australia. In India, BPO is a youthful industry in more ways than one. Not only is it a recent novelty on the Indian scene, but it is also reliant upon a vast mixed gender labour force of young, mainly unmarried, university graduates. It is very rare indeed to encounter non-managerial workers over the age of 30 in the industry. Employment largely takes place during unsociable hours (that is, night shifts) with an average nine hour working night. Adding often considerable commuting times onto this leaves little time for the leisure and social activities that are often associated with a balanced life. Moreover, participation in the BPO economy means acceptance of these conditions. Alternatives, such as in the form of part-time work or work and study options are mainly impractical in the large conurbations where the industry is located, owing to the logistical challenges of transporting employees to their work sites. Given these arrangements it is easy to appreciate that work may assume social and cultural dimensions that are accentuated.

Meanwhile, the individuation of work in the BPO setting helps to explain why workers in the sector look more favourably upon such practices as performance competitions. Variable pay or performance-related remuneration seems to play a larger role in the BPO organisations that we studied than in the Australian case studies. Under such circumstances, it is understandable that workers would be more willing to engage with such incentive schemes if they come to constitute a significant proportion of take-home pay.

Such levels of engagement with organisational socialisation/identity do appear to have an influence on workers' attitudes towards their employment as is illustrated by the responses in the bottom quadrants of Table 10.3. First, there appears to be greater levels of trust on the part of the Indian cohort in the good intentions of their employers' vis-à-vis the workforces. Conversely, BPO workers are less likely to register the existence of adversarial relationships between labour and management in these workplaces. Just over a third of the Indian sample, which is not necessarily an insignificant proportion, would characterise employment relationships at their establishments as adversarial, whereas just over half of the Australian sample is willing to lend this characterisation to their workplace. Organisational identification is strong in both locales, although it appears more robust in the Indian BPOs. Here, just over three-quarters of the sample claims to strongly identify with the mission and goals of the employing organisation, compared to just under 60 per cent of the Australian sample. However, the implications of this are more profound in the Indian case. Here employment provides a key source of identity for a far greater proportion of those sampled than is the case in the Australian case study organisations. While approximately one-third of the Australian sample *strongly/ agreed* that their work constituted an important element of self-definition, just as many *strongly/disagreed* with this statement. Within the BPO organisations almost double the proportion consider their current employment to be a key anchor for self-identity (65 per cent of the sample), while very few are prepared to write their employment off in terms of its meaning for the self.

These findings lend support to those who have drawn our attention to the ethos of professionalism within which ITeS/BPO has wrapped itself (D'Cruz and Noronha 2006, 2007). It is not only that BPOs are strong on culture, arguably so are some of the Australian organisations included in this study. Rather, Indian BPO workers are also quite receptive to the messages which these new transnationals are broadcasting. As we have suggested, this is partly a function of the specific labour force demographic that populates the industry (young, aspirant) and partly a function of the conditions under which it labours (long, unsociable hours). It is also a function of the novelty of BPO and the absence of contending voices/identity anchors such as trade unions. There are now signs that the novelty factor is beginning to wear thin (see Budhwar et al., in this volume) just as there are indications that the unitarism associated with the employment relations of BPO may be on the way to being challenged (see Taylor et al., in this volume). These developments will pose new challenges for HR practices which so far have mainly been preoccupied with recruitment, selection and retention.

Does identification with the employing organisation and the subjectivities that are fostered by it influence work effort? The final three entries in Table 10.3 broach this matter by posing questions pertaining to discretionary effort. First, workers were asked whether they would be willing to help the organisation out by working extra hours *without* receiving overtime or premium rates of pay. Here the results are mixed. A somewhat greater proportion of Australian CSRs indicate they would not be willing to make such a sacrifice *while* a slightly greater proportion of the Australian respondents also indicate that they would. The BPO workers are about twice as likely to be undecided on this question. In response to other questions, workers in BPO are more inclined to agree that they would be willing to stay late to complete work, while indicating that they are less likely to avoid taking on work just before breaks or the end of a shift. Overall, there is some suggestion that discretionary work behaviours are greater in the Indian case, however, this is qualified and the correlations are considerably more modest than is the case with the questions pertaining to organisational identification.

The Indian sample is marginally less likely to agree to working extra hours to help out. In the context of nine hour working days, plus often lengthy commuting times this is understandable. Meanwhile, within existing labour processes, BPO workers are somewhat more likely to concur with discretionary work actions. Staying late after a shift to complete work may not be a large issue for some, who are dependent upon company transportation to return home and the periods of waiting around that is often entailed until such transportation is organised. In other words, tokens of discretionary work effort do not seem to be an issue, however, greater commitments such as working additional hours runs into greater opposition, a sign perhaps that existing arrangements are already fully capitalising on the goodwill of this workforce.

CONCLUSIONS

This chapter has attempted to shine a different light on the phenomenon of BPO by undertaking a comparative analysis in terms of work processes, skill and identity. On the surface, call centres in the West and in India mainly resemble one another with similar, or in some cases identical, socio-technical systems and similar HR practices. What are starkly different are the contexts under which such work is carried out. In countries such as Australia, most call centre work is performed as an internal operation in specific firms and public sector organisations. In these terms, call centres constitute a new labour process for the delivery of informational services to various publics. Outsourcing on a massive scale, such as we encounter in India, represents nothing less than the creation of a new industry that makes use of these labour processes. This forms the link in new transnational business-to-business relationships that provides substance to our notions of globalisation. This shift has implications for work and those who undertake it.

The findings presented in this chapter suggest that info-service labour processes are experienced as more intensive in BPO operations than in the call centres that were studied in Australia. Moreover, while we argue that the work of the BPO 'process executive' is no less skilled than that which is undertaken in a typical Australian call centre, it is skilled in different ways. Work is potentially both broader, with more variety, but at the same time it is more tightly controlled and monitored. When combined with the demographic of the BPO workforce (young and highly educated), this represents a potentially powerful contradiction. Finally, as an industry *sui generis*, BPO providers have had a largely free hand in creating unique corporate cultures that have offered initial attractions and which have been free of contending interpretative frameworks. Once again, this differs from the Western situation where workers may be covered by union organisations that have long histories of representing workers in specific industries and which carry over to new call centre operations.

With high levels of work expectation, control and actual work intensity *burning out* existing workforces and *burning through* potential workforces remains more than a theoretical possibility. Our argument is that the conditions that give rise to this are macro and structural in nature. They are part of the essence of globalisation founded upon new forms of global competition and the insertion of a specific labour market into this juggernaut. From this perspective, the role of HRM in providing industry solutions for BPO may be distinctly limited.

ACKNOWLEDGEMENTS

The authors would like to thank the Service Industry Research Centre, Griffith University, for providing seed funding through which data collection for this research was made possible.

NOTE

1. For readability the original five Likert response categories have been aggregated into three cells, with strongly disagree, disagree responses being combined and strongly agree and agree responses being combined.

REFERENCES

Batt, R. 1999. 'Work Organization, Technology and Performance in Customer Service and Sales', *Industrial and Labor Relations Review*, 52(4): 539–64.

Batt, R. 2000 'Strategic Segmentation in Front-line Services: Matching Customers, Employees and Human Resource Systems', *International Journal of Human Resource Management,* 11(3): 540–61.

———. 2002. 'Managing Customer Services: Human Resource Practices, Quit Rates, and Sales Growth', *Academy of Management Journal,* 45(3): 587–97.

Batt, R. and L. Moynihan. 2002. 'The Viability of Alternative Call Centre Production Models', *Human Resource Management Journal,* 12(4): 14–34.

Batt, R., V. Doellgast, and H. Kwon. 2008. 'Employment Systems in the United States and Indian Call Centre', in M. Thite and B. Russell (eds), *The Next Available Operator: Managing Human Resources in Indian Business Process Outsourcing Industry,* pp. 217–52. New Delhi: Sage.

Bhatnagar, J. 2007. 'Talent Management Strategy of Employee Engagement in Indian ITES Employees: Key to Retention', *Employee Relations,* 29(6):640–63.

Budhwar, P., A. Varma, V. Singh, and R. Dhar. 2006. 'HRM Systems of Indian Call Centres: An Exploratory Study', *International Journal of Human Resource Management,* 17(5): 881–97.

Budhwar, P., N. Malhotra, and V. Singh. 2008. 'Work Processes and Emerging Problems in Indian Call Centres', in M. Thite and B. Russell (eds), *The Next Available Operator: Managing Human Resources in Indian Business Process Outsourcing Industry,* pp. 59–82. New Delhi: Sage.

Callaghan, G. and P. Thompson. 2001. 'Edwards Revisited: Technical Control and Call Centres', *Economic and Industrial Democracy,* 22(1): 13–37.

Carroll, W. and T. Wagar. 2008. 'Strategic Human Resource Management in Outsourced Call Centres in India and Canada', in M. Thite and B. Russell (eds), *The Next Available Operator: Managing Human Resources in Indian Business Process Outsourcing Industry,* pp. 279–310. New Delhi: Sage.

Das, G. 2002. *India Unbound: From Independence to the Global Information Age.* New Delhi: Penguin.

D'Cruz, P. and E. Noronha. 2006. 'Being Professional: Organisational Control in Indian Call Centres', *Social Science Computer Review,* 24(3): 342–61.

———. 2007. 'Technical Call Centres: Beyond "Elec-tronic Sweatshops" and "Assembly Lines in the Head"', *Global Business Review,* 8(1): 53–67.

Eisenhardt, K. 1989. 'Agency Theory: An Assessment and Review', *The Academy of Management Review,* 14(1): 57–74.

Frenkel, S., M. Tam, M. Korczynski, and K. Shire. 1998. 'Beyond Bureaucracy? Work Organization in Call Centres', *The International Journal of Human Resource Management,* 9(6): 957–79.

Frenkel, S., M. Korczynski, K. Shire, and M. Tam. 1999. *On the Front Line.* Ithaca: Cornell University Press.

Friedman, T. 2005. *The World is Flat.* New York: Farrar, Straus and Giroux.

Government of India. 2003. *Task Force on Meeting the Human Resources Challenge for IT and IT enabled Services.* New Delhi: Ministry of Communications and Information Technology, Department of Information Technology.

Government of India. www.*censusindia.net*

Hockschild, A. 1983. *The Managed Heart: Commercialization of Human Feeling*. Berkeley: University of California Press.

Kamdar, M. 2007. *Planet India*. New York: Scribner.

Kinnie, N., S. Hutchinson, and J. Purcell. 2000. '"Fun and Surveillance": The Paradox of High Commitment Management in Call Centres', *International Journal of Human Resource Management*, 11(5): 967–85.

Korczynski, M. 2001. 'The Contradictions of Service Work: The Call Centre as Customer-oriented Bureaucracy', in A. Sturdy, I. Grugulis and H. Willmott (eds), *Customer Service: Empowerment and Entrapment*, pp. 79–101. Houndmills: Palgrave.

———. 2002. *Human Resource Management in Service Work*. Houndmills: Palgrave.

———. 2003. 'Communities of Coping: Collective Emotional Labour in Service Work', *Organization*, 10(1): 55–79.

Korczynski, M., K. Shire, S. Frenkel, and M. Tam. 2000. 'Service Work in Consumer Capitalism: Customers, Control and Contradictions', *Work, Employment and Society*, 14(4): 669–87.

KPMG. 2004. *Strengthening the Human Resource Foundation of the Indian IT Enabled Services/IT Industry*. Mumbai: KPMG.

Mirchandani, K. 2008. 'Transnationalism in Indian Call Centres', in M. Thite and B. Russell (eds), *The Next Available Operator: Managing Human Resources in Indian Business Process Outsourcing Industry*, pp. 83–111. New Delhi: Sage.

Ofreneo, R., C. Ng, and L. Marasigan-Pasumbal. 2007. 'Voice for the Voice Workers: Addressing the IR Concerns in the Call Center/BPO Industry of Asia', *The Indian Journal of Industrial Relations*, 42(4): 534–57.

Raman, S., P. Budhwar, and G. Balasubramanian. 2007. 'People Management Issues in Indian KPOs', *Employee Relations*, 29(6): 696–710.

Russell, B. 2002. 'The Talk Shop and Shop Talk: Employment and Work in a Call Centre', *Journal of Industrial Relations*, 44(4): 467–90.

Russell, B. and Thite, M. 2008. 'The Next Division of Labour: Work Skills in Australian and Indian Call Centres', *Work, Employment and Society*, 22(4): 615–34.

Shah, V. and R. Bandi. 2003. 'Capability Development in Knowledge Intensive IT Enabled Services', *European Journal of Work and Organizational Psychology*, 12(4): 418–27.

Sheshabalaya, A. 2005. *Rising Elephant*. New Delhi: Macmillan.

Srivastava, S. and N. Theodore. 2006. 'Offshoring Call Centres: The View from Wall Street', in J. Burgess, and J. Connell (eds), *Developments in the Call Centre Industry*, pp. 19–35. Abingdon, OX: Routledge.

Taylor, P. and P. Bain. 2004. 'Call Centre Outsourcing to India: The Revenge of History?', *Labour and Industry*, 14(3): 15–38.

Taylor, P. and P. Bain. 2005. '"India Calling to the Far Away Towns": The Call Centre Labour Process and Globalisation', *Work, Employment and Society*, 19(2): 261–82.

———. 2006 'Work Organisation and Employee Relations in Indian Call Centres', in J. Burgess and J. Connell (eds), *Developments in the Call Centre Industry*, pp. 36–57. Abingdon, OX: Routledge.

Taylor, P., P. D'Cruz, E. Noronha, E., and D. Scholarios. 2008. 'Union Formation in the Indian Call Centre/BPO Industry' in M. Thite and B. Russell (eds), *The Next Available Operator: Managing Human Resources in Indian Business Process Outsourcing Industry*, pp. 145–81. New Delhi: Sage.

Thite, M. and B. Russell. 2007 'India and Business Process Outsourcing', in J. Burgess and J. Connell (eds), *Globalisation and Work in Asia*, pp. 67–92. Oxford: Chandos Publishing.

11

Strategic Human Resource Management in Outsourced Call Centres in India and Canada

Wendy Carroll and Terry Wagar

INTRODUCTION

There has been much debate since the 1990s about the impact of outsourced call centre operations on an organisation's performance. Central to this discussion has been the decision to outsource call centre operations to various locations both within and outside of the country in which customers are being served. For example, India and Canada are among some of the top outsourcing destinations for companies in the United States (US) and the United Kingdom (UK), and each of these regions has experienced significant economic growth as a result of this trend. Although much attention has been focused on issues pertaining to the effects of outsourcing, there has been less empirical research to date to examine the phenomenon from a human resources management (HRM) perspective (Batt et al. in this volume).

Research examining differences between in-house and out-sourced employment models has shown evidence that the latter is typified as having lower levels of compensation, benefits and job discretion and higher levels of standard-isation and performance monitoring (ibid.). These controls are evidenced in practices such as scripting, where outsourced call centre operations are often heavily scripted, contributing to a more complicated and intensified employee–customer interaction. For example, both Indian and Canadian employees working in outsourced call centre operations may be scripted to conceal their geographic location and national identity when speaking to customers (Carroll et al. forthcoming; Mirchandani, this volume; Poster 2007). In general, these low-cost systems are reported to have higher levels of employee turnover (Batt and Moynihan 2002) and research attention has increased in this area (Batt 2002; Deery et al. 2002; Holman 2002). In addition, attention by researchers and practitioners on the supervisors role in relation to employee turnover (Wilk and Moynihan 2005) has also triggered an examination of a supervisory skills gap (Agrawal and Thite 2003, 2006). Such research has provided important guidance for future work in this area.

To offer further insight about these issues, this chapter provides empirical evidence from a comparative study of an organisation with outsourced call centre operations in India and Canada. The aim of this study is to provide us with a macro-level understanding of the HRM system. In other words, we will examine the HRM system of practices and the ways in which it is impacted by an organisation's business strategy and culture. The study focuses on managers' perceptions of this alignment given the importance of their role in influencing employee turnover. More specifically, this chapter will focus on two questions. First, what are the similarities and differences in strategic human resource management (SHRM) when we consider one outsourced call centre organisation, operating at two sites? In other words, do differences in macro HR alignment within an organisation's business unit levels affect the implementation and outcomes related to HRM principles and practices? Some preliminary findings from this study indeed reveal an overall difference in macro HR alignment and associated firm performance when examining HRM practices, organisational culture and firm performance. Second, this study explores what factors contribute to retention in each of the call centres. The study shows evidence of similarities and differences in manager perceptions and also provides interesting results relating to their intention to stay with the organisation.

DESTINATIONS OF CHOICE FOR CALL CENTRE OUTSOURCING

Outsourcing call centre operations has become an integral strategy for many organisations focused on reducing costs and improving service response time (Metagroup 2005). Over 50 per cent of the organisations that participate in business process outsourcing (BPO) report reduction of costs as the number one reason for choosing this approach. To date, customer service reflects the largest component of BPO, representing 34 per cent of total BPO (Metagroup 2005). With the rapid advancements in technology since the 1980s, outsourcing has become relatively unlimited by geographic location whilst driven by factors such as labour availability, costs and skills. As a result of this trend, India and Canada are among the top five countries in the world experiencing major growth in BPO of call centre operations (Aberdeen-Group 2003). While Canada is considered a domestic or nearshore solution for North American firms developing outsourcing[1] strategies, India represents an offshore solution.

The demand for outsourcing call centre work is expected to grow with the continued focus of North American operations to become more cost-effective (Herald 2006). As a result, it is anticipated that these organisations will emphasise strategies with thrusts towards optimising self-service channels and increasing outsourcing options. These trends are supported by future projections, which suggest that the US call centre market alone over the next five years will decrease in agent positions and centres due to increased use of customer self-service channels and outsourcing in both near and offshore locations (Datamonitor 2004).

The growth of the call centre service delivery model since the 1990s has resulted in a phenomenal increase in call centre agent employment in numerous locations. Initially this growth was concentrated in the US and UK. However, with the rapid advancements and acceptance of self-serve technologies (Bremner et al. 2005), along with consolidation efforts and outsourcing, this number is expected to decrease within the US leaving India and Canada as two of several countries positioned as recipients of this growth over the next five years (Datamonitor 2004; Herald 2006). For example, Canada is expected to become the recipient of a significant number of the approximate 176,000 call centre agent positions to be created in North America by 2008 (Datamonitor 2004). Similarly, information technology (IT)-BPO positions (which include call centre work) in India are expected to grow to 1.6 million positions by 2010 (NASSCOM 2006, 2007).

Motivation to establish operations in other countries has been driven predominantly by cost but also by reasons such as labour availability, highly educated workforces and highly skilled workers. When considering Canada as an outsourcing partner, reasons such as a highly educated workforce, highly developed infrastructure (including roads and communication), highly stable political environment and highly developed cultural relationships with the US are frequently cited. However, BPO operations in other countries have also grown over the past decade as well. To date, most of the BPO services in countries such as India or China comprise call centre services and account for 65 per cent of offshore BPO, with an additional 15 per cent accounted for in email and chat services and 20 per cent in back-end processing (Karamouzis et al. 2004). Although key issues such as privacy and job exporting to other countries continue to be debated, call centres remain a significant presence in the offshore outsourcing market in India.

As North American companies consider BPO alternatives, Canada will be faced with competitive pressures relating to cost in comparison to offshore providers located in other countries (Bremner et al. 2005). With the increasing value of the Canadian dollar compared to the US dollar, many North American organisations are developing multi-location outsourcing strategies.

In these cases, organisations are selecting outsourcing partners with domestic, nearshore and offshore capacity in order to distribute the work to balance risks, while still achieving cost-effectiveness. Thus, both India and Canada continue to be among the top players for call centre outsourcing strategies.

EFFECTS OF HRM IN OUTSOURCING ENVIRONMENTS

According to the results reported in a study by Data Vantage (Vencat 2006), for every US$ 1 billion of annual revenue a company makes, it may be losing US$ 250 million in potential sales due to call centre interactions. This study suggests that customers who are having or have had a poor experience are negatively impacted in current and future buying decisions. These results are beginning to signal a need for organisations to develop customer experience management strategies to protect eroding revenues. However, central to understanding the employee–customer interaction phenomenon is the call centre business process model with its accompanying HRM practices.

Both in-house and outsourced call centres have the distinct element of intense customer interaction and regimented standard operational practices (Gans et al. 2003). Effects of work organisation and HR practices in both mass and high commitment call centre service models have revealed differences in employee and organisational outcomes (Batt 2002). Specifically, mass model environments that emphasise cost and profit are found to be more closely regulated while interactions with customers are often scripted, with restrictive instructions for conversations with transnational customers for outsourced employees (Mirchandani, in this volume). In addition, within such environments, higher levels of employee turnover and burnout are reported and at times shortages of willing candidates to enter call centre businesses exist (Deery et al. 2002; Mirchandani, in this volume). Yet des-pite these negative impacts on firm performance, the outsourced call centre model continues to develop into a highly routine and repetitive work environment that struggles to attract and retain employees regardless of geography.

EXAMINING STRATEGIC HR ALIGNMENT

Given the focus on outsourced business service models to be cost-effective, our study will take a closer examination of call centres from a SHRM alignment perspective. In the 1980s, management researchers began to shift the focus of research questions from more micro HR questions relating to individual HR practices, to include more macro questions of HR alignment with such areas as business strategy. Business strategy in the SHRM literature predominantly uses as a basis Porter's model (1981), which highlights a business emphasis on either cost or differentiation. A cost strategy is characterised by thrusts such as reducing costs, ensuring low response times and providing lower cost services, whereas a differentiation strategy is focused on quality and innovation that highlights characteristics such as improving the quality of service, customising products, developing new techniques and producing products for highly segmented markets. SHRM researchers generally agree that an organisation's HRM and business strategy alignment has an effect on its performance.

In a 2006 overview of SHRM research, Becker and Huselid (2006) positioned strategy implementation as a major element in the SHRM relationship. Although most researchers accept business strategy as a key relationship, it has also been argued that there are other intermediate relationships that must be considered in the SHRM alignment. For example, Bowen and Ostroff (2004) echoed a call from Ferris et al. (1999) for more research on intermediate linkages to further our understanding of the relationship between HRM and performance. This gap in the literature has been acknowledged by several conceptualisations emphasising the centrality of organisational culture and climate as intermediate linkages (Bowen and Ostroff 2004). Although these works have provided theoretical frameworks to further examine such linkages, less empirical work has been done to test the models.

This comparative study between call centre business units in India and Canada will specifically consider the relationship between the macro HR alignment, including business strategy, culture, HR practices and firm performance. A discussion about organisational culture will follow to provide the background about the ways in which it applies to this study and the approach used to measure it in organisations.

CULTURE AS A LINKAGE

An important consideration about culture emerges from suggestions that it provides the essential framework from which organisational business strategy is operationalised (Barney 1986). This emphasis on culture has been identified as a driver of HRM practices (Dyer and Ericksen 2005) that reinforces cultural norms (Bowen and Ostroff 2004). Recent reviews of culture's relationship to SHRM suggest that it plays a significant role in strategy implementation for sustaining competitive advantage and contributing to firm performance (Dyer and Ericksen 2005; Roberts and Hirsch 2005; Roehling et al. 2005). Thus, an examination of the relationships among business strategy, organisational culture and HRM will provide some valuable insights about the effects on firm performance.

Organisational culture and culture change have received increasing attention since the early 1980s from both quantitative and qualitative researchers. Qualitative researchers argue that quantitative approaches to assessing organisational culture are limited because the methods are unable to reveal the more deeply hidden aspects of culture (Denison 1996). However, other researchers have endorsed quantitative approaches because of the ability to make the field of organisational culture more accessible through the use of survey methods.

To that end, there are three frequently cited and commonly used quantitative methodological approaches to culture in organisational studies which include Hofstede's global dimensions model (1983), Kets de Vrie's five dysfunctional type model (1986) and Cameron and Quinn's competing values framework (2006). For individual studies, the literature to date has predominantly made use of the competing values framework. This framework has been empirically tested and recently further validated (see Cameron and Quinn 2006; Kwan and Walker 2004). The competing values framework will be used to examine the organisational culture within each of the business units in these call centres. However, we think it is important for us to first recognise the differences in cultural values between India and Canada before examining more in-depth the organisational culture of the two work sites in the study. Therefore, we will first explore Hofstede's model to understand the differences between India and Canada before we discuss the competing values framework used in this comparative study.

In the early 1980s, Hofstede (1983) created a model of national cultural dimensions for organisations which was tested across international boundaries. The model examines and empirically tests the differences between cultures in various countries around the world. Although Hofstede's work has been expanded by the GLOBE research project team to nine dimensions, the discussion for the purposes of this study will focus on Hofstede's original dimensions. When comparing India and Canada using this model, we note the two most extreme differences in the dimensions of individualism and power distance when using the online Hofstede cultural assessment tool (ITIM-International 2007). The following offers a brief description of each of these two dimensions as well as some comparative commentary.

Individual/collectivism focuses on the extent to which individuals are encouraged towards groups by both societal and organisational institutions. Countries where these institutions are less orientated towards group integration are considered to be more individualistic, whereas countries where individuals are more orientated towards group integration are considered to be collectivistic. When examining India and Canada we find that Canada is more individualistic and India is more collectivistic.

Power distance examines the differences in the ways that members of a society and organisation perceive the distance of power. Power distance examines the differences in perceptions of individuals in various cultures about the equal distribution of power. When examining India and Canada we note that power distance is higher for India than for Canada. In other words, people in India perceive the distribution of power to be less equal than people in Canada.

Hofstede's model offers us a backdrop to understand some of the underlying differences in organisational cultural orientation. These are important considerations when comparing two organisations from different countries, such as India and Canada, in relation to HR practices.

To provide us with a deeper analysis of the organisational cultures within each of these business units, we employ Cameron and Quinn's (2006) competing values framework. Through the use of the organisational cultural assessment instrument (OCAI), an organisation's overall cultural profile and dominant characteristic traits can be assessed through a self-reported survey method. The model considers two sets of competing values. The first represents the values relating to the degree of control an organisation exercises on the one hand to the degree of flexibility it offers on the other. The second dimension of this model contrasts the degree to which an organisation has an internal versus and external focus. Using these dimensions, the OCAI competing values framework offers a differentiation of organisational cultures on the basis of four culture types, namely, clan, hierarchy, adhocracy and market. These culture types cluster around a set of core values which can be represented by a framework as shown in Figure 11.1.

These four main culture types each have notable characteristics which distinguish one from another. In studies conducted using this approach to measuring organisational culture, it is

Figure 11.1:   The Competing Values Framework

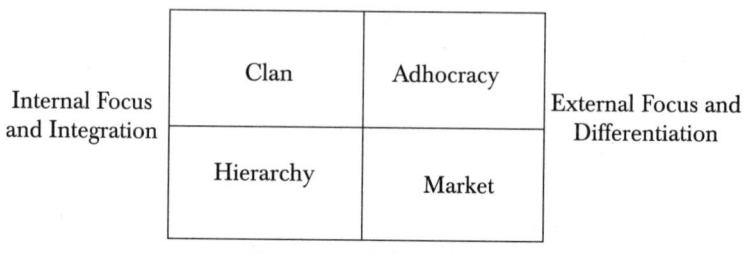

Flexibility and Discretion

	Clan	Adhocracy	
Internal Focus and Integration			External Focus and Differentiation
	Hierarchy	Market	

Stability and Control

Source: Cameron and Quinn (2006).

typical that a company will have one dominant culture type and demonstrate varying degrees of each of the other types. The four culture types are further defined based on six key dimensions which include the dominant characteristics of the culture, the type of organisational leadership, the approach to management of employees, the organisational glue, the strategic emphasis and criteria for success of the organisation. Table 11.1 provides a brief overview of the characteristics for each of the culture types and the six key dimensions.

By using the OCAI we were able to gather information about the managers' perceptions of organisational culture through the use of a quantitative survey. This approach provided us with a basis to explore the organisational culture and HRM.

EXAMINING MANAGER PERCEPTIONS IN CALL CENTRES

In this chapter, we report manager perceptions of HRM, business strategy, organisational culture and firm performance. The managers within the business units included team leaders, operation managers and directors. Examining manager perceptions contribute to our understanding of HRM and the effectiveness of its implementation in two ways. First, there has been much

Table 11.1: Key Dimensions of OCAI

	Clan	Hierarchy	Adhocracy	Market
Brief description	A social environment where employees work well together in teams.	A strong focus on rules, processes and procedures.	An innovative, creative environment which encourages risk-taking.	A results-orientated approach with an emphasis on growing the market.
Dominant characteristic	Internal/flexibility, personal place.	Internal/control, formal rules.	External/flexibility, risk-taking.	External/control, competitive.
Organisational leadership	Leaders focus on mentoring and facilitating.	Leaders are good coordinators and organisers.	Leaders are innovative, risk-takers who are entrepreneurial.	Leaders are results-orientated, competitive and hard driving.
Management of employees	Emphasis on teamwork and participation.	Focused on stability, job security and conformity.	Encourages individual risk-taking and innovation.	High demand for achievement.
Organisational glue	High levels of employee loyalty and mutual trust.	An efficient operation with formal rules and procedures.	Emphasis on developing new and creative ideas.	Goal-orientated, getting the job done.
Strategic emphasis	A trusting environment, highlighted by cooperation and openness.	Emphasis on keeping the operation running efficiently.	Looking for new opportunities and welcoming new challenges.	Gaining new market share and reaching targets.
Criteria for success	Highlights a concern for people and customers.	Emphasis on reliability and dependability.	Success is defined as being first with new ideas, products and services.	Being a market leader.

Source: Cameron and Quinn (2006).

discussion in the SHRM literature about single response bias from studies conducted using a single manager response from each organisation (Datta et al. 2005; Wright et al. 2001). Through a multiple case study of two separate business units as conducted here, we are able to examine multiple manager responses for consistency of responses among managers. Second, it has been argued that managers are central to the effective implementation of HRM practices and employee retention for call centre employees (Fleischer 2007). The skills vacuum for managers in IT-BPO has been noted in India (Agrawal and Thite 2003, 2006) and North America (Levin 2006), which highlights an important focus for firm performance outcomes in these environments. Thus, examining manager perceptions of HRM is helpful to understand their satisfaction as employees and intent to stay with an organisation which, in turn, may affect the retention of call centre agents.

METHODOLOGY

With the rapid development of call centres in both India and Canada, issues relating to HR performance such as turnover, absenteeism and stress have been very important. Our study aims to explore the differences between HR practices in an Indian and a Canadian call centre. Through an examination of organisational culture using Cameron and Quinn's competing values framework, a closer look at the differences between the two environments will be discussed.

The two call centres involved in this study were owned by the same company, which operates outsourced services for clients in North America. This call centre outsourcer provides an array of front and back-end processing relating to customer service, technical support, sales and data input for a wide range of industries. More specifically in this case, the business units within each of the call centre organisations in the case study provided services for a North American client in the telecommunications sector.

In the development of this project, interviews were conducted face to face or via telephone conference calls with managers to arrange for the administration of the study. A survey approach to data collection was used, which included the distribution of an electronic survey to customer service representative (CSR) employees and managers in both call centres. Participation in the survey was voluntary and results were gathered directly by the researchers. Data collection commenced in May 2007 and ended in September 2007.

Sample Characteristics

Although data collected were for both employees and managers at both call centre locations, only the manager responses will be discussed in this chapter. We received useable responses from 28 managers at the India call centre (46 per cent response rate) and 61 managers at the Canadian centre (75 per cent response rate). Managers in both call centres included team leaders, operations managers, support managers and senior managers (director level). With reference to the gender of the managers, 33 per cent of the Canadian sample and 11 per cent of the Indian sample were female. Approximately 28 per cent of the managers from Canada and 79 per cent of the managers from India reported having previous call centre experience.

When considering age, the managers from India were somewhat younger, with 47 per cent indicating that they were 24 years of age or younger (compared with 32 per cent for the Canadian sample). About 26 per cent of the Canadian managers and 11 per cent of the Indian managers responded that they were 30 years of age or older. None of the managers stated that they were at least 50 years of age. In terms of service, 33 per cent of the Canadian managers and 32 per cent of the Indian managers had less than one year of service, while 18 per cent of the Canadian sample and 4 per cent of the Indian sample had more than five years of service.

MEASURES AND PRELIMINARY FINDINGS

Business Strategy

Using scales developed based on Porter's (1981) model, 12 questions were asked of survey participants to assess perceptions of business strategy as cost or differentiation (quality or innovation) focused. For each question, respondents were to indicate the degree of importance to the organisation (1 = not at all important; 5 = very important).

The business strategy results were lower for both cost and differentiation strategies for Canada than for India. Most notably, these results were reflected in the scores for differentiation (see Figure 11.2). The average scores for each of the centres are given in Figure 11.2. As can be noted, the Indian centre's perception of the organisational business strategy as differentiated was rated at an average score of 4.29 whereas the Canadian centre rating for the same was 3.90. The t-test results indicated that the difference between the two means was significant at $p < 0.05$.

Figure 11.2:   Business Strategy

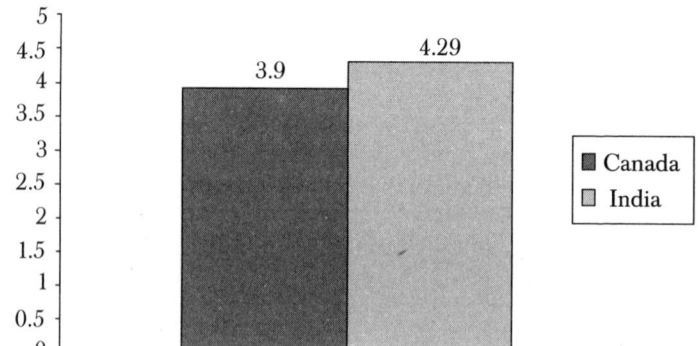

Human Resource Management

In an effort to learn more about HRM issues, we asked a series of questions addressing five HRM functions: (*a*) recruitment and selection; (*b*) training; (*c*) job design; (*d*) employee involvement; and (*e*) compensation. For each question, respondents were to indicate the degree of importance to the organisation (1 = not at all important; 5 = very important). The questions were adapted from a number of previous studies including Bae and Lawler (2000), Michie and Sheehan (2005) and Hoque (1999).

For each of the five HRM functions, we had a minimum of five questions and the Cronbach alphas ranged from 0.81 to 0.95. The measures in this study focused primarily on HRM principles (Colbert 2004) with some emphasis on policy and practices. Sample items are provided in Table 11.2:

Table 11.2: Sample HR Items

HRM Function	*Sample Question*
1. Recruitment and selection	Make a great effort to select the right person.
2. Training	Place a high priority on training.
3. Job design	Have broadly defined jobs requiring a variety of skills.
4. Employee involvement	Encourage employees to make suggestions for improvements within the workplace.
5. Compensation	Closely tie pay to individual and group rewards.

Summary results for the two call centres are provided in Figure 11.3. For all five of the HRM measures, the call centre in India had higher scores. The gap between the scores ranged from a low of 0.38 on the measure of training to a high of 0.63 on the measure associated with job design. For three of the measures (recruitment and selection, job design, and compensation), the t-test results were significant at $p < 0.01$. The employee involvement measure was significant at $p < 0.05$ while the training variable was significant at $p < 0.10$.

Figure 11.3:   Importance of HRM

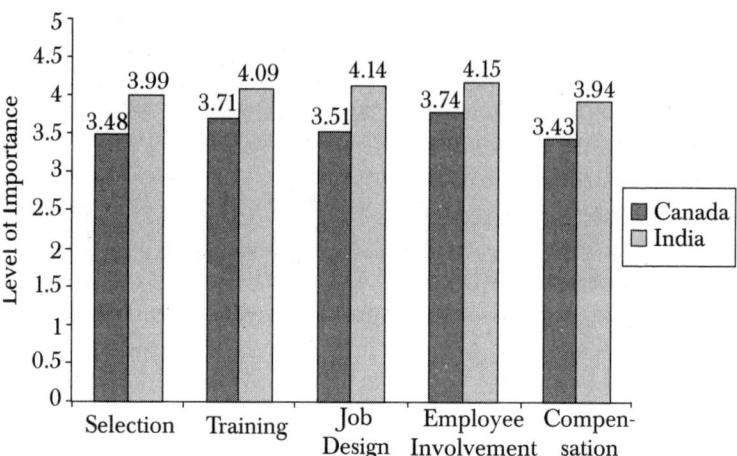

Organisational Culture

As noted previously, we used the OCAI (Cameron and Quinn 2006) to measure organisational culture. Each of the six questions addressed the different dimensions of culture discussed earlier which include dominant characteristics, organisational leadership, management style, organisational glue, strategic emphasis and criteria for success.

For each question, participants were asked to consider four statements (each of which addressed one of the four cultural types–clan, hierarchy, adhocracy and market culture) and distribute a total of 10 points among the four statements. Assigning half points were permitted and we had a built-in calculator to ensure that the total added to 10. For instance, a manager who perceived that the organisation had a strong market culture, a moderate hierarchical culture and weak clan and adhocracy culture might assign 6 points to the market culture statement, 3 points to the hierarchical culture statement, and 0.5 points to each of the clan and adhocracy culture statements.

The average scores for the four culture types are provided in Figure 11. 4. Assuming the four culture types were distributed equally, the average score would be 2.50. Note that the highest

Figure 11.4: Organisational Culture

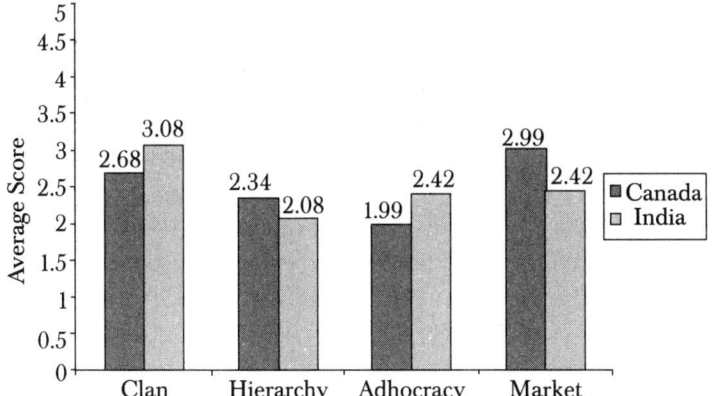

mean score for the call centre in India was for the clan culture measure while in Canada, the highest average score was for a market culture. The Indian centre had a higher score than the Canadian centre when considering the adhocracy culture while the Canadian centre had a higher score on the hierarchy culture measure. The t-test results for the adhocracy and market cultures were significant at $p < 0.01$ while the hierarchy and clan cultures were significant at $p < 0.05$.

Performance Measures

Building on previous work, subjective perceptual measures were adapted from several previous studies (Huselid et al. 1997; Wall et al. 2004). We had managers provide their perceptions concerning various aspects of organisational performance, which included three scales to measure overall employee satisfaction, operational performance and financial performance. Each of the three scales had at least three items and the reliabilities ranged from 0.85 to 0.89. The items making up the scales were measured using a 5-point scale (1 = very low; 5 = very high). While we relied on perceptual measures of performance, there is evidence that perceptual and objective performance measures may be related (Wall et al. 2004).

In addition to the three measures of performance described here, we also asked a number of single-item questions (see Figure 11.5). Again, each of these questions was measured on a 5-point scale with the same anchors (1 = very low; 5 = very high). When we examine the results from Figure 11.5, we observe that employee satisfaction was noticeably lower in the Canadian call centre (a difference of more than 1 full point).

There was virtually no difference between the two centres when considering employee turnover. Both the Canadian and Indian average scores indicated that turnover was fairly high

Figure 11.5: HR Performance

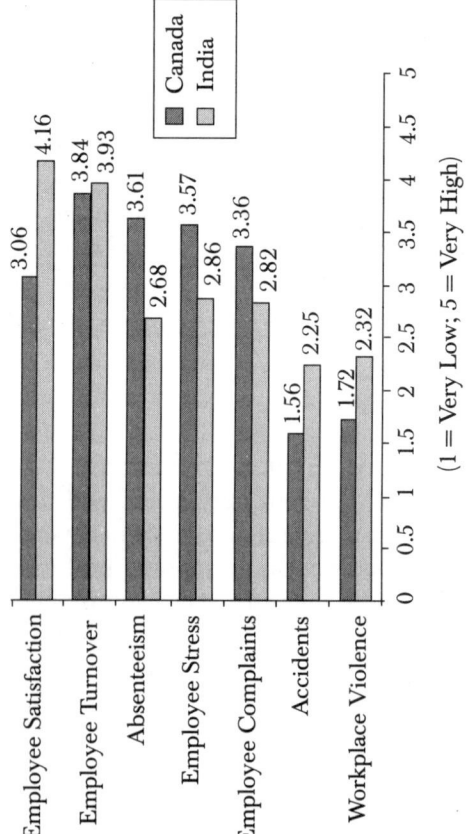

(just below the 4.0 mark on the 5-point scale) which is consistent with objective measures of turnover for both centres. On the one hand, absenteeism was higher at the Canadian centre with scores of higher levels of stress and employee complaints. On the other hand, managers at the call centre in India reported higher incidents of workplace accidents and workplace violence.

Intention to Stay

In light of the importance of retaining valued employees in a call centre environment, we asked respondents to indicate how long they intended to stay with their current employer. While much of the past research has focused on quit behaviour and intention to quit, our question was framed as an intention to stay with the organisation based on discussions with representatives from the centres. In other words, the question asked employees how long they intended to continue to work with the organisation.

As observed in Figure 11.6, approximately 13 per cent of the managers in the Canadian sample and about 7 per cent in the Indian sample responded that they intended to stay with the employer for less than one year. When we consider the 1 to –2 years and 3 to 5 years categories, the results indicate that a greater percentage of managers from the call centre in India intend to stay for 1 to 5 years. However, 54 per cent of Canadian managers (compared with only 32 per cent of managers from India) reported that they intended to stay more than five years with the employer. When comparing Canadian and Indian managers, the Chi square test was only moderately significant ($p < 0.10$).

Initial analyses indicated a positive correlation between both age and length of service and projected stay with the call centre. Also, the level of investment in HRM and a higher score on the employee satisfaction scale were related with intention to stay. However, a perception that the culture was hierarchical was associated with a shorter projected stay.

Figure 11.6: Intention to Stay

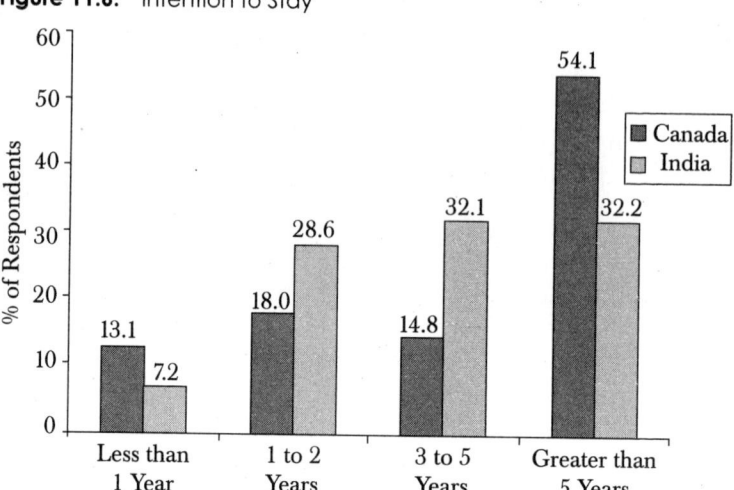

Discussion and Conclusion

Preliminary results from this comparative study reveal some important findings. It is interesting to note the few similarities between the two workplaces versus the differences. Some of the important findings from this study are provided in Table 11.3.

For example, perceptions about operational and financial performance are rated high for both centres, with the Indian centre being slightly higher. In general, managers in the Indian call centre perceived the importance of HRM and HR performance outcomes to be higher relative to their counterparts in the Canadian call centre. Although practices vary to some extent between the two countries (for instance, the wage level, holidays and shifts), the underlying principles of HRM within the organisation are similar. For example, many of the practices relating to training and job design are the same for both centres to ensure that the client service is consistently delivered. However, areas such as selection and compensation differ in both areas. In Canada, the wages associated with call centre work are perceived as low and the employment is considered short term. Conversely, the compensation structure for call centre jobs in India

Table 11.3: Summary of Study Findings

	India	*Canada*
Business strategy–Primary[1]	Differentiation.	Differentiation.
Culture–dominant characteristic	1. Clan. 2. Adhocracy and market. 3. Hierarchy.	1. Market. 2. Clan. 3. Hierarchy. 4. Adhocracy.
HR performance	1. Higher workplace violence. 2. Higher workplace accidents. 3. Higher employee satisfaction.	1. Higher stress. 2. Higher absenteeism. 3. Higher complaints.

Note: [1]For business strategy, primary refers to the higher average mean score between cost and differentiation business strategy types.

is relatively high compared to other available work which may explain some of the perceptual differences in compensation.

Some other differences between HR approaches hinge on practices in place to deal with issues in India relating to areas such as transportation and hours of operation. For example, employees in Indian call centre operations usually work during the night in order to service customers in North America. As a result, many call centre organisations provide employees with transportation to and from work. This practice is, in fact, in place in the centre studied. In a fictional account of call centres in India based on interviews with calling agents, the experience of the commute to and from work in a Toyota Qualis with a group of co-workers seems to be an integral part of the experience (Bhagat 2007). This practice is reinforced in another account by an Indian calling agent who discusses the commuting experience and connections with co-workers created (Yadav 2007). The centre studied in this chapter also has other practices in place to support employees working a fixed night shift. These practices include the provision of meals, break snacks and refreshments. Although the hours of work for the employees are less desirable, the practices supporting the employees, along with a higher wage rate compared to other employment in the area, may contribute to creating an overall perception of higher HRM. However, it should also be noted that although the perceptions of HRM is higher for managers in India, the percentage of managers who intend to stay longer than five years is lower in India (32 per cent) compared to Canada (54 per cent).

Another notable area of difference concerns the perceptions relating to employee HRM outcomes. On the one hand, the Canadian centre tends to be lower in areas of employee satisfaction (morale and quality of work) and higher in areas of employee withdrawal and problems (employee complaints, absenteeism, stress). These findings may be symptomatic of a tighter focus on the management of human capital due to the higher cost of labour and greater client pressures to achieve lower costs. Yet, even with this difference, perceptions of turnover are high for both centres. On the other hand, the perception of incidents of workplace violence and accidents by managers in India is higher. Although both the Canadian and the Indian perceptions of these two items were low, the Indian managers' scores were almost a half point higher than their Canadian counterparts.

The area of workplace violence requires further examination to determine what factors are influencing these perceptions in both Canada and India. For example, perhaps the customer–employee interaction is perceived as more intense or aggressive. In previous work in this area, an examination of Indian call centres suggests different forms of resistance by managers, employees and customers in transnational workforces (Mirchandani, this volume). This research finds an approach of 'bluffing' with customers used by call agents. As described in the study, bluffing is a tactic used by CSRs to achieve their key performance measures by suggesting solutions to customers that do not address the problem but results in a completed call without impacting the agent's quality performance. The use of such a tactic may intensify the customer interactions and potentially escalate, creating a more aggressive interaction. In a study by Poster (2007), extremely aggressive behaviour towards CSRs was noted at least hourly. The issue of workplace violence requires further research to help us better understand the phenomena, especially since we are comparing the same customers interacting with two separate geographic locations about the same services. The final area of note is the difference in dominant culture types between the two centres. While the Canadian centre had a primary focus on a market type culture, which is more results oriented, the most dominant type of culture at the Indian centre was a clan culture, which is more social. The market culture type is consistent with past works that suggest that outsourcers are more focused on cost control (see Batt et al. 2006). Both centres rated the rules and process hierarchy culture type lower than most of the other culture types. However, it should be noted that for Canada the lowest culture type was adhocracy, which is highlighted by innovation and creativity. In both centres, managers who perceived the culture as clan type were more likely to stay longer with the organisation as compared to employees who perceived the culture as being more hierarchical.

In terms of future research, there is a need to examine perceptions of both managers and employees at the establishment level. The Canadian component of our study examined the attitudes of CSRs and the results suggest that manager and employee perceptions differ noticeably. For example, the managers' perceptions of HR performance outcomes were higher in almost every category relating to employee satisfaction compared to employee (CSR or calling agent) ratings of the same. However, the ratings of employee withdrawal behaviours such as turnover, absenteeism and complaints were high for both the managers and employees. Further, manager and employee perceptions of different cultural dimensions, such as management of employees, differed (managers perceived it as a clan type whereas employees saw it as a market type). A smaller sample of employees was surveyed in India and preliminary findings suggest a similar pattern of results. Thus, a more comprehensive study examining the differences between the two countries in terms of the effects of HRM and organisational culture is recommended.

Our study is helpful in revealing the similarities and differences in SHRM alignment of two centres in the same organisation that are operating in different geographic settings. Although the sample size in this study is small, the results assist us in developing a deeper understanding of the application of HRM in different countries. More importantly, the findings highlight the need to examine each of these operations separately to develop a more comprehensive view of SHRM alignment at the establishment level of organisations.

NOTE

1. Definitions for outsourcing: *domestic outsourcing* is when the company and the third-party service provider are located within the same country; *near-shore outsourcing* is when the third-party service provider is in another country yet is deemed to be a commutable distance from the main company it provides services for; *offshore outsourcing* is when there is a large distance geographically between the main company and the third-party service provider; *homeshoring* is a recent trend of relocating call centre work from near or offshore outsourcing arrangements to domestic locations using work-at-home programmes.

REFERENCES

Aberdeen-Group. 2003. *The Outsourced Customer Contact Center: Key Findings in Global Contact Centre Outsourcing Services, 2003–2004.* Boston, Massachusetts: Aberdeen Group.

Agrawal, N.M. and M. Thite. 2003. 'Human Resource Issues, Challenges and Strategies in the Indian Software Industry', *International Journal of Human Resource Development and Management,* 3: 249–64.

———. 2006. 'Nature and Importance of Soft Skills in Software Project Leaders', *Asia Pacific Management Review,* 11: 405–13.

Bae, J. and J.J. Lawler. 2000. 'Organizational and HRM Strategies in Korea: Impact on Firm Performance in an Emerging Economy', *Academy of Management Journal,* 43: 502.

Barney, J.B. 1986. 'Organizational Culture: Can it be a Source of Sustained Competitive Advantage?', *Academy of Management Review,* 11: 656–65.

Batt, R. 2002. 'Managing Customer Services: Human Resource Practices, Quit Rates, and Sales Growth', *Academy of Management Journal*, 45: 587.

Batt, R., V. Doellgast, and Hyunji Kwon. 2008. 'Employment Systems in Call Centers in the United States and India', in Mohan Thite and Bob Russell (eds), *The Next Available Operator: Managing Human Resources in Indian Business Process Outsourcing Industry*, pp. 217–52. New Delhi: Sage.

Batt, R. and L. Moynihan. 2002. 'The Viability of Alternative Call Centre Production Models', *Human Resource Management Journal*, 12: 14.

Becker, B.E. and M.A. Huselid. 2006. 'Strategic Human Resource Management: Where do we go from here?', *Journal of Management*, 32: 898–925.

Bhagat, C. 2007. *One Night at the Call Centre*. Great Britain: Black Swan.

Bowen, D.E. and C. Ostroff. 2004. 'Understanding HRM-Firm Performance Linkages: The Role of the Strength of the HRM System', *Academy of Management Review*, 29: 203–21.

Bremner, J., J. Westcott, and S. Ruest. 2005. *eBusiness Killed the Call Centre Star*. Toronto, Ontario: IDC.

Cameron, K.S. and R.E. Quinn. 2006. *Diagnosing and Changing Organizational Culture*. San Francisco: Jossey-Bass.

Carroll, W, J. Helms-Mills, and A. Mills. Forthcoming. Managing Power and Resistance: Making Critical Sense of Call Centre Management, *Gestion 2000*, special issue.

Colbert, B.A. 2004. 'The Complex Resource-based View: Implications for Theory and Practice in Strategic Human Resource Management', *Academy of Management. The Academy of Management Review*, 29: 341.

Datamonitor. 2004. *The Vertical Guide to Contact Centers in North America*. Datamonitor.

Datta, D.K., J.P. Guthrie, and P.M. Wright. 2005. 'Human Resource Management and Labour Productivity: Does Industry Matter?', *Academy of Management Journal*, 48: 135–45.

Deery, S., R. Iverson, and J. Walsh. 2002. 'Work Relationships in Telephone Call Centres: Understanding Emotional Exhaustion and Employee Withdrawal', *Journal of Management Studies*, 39: 471–96.

Denison, D.R. 1996. 'What is the Difference between Organizational Culture and Organizational Climate? A Native's Point of View on a Decade of Paradigm Wars', *Academy of Management. The Academy of Management Review*, 21: 619.

DeVries, M. F. R. K. and D. Miller. 1986. 'Personality, Culture and Organization', *Academy of Management Review*, 11(2): 266–79.

Dyer, L. and J. Ericksen. 2005. 'In Pursuit of Marketplace Agility: Applying Precepts of Self-organizing Systems to Optimize Human Resource Scalability', *Human Resource Management*, 44: 183.

Ferris, G.R., W.A. Hochwarter, M.R. Buckley, G. Harrell-Cook, and D.D. Frink. 1999. 'Human Resource Management: Some New Directions', *Journal of Management*, 25: 385.

Fleischer, J. 2007. 'Why Mentoring is the Best Defense against Agent Turnover', *Call Centre Magazine* (San Francisco), 20: 56.

Gans, N., G. Koole, and A. Mandelbaum. 2003. 'Telephone Call Centers: Tutorial, Review, and Research Prospects', *Manufacturing and Service Operations Management*, 5: 79.

Herald, D. 2006. 'Relocating the Back Office–Offshoring–The Benefits of Offshoring', NASSCOM. Available online at: http://www.nasscom. in/Nasscom/templates/NormalPage.aspx?id=736 (accessed in February 2008).

Hofstede, G. 1983. 'National Cultures in Four Dimensions: A Research-Based Theory of Cultural Differences among Nations', *International Studies of Management and Organization*, 13: 46.

Holman, D. 2002. 'Employee Wellbeing in Call Centres', *Human Resource Management Journal*, 12: 35.

Hoque, K. 1999. 'Human Resource Management and Performance in the U.K. Hotel Industry', *British Journal of Industrial Relations*, 37: 419–43.

Huselid, M.A., S.E. Jackson, and R.S. Schuler. 1997. 'Technical and Strategic Human Resource Management Effectiveness as Determinants of Firm Performance', *Academy of Management Journal*, 40: 171.

ITIM (Intercultural Management)-International. 2007. 'Hofstede's Cultural Dimensions'.

Karamouzis, F., A. Young, P. Iyengar, R. Terdiman, I. Marriott, and R.H. Brown. 2004. *Gartner's Global Offshore Sourcing Predictions*. Gartner.

Kwan, P. and A. Walker. 2004. 'Validating the Competing Values Model as a Representation of Organizational Culture through Inter-institutional Comparisons', *Organizational Analysis*, 12: 21.

Levin, G. 2006. 'The Often-Ignored Art of Supervisor Selection–With so Much of a Center's Success Hinging on Supervisor Performance, it Makes Sense to Dedicate Time and Effort to their Selection and Mentoring', *Call Center Magazine*, 19: 32.

Metagroup. 2005. *Business Process and Transformational Outsourcing: Current State, Future Directions.* Stamford, Connecticut: Metagroup.

Michie, J., and M. Sheehan. 2005. 'Business Strategy, Human Resources, Labour Flexibility and Competitive Advantage', *Human Resource Management*, 16: 445–64.

Mirchandani, K. 2008. 'Transnationalism in Indian Call Centres', in Mohan Thite and Bob Russell (eds), *The Next Available Operator: Managing Human Resources in Indian Business Process Outsourcing Industry*, pp. 83–111. New Delhi: Sage.

NASSCOM. 2006. *Indian IT–BPO Sector.* New Delhi: NASSCOM.

———. 2007. 'Global Trends that will Drive India's IT-BPO Industry (2007–2010)' Available online at:http://74.125.45.104/custom?q=cache:hiyOms AVsGgJ:www.nasscom.in/upload/51054/Executive%2520Summary. pdf+Global+trends+that+will+drive+Indian+IT-BPO+industry+

2006&hl=en&ct=clnk&cd=1&client=google-coop-np (accessed in February 2008).

Porter, M.E. 1981. 'The Contributions of Industrial Organization to Strategic Management', *Academy of Management. The Academy of Management Review*, 6(4): 609.

Poster, W.R. 2007. 'Who's on the Line? Indian Call Centre Agents Pose as Americans for U.S. Outsourced Firms', *Industrial Relations*, 46: 271–304.

Roberts, R. and P. Hirsch. 2005. 'Evolution and Revolution in the Twenty-first Century: Rules for Organizations and Managing Human Resources', *Human Resource Management*, 44: 171.

Roehling, M.V., W.R. Boswell, P. Caligiuri, D. Feldman, M.E. Graham, J.P. Guthrie, M. Morishima, and J.W. Tansky. 2005. 'The Future of HR Management: Research Needs and Directions', *Human Resource Management*, 44: 207.

Vencat, E.F. 2006. 'Call Centers: A Friendly Touch', *Newsweek*, 16 October 2006, international edition.

Wall, T.D., J. Michie, M. Patterson, S. Wood, M. Sheehan, C.W. Clegg, and M. West. 2004. 'On the Validity of Subjective Measures of Company Performance', *Personnel Psychology*, 57: 95–118.

Wilk, S.L. and L.M. Moynihan. 2005. 'Display Rule "Regulators": The Relationship between Supervisors and Worker Emotional Exhaustion', *Journal of Applied Psychology*, 90: 917.

Wright, P.M., T.M. Gardner, L.M. Moynihan, H.J. Park, B. Gerhart, and J. Delery. 2001. 'Measurement Error in Research on Human Resources and Firm Performance: Additional Data and Suggestions for Future Research', *Personnel Psychology*, 54: 875.

Yadav, M. 2007. *Winning at Call Centre: Confessions of a Calling Agent*. New Delhi: Wisdom Tree.

ABOUT THE EDITORS
AND CONTRIBUTORS

Editors

Mohan Thite is Senior Lecturer at Griffith Business School, Griffith University, Brisbane, Australia. He has over 20 years experience as a human resources professional, both in industry and academia. He is a Fellow of the Australian Human Resource Institute. His research interests include strategic human resource management (HRM) in the knowledge economy, HRM in the Asia-Pacific region, HRM in multinational corporations from emerging economies and HRM in Indian business process outsourcing (BPO). His publications include a book on *Managing People in the New Economy* (Sage), a forthcoming book on Human Resource Information Systems and articles in international journals.

Bob Russell is Associate Professor at Griffith Business School, Griffith University, Brisbane, Australia. He is the author of books on industrial relations in Canada and work transformation in the mining industry. Currently he is conducting research on call centres, information and globalisation. This material has appeared in Australian and international journals including the *Journal of Industrial Relations, Work, Employment and Society* and *New Technology, Work and Employment*. Bob is currently completing another single-authored book on info-service work.

CONTRIBUTORS

John Arnold is Professor of Organisational Behaviour at the Business School, Loughborough University, United Kingdom. His interests span all areas of careers and their management, especially personal development and adjustment, work role identities and transitions, and the impact of career management interventions such as mentoring, development centres and succession planning. He has conducted many research and consultancy projects in these areas and published widely across a range of applied social science journals, such as the *Journal of Vocational Behavior, Human Relations* and *Work, Employment and Society.* John is the editor of the leading European applied psychology journal, the *Journal of Occupational and Organizational Psychology.*

Rosemary Batt is the Alice Cook Professor of Women and Work at the Industrial and Labour Relations (ILR) School, Cornell University. She received her BA from Cornell University and her PhD from the Sloan School of Management, Massachusetts Institute of Technology. She is co-coordinator of the Global Call Center Research Project (www.globalcallcenter.org). Her work has appeared in journals such as the *British Journal of Industrial Relations, Industrial and Labor Relations Review, Industrial Relations, International Journal of Human Resource Management* and *Academy of Management Journal.* She is co-editor of the *Oxford Handbook on Work and Organization* and co-author of *The New American Workplace* (Cornell University Press).

Pawan Budhwar is Professor of International HRM and Head of Work and Organisational Psychology Group at Aston Business School. He is also the Director for the Aston India Foundation for Applied Business Research and Aston Centre for HRs. Pawan has published extensively in the fields of HRM, organisational behaviour and international HRM with specific emphasis on India. His main research interests are in the areas of international HRM, cross-cultural management, management in emerging markets and work processes in Indian call centres. Pawan's work has appeared in journals like *OBHDP, Organization Studies, Journal of Organisational Behaviour, International Journal of Human Resource Management, Human Resource Management Journal, MIR, International Business Review, HRM Review, BJM, IJMRs* and *Thunder Bird International Business Review*. He has also written and co-edited books on HRM in the Asia-Pacific region, HRM in the Middle-East, HRM in developing countries and performance management around the globe. He is the Senior Associate Editor of the *British Journal of Management* and Associate Editor of the *International Journal of Cross Cultural Management*.

Wendy Carroll is Associate Professor of Management at the University of Prince Edward Island. Her research focuses on strategic HRM and the effects of technology in the workplace. Prior to entering academia, Wendy worked in industry in a variety of management and executive roles. Wendy has a specific interest in contact centres in Canada of which she draws on her 20 years of experience in the field. Her research is primarily focused in the areas of the future of work, employee relations and global workforces.

Laurie Cohen is Professor of Organisation Studies at the Business School, Loughborough University, United Kingdom. Her research focuses on professional work and career, with a particular interest in the ways in which individuals account for their career experiences. She has conducted projects in a variety of occupational sectors, including research science, solicitors and architects and, most recently, financial services, where the focus has been on the career perceptions and experiences of customer service workers based in the UK and India. Central to her work is an interest in language and meaning making.

She has published widely in social science journals including *Organization Studies, Organization, Human Relations, Work, Employment and Society* and the *Journal of Vocational Behavior.*

Premilla D'Cruz, PhD, is currently Assistant Professor, Organisational Behaviour, at the Indian Institute of Management, Ahmedabad. Her research interests include emotions in organisations, workplace bullying, self and identity, organisational control, and ICTs and organisations.

Virginia Doellgast is a Lecturer in Comparative Human Resource Management in the Department of Management, King's College London. Her research focuses on the effects of contemporary changes in national industrial relations on job quality in more poorly regulated industry sectors. Recent projects include a comparison of organisational and work restructuring in the United States and German telecommunications industries and a comparative study of HRM and employment relations in the global call centre industry. Virginia's work has been published in *Industrial Relations*, the *British Journal of Industrial Relations* and the *European Journal of Industrial Relations.*

Amal El-Sawad is a Lecturer in Human Resource Management at the Business School, Loughborough University. She began her career as a personnel practitioner working in both the private and public sector. She is a member of the Chartered Institute of Personnel and Development. Her current research interests include the leadership and management of schools in international/multicultural contexts and the relationships between career development and organisational development. She has published in journals such as *Human Relations*, the *Journal of Occupational and Organizational Psychology* and *Group and Organization Management.*

Nandita Gurjar is Vice President and Global Head of Human Resources for the Infosys Group of companies. In this position, she is responsible for steering HR strategy for all the Infosys companies which include Infosys Technologies, Infosys BPO, Infosys Consulting and subsidiaries Infosys China and Infosys Australia. Over the past years, Nandita has been invited to various international and India forums to talk about and share her experiences in managing HR for a large growth BPO company.

Hyunji Kwon is research fellow at the Korea Labour Institute, Seoul, Korea. She received her BA in sociology from Ewha Women's University and PhD from the School of Industrial and Labor Relations, Cornell University. Her research interests include changes in employment relations in the customer service sector. Specifically, she has been working on changes in internal labour markets and labour-management relationship in the financial industry, employee outcomes in emerging call centres and flexible labour in various service sectors.

Neeru Malhotra is Lecturer in Marketing at Aston Business School, Aston University, Birmingham, UK. The focus of Neeru's research is in the area of services marketing, within which her research interests are internal marketing, service quality management and strategy. She is particularly interested in an inter-disciplinary approach towards research on service quality management, especially in the banking and call centre industries. Neeru has published in many internationally recognised journals, such as the *International Journal of Service Industry Management, Journal of Services Marketing, Service Industries Journal, International Journal of Human Resource Management* and the *Journal of Marketing Management.* She is a Fellow of HEA and member of the Aston India Foundation for Applied Business Research. She is the co-editor of a forthcoming 'Call Centres' special issue in the *Journal of Services Marketing* and is an Editorial Board Member of the *International Journal of Pharmaceutical and Healthcare Marketing.*

Kiran Mirchandani is an Associate Professor at the Ontario Institute for Studies in Education of the University of Toronto.

About the Editors and Contributors **311**

She has published on home-based work, telework, contingent work, entrepreneurship, transnational service work and self-employment. Her articles have appeared in journals such as *Gender and Society, Global Networks, Qualitative Methods* and *Gender, Work and Organization.* She teaches in the Adult Education and Community Development Programme (workplace learning and change focus) and offers courses on gendered and racialised processes in the workplace; critical perspectives on organisational development and learning; and technology, globalisation and economic restructuring.

Ernesto Noronha, PhD, is a faculty member of the Indian Institute of Management, Ahmedabad, where he teaches organisational behaviour. His research interests include ethnicity and diversity at work, labour relations, downsizing, organisational control, and ICTs and organisations. He has extensively studied the Indian ITES-BPO industry and labour issues in Indian ports. His other important work includes headload workers in Kerala and ethnicity in Indian organisations.

Dora Scholarios is a Reader in Organisational Behaviour in the Department of Human Resource Management at the University of Strathclyde. Her research interests are in the areas of employee well-being, recruitment, assessment and selection.

Virender Singh is a Reader in Marketing at the Institute of Management Studies and Research (IMSAR) at MD University, Rohtak, India. His main research interests are in the fields of marketing, consumer behaviour and management of people in the Indian context. His work has appeared in journals like the *International Journal of HRM, Employee Relations* and the *South Asian Journal of Management.*

Phil Taylor is Professor of Work and Employment Studies at the University of Strathclyde in Glasgow. For more than a decade he has researched and published extensively on diverse aspects of the call centre phenomenon and more recently has completed several studies on offshoring to India. Other research interests include occupational health and safety, prison privatisation and trade union organisation. He was a lead member of a major multi-disciplinary, cross-institutional project funded by the ESRC under its 'Future of Work Programme'. He became co-editor of the journal *Work, Employment and Society* in January 2008.

Terry Wagar is a Professor of Human Resource Management and Industrial Relations in the Department of Management at Saint Mary's University in Halifax, Canada. Dr Wagar is co-author of *Canadian Human Resource Management: A Strategic Approach.* In 2006, he received the IPMA (Canada) President's Award for his contributions to HRM. His research is primarily in the areas of HRM, employment law, industrial relations and organisational restructuring.

Catriona Wallace is the Managing Director of callcentres.net, a contact centre research, analyst and online publishing company, based in Singapore and Sydney. Dr Wallace is regarded as the leading analyst for the contact centre and outsourcing sectors in the Asia-Pacific region. Dr Wallace has a BA, MA and PhD in Organisational Behaviour from the Australian Graduate School of Management (AGSM). Dr Wallace also lectures on the MBA programme at the AGSM, has published numerous articles related to the contact centre and outsourcing sectors, and is the author of the book titled, *The Complete Guide to Call and Contact Centre Management.*

INDEX